St. Martin's Paperbacks True Crime Library Titles
by Diane Fanning

Through the Window

Into the Water

WRITTEN IN BLOOD

A True Story of Murder and a Deadly 16-Year-Old
Secret that Tore a Family Apart

DIANE FANNING

St. Martin's Paperbacks

WRITTEN IN BLOOD

Copyright © 2005 by Diane Fanning.

Poem on p. v, "Acension," © 1987 by Colleen Corah Hitchcock. Used with the author's permission and sincere condolences to the family and friends of Elizabeth McKee Ratliff and Kathleen Hunt Peterson.

ISBN: 0-312-99403-6
EAN: 80312-99403-7

Printed in the United States of America

St. Martin's Paperbacks edition / February 2005

St. Martin's Paperbacks are published by St. Martin's Press, 175 Fifth Avenue, New York, NY 10010.

10 9 8 7 6 5 4 3 2 1

This book is dedicated to the memory of two
extraordinary women—
Elizabeth McKee Ratliff and Kathleen Hunt Peterson

Ascension

*And if I go,
while you're still here...
Know that I live on,
vibrating to a different measure
—behind a thin veil you cannot see through.
You will not see me,
so you must have faith.
I wait for the time when we can soar together again,
—both aware of each other.
Until then, live your life to its fullest.
And when you need me,
Just whisper my name in your heart,
...I will be there.*

Acknowledgments

This book would not have been possible without the insight and assistance of many people. I express my gratitude to the family members of Elizabeth Ratliff and Kathleen Peterson who shared their stories with me: Caitlin Atwater, Fred Atwater, Margaret Blair, Rosemary Kelloway, Lori Campell, Veronica Hunt and Candace Zamperini. And to the others who felt the pain of these deaths: Randy Durham, Barbara Malagnino, Donna Carlson Lindahl, Pat Finn, and Patty Peterson.

I deeply appreciate the assistance I received from so many Durham County officials—District Attorney Jim Hardin, Assistant District Attorney Freda Black, Jury Clerk Susan Cowen, Victim-Witness Legal Assistant Leslie Hearn, Deputy Brian Mister, Sergeant Vicky Menser and Dee Johnson of the sheriff's department, Jay Rose and Mickey Tezai of the Durham County Emergency Medical Services. A very special expression of gratitude to the angel of the courthouse, Court Clerk Angie Kelly—I would have been lost and bewildered without your help and hospitality.

Thanks, too, to Investigator Art Holland, SBI Agent

Duane Deaver, Dr. Deborah Radisch and to my new friend, Carolyn Hardin.

Thanks to Nancy Perry at the Duke Archives and Elizabeth Dean in the university's Special Collections library.

I appreciate the hard work of all the jurors, but in particular want to thank the three who shared their experience with me: Kelli Colgan, Bettye Blackwell and Richard Sarratt.

I appreciate the help of Tom Ewing at the Educational Testing Services in Princeton, New Jersey, and forensic pathologist John Cooper, Jr., in California. In my home state of Texas, thanks to Andy Krueger of Krueger Legal Services, Beverley Horne of the Writers' League of Texas, Susie Adkins at Cedarvale Cemetery in Bay City and Ron Friesenhahn, my favorite attorney in New Braunfels—maybe, the whole state.

I send my gratitude to Peter Eichenberger, David Perlmutt, Defense Attorney Tom Maher, Maureen Berry, Marlo Kinsey and Attorney Jay Trehy, as well. And to those of you who helped me but asked to remain anonymous, you know who you are and I appreciate you.

Finally, a huge thanks to my agent, Jane Dystel, and to St. Martin's executive editor Charles Spicer, and my editor, Emily Drum. You made this book possible.

And a special thank you to my husband, Wayne, for his infinite patience and support and to my daughter, Liz, whose wedding plans I neglected until I finished this book.

THE STAIRWELL

"The chance of a criminal getting caught is only slightly better than getting hit by lightning."

—Michael Peterson, *The Herald-Sun*, July 1999

1

For Mary Allen, December 9, 2001, started as a long and lonely shift in the 9-1-1 call center in Durham, North Carolina. Another night spent on the outskirts of tragedy, aware of its presence but barely touched by its shadows.

At 2:40 A.M., she responded to an incoming call. Mary had no idea that she just took the first step onto the world stage of a long-playing drama.

"Durham 9-1-1. Where is your emergency?"

Breathing heavy, Michael Peterson responded: "1810 Cedar Street. Please!"

"What's wrong?" Mary asked.

"My wife had an accident. She's still breathing!"

"What kind of accident?"

"She fell down the stairs. She's still breathing! Please come!"

"Is she conscious?"

A bewildered Peterson did not seem to understand the question. "What?"

"Is she conscious?" Mary repeated.

"No, no, she's not conscious. Please!"

"How many stairs did she fall down?"

"What? Huh???"

Calmly, Mary repeated the question. "How many stairs did . . ."

"The back stairs!"

"How many stairs?"

"Oh, ah, ah . . ." His voice quaked with each syllable.

"Calm down, sir. Calm down."

Without warning, the heavy breathing ceased and Peterson responded in an off-hand manner, "Oh, fifteen, twenty. I don't know." Then the hysterical tone consumed his voice again. "Please! Get somebody here, right away. Please!"

"Okay, somebody's dispatching the ambulance while I'm asking you questions."

"It's off of a . . . It's in Forest Hills! Okay? Please! Please!"

"Okay, sir," she continued as Peterson whimpered. "Somebody else is dispatching the ambulance. Is she awake now?"

"Oh my," he moaned.

"Hello?"

"I didn't mmmm . . ." Peterson's words disintegrated into an inarticulate blur of noise.

"Hello?" Allen asked again.

He whispered, "Breathe. Oh, God." Incomprehensible mumblings burbled on the line. "Breathe," he whispered again. All Mary could hear now were strained and rapid inhalations and exhalations that sounded like the panting of a dog.

Then there was silence—followed by the blare of a dial tone that mocked Mary's efforts to assist.

· · ·

Elizabeth Poole's dispatch scratched out on the airways. "See an unconscious person 1810 Cedar Street. Engine 5, Medic 5. Unconscious person, 1810, 1-8-1-0 Cedar Street from East Oak Drive to Sycamore Street. Female fell down, fifteen to twenty stairs, hysterical caller is not able to give much further information, just advised it was accidental. OPS channel 2, OPS 2, Engine 5."

From their vehicle, Jayson Crank and Andrew Johnson of the Durham Fire Department responded, "Engine 5 is 10-17."

"10-4, no further," signaled Elizabeth. "Medic 5, did you copy your call to 1810 Cedar Street?"

"10-4, en route," came loud and clear from the EMS vehicle bearing Jay Rose and Ron Paige.

"Medic 5, 10-4."

At 2:46 A.M., Michael Peterson called in again. Once again, Mary Allen answered, "Durham 9-1-1. Where is your emergency?"

"Where are they?" Michael Peterson gasped. "This is 1810 Cedar—wh . . . She's not breathing! Please! Please, would you hurry up!"

In response, dispatcher Linda Gant sent out a Code 5 message indicating that the patient's condition was critical. This change of status meant Durham police were now on their way to the scene, too.

"Sir?" Mary asked.

His voice jumped up an octave. "Can you hear me?"

"Sir? Sir?"

"Yes."

"Calm down. They're on their way. Can you tell me for sure she's not breathing?"

A small click was the only answer she received.

"Sir . . . ?"

A dial tone echoed in her ear. "Hello . . . ? Hello . . . ?"

Over the next few hours, each person entering 1810 Cedar Street was shocked by the copious amount of blood. Blood on the walls. Blood on the floor. Blood on Kathleen.

Blood. A word that Michael Peterson left unspoken.

2

Two minutes after receiving the call, Jay Rose and Ron Paige were on their way, with Paige behind the wheel. Their siren split the silence of the night. They divided up the duties they needed to perform on the scene. Rose's responsibilities were greater because it was his turn to ride in the back when transporting the patient to the hospital. A couple of minutes later, they barreled their cumbersome vehicle down the narrow roads of the exclusive neighborhood of Forest Hills and killed the siren.

A Christmas wreath hung on the front door of 1810 Cedar Street, obscuring the house number. The truck shot past the residence. As soon as they saw the street number on the next mailbox, they realized their mistake. Paige turned the truck around and pulled into the Petersons' circular drive. This was no ordinary house call—the EMS responders arrived at a million-dollar mansion with a magnificent swimming pool and other trappings of a wealth they would never know.

From the back of the truck, Paige grabbed the Thomas Pack, a bag filled with equipment, Band-Aids, pads and other medical supplies needed for emergency treatment. Rose snatched up the Life Pack, consisting of a monitor to determine the electrical activity of the heart and a defibrillator. They rushed down the elegant slate sidewalk.

By curious coincidence, Todd Peterson, Michael's adult son, arrived at the same time as the first responders. He brushed past them and into the open door of the home. Paige and Rose heard a man sobbing inside as they approached the entrance.

Walking over a burgundy, gold and black rug, they saw the bottom half of Kathleen's body protruding from the stairway to the left. Michael Peterson crouched over her body crying. No one was making any attempt to administer CPR, cardio-pulmonary resuscitation, a standard first aid procedure.

The paramedics were prepared for broken bones or paralysis from a broken neck. They were not prepared for what they found. In his career, Rose had responded to thirty or forty falls and he never once saw so much blood. He was stunned. It looked more like the scene of a massacre than a tumble down the stairs.

Kathleen's body sprawled across the hardwood floor of the hallway, her legs spread wide. Drying blood covered the soles of her bare feet. A red-splattered roll of paper towels lay by her left foot. Next to the roll and a few wadded used towels, sat one of Michael Peterson's athletic shoes—splatters of blood standing out in sharp relief on the white leather.

Dried blood splotched over both legs of Kathleen's gray sweatpants. Between her spread legs, a pair of blood-spotted socks lay on the floor. At her hip and waist area, her pants were soaked to capacity with a dark, wet red.

A scarlet pool flowed across the floor from under her body.

Bloodstained, half-clenched hands rested in an awkward position in her lap. Her shoulders contorted at an artificial angle against a bottom step. Her head fell backward—leaving her neck exposed as if on a sacrificial altar. The expression that greeted the emergency responders was one of abject horror.

Dried blood caked her hair in clumps as it lay on a stack of bright red towels—their original snowy whiteness disguised by a recent baptism in blood. All around her, dark red smears and spatter covered the stairs and the doorjamb and rose up high on the walls.

On the way to their patient, the paramedics asked her age and how long it had been since her fall. Mike Peterson only said, "I just went outside to turn out the lights and came in." Then he wandered away from the stairwell and into the kitchen.

Behind the paramedics, men from the Durham Fire Department entered the house. Firefighter Jayson Crank was the first one in. He turned and pulled back the door for the others to enter. He noticed a smear of blood on the inside of the door beneath the spot where his fingers held it. But no blood lifted to his gloves—it was too dry to transfer.

The fire department personnel did not go near the body. They stood three abreast between the entranceway and the stairwell, blocking Kathleen's body from view and preventing any civilians from entering the area from that direction.

The emergency medical technicians knelt beside Kathleen—Rose on the right side, Paige on the left. The coppery scent of spilled blood permeated the air they breathed. They worked the rapid assessment protocol with efficiency and with few words exchanged. Each man moved in rhythm to the actions of the other as if each step were choreographed for the stage. Their instinctive timing and teamwork were impeccable.

Kathleen's pupils were dilated to 6 mm, indicating a lack of oxygen to the brain. There was no verbal activity from their patient, no motor response, no spontaneous eye movement. They determined her level of consciousness score was 3 of 3—the lowest possible score on the Glasgow Coma Scale. Kathleen had no pulse, no respiration, no blood pressure.

Paige put cardiac monitor leads on Kathleen just as he heard Todd Peterson say, "She's dead, Dad. The paramedics are here."

Todd may have made his assessment a bit quicker than the professionals on the scene, but he was right. No response registered on the cardiac monitor. There was zero electrical activity from her heart. Kathleen Peterson was dead—"very dead" according to Ron Paige. And it appeared as if she was dead long before Paige and Rose ever got the call to respond.

Paige stood guard by the body while Rose sought out Michael Peterson. He found him outside on the patio by the pool. The newly widowed husband was no longer crying. He was barefooted, wearing a tee shirt and shorts, and covered in blood. Small drops were scattered up and down his arms and legs and on his hands. Although his shirt was a dark navy blue, the large amount of blood on its surface was still obvious. On his khaki shorts, large red stains created a more dramatic contrast on both the front and back sides. All the blood on Michael Peterson appeared to be dry.

Rose asked Mike for Kathleen's birth date. Peterson just gave him a blank stare. When asked for her medical history, Peterson did not respond.

Rose returned to Kathleen's side. The two paramedics stayed by the body protecting her and the scene until they were relieved by Durham police officers.

Corporal Juanita McDowell and Officer Victor Figueroa of the Durham Police Department were the first officers on the scene. They entered the house where the emergency medical technicians were still checking for vital signs. McDowell saw Michael Peterson in the kitchen area with Todd's arm around his shoulders.

The officers saw a chair lift attached to the wall of the stairwell. The seat was folded up, but still they wondered if it played a role in the incident. They also made the mistaken assumption that Kathleen was disabled. They did not know the lift had been installed by the previous owner and simply was never removed by the Petersons.

In less than ten minutes McDowell knew that this scene did not look like a typical accidental fall. There was too much blood—and it no longer had the sheen she always saw where the blood was freshly spilled. She called the criminal investigations division on her radio.

Avoiding the stairwell area, McDowell walked the long way around to the kitchen and asked Todd Peterson for a telephone. He stepped to the edge of the stairway and plucked a portable phone off a step there before

Paige or Rose had a chance to object. McDowell then put Todd and Mike out on the patio.

At the door, firefighters contended with the arrival of Todd Peterson's friends, Ben Maynor, and Heather Whitson. Todd phoned Maynor minutes earlier and told him to come to the house, and to bring Heather, a medical resident at Duke University.

In a loud voice, an intoxicated Maynor insisted, "Get out of the way. Get out of the way. She's a doctor, she can help."

The firefighters turned to the sober Whitson, dressed in a burgundy top and black pants for the casual holiday party she had just abandoned. "I'm a doctor. Is there anything I can do?"

"No. It's too late for that. You need to wait outside."

Todd came to the door and intervened. Telling the firefighters it was all right, he ushered Ben and Heather inside. "Please look at my dad, Heather," Todd requested. "He is in shock."

The medical resident went out on the patio where Michael Peterson sat with a blank look on his face. At her arrival, he stood up and paced back and forth, crying and moaning.

The Petersons' two English bulldogs, who had been placid earlier, were now growling at the emergency responders and trying to push their way into the house. At McDowell's request, Christina Tomasetti, who had arrived at the house with Todd Peterson, corralled the dogs and put them in a closed room.

Christina caught a glimpse of Kathleen Peterson at the foot of the stairs. She jerked her head away from the bloody scene. She had no desire for a closer look. As she put the dogs in the den, she learned that Kathleen was dead.

McDowell stepped outside and awaited the arrival of the investigators.

1810 Cedar Street was now a crime scene.

3

ID Tech Dan George knocked on the closed side door and was told to come in. From the kitchen, he observed the victim from a distance of four or five feet. He saw large quantities of blood all over the floor, the wall and the victim's hands and feet. He realized that the blood on the floor was congealed and what was on the wall was smeared and dried. To his experienced eye, the evidence did not appear to point to an accidental fall. He left the house to contact the criminal investigation division (CID).

As he exited, he saw a drop of blood on the slate porch. He went to his car to get a flashlight and continued his search for more blood. He found a trace on the mortar between the bricks of the sidewalk about six feet away from where he saw the first drop. He put small pieces of paper by the blood and moved a planter into the path to avoid inadvertent trampling of the evidence.

Todd Peterson came out of the house to move his car. McDowell asked him, "Is the victim handicapped?"

"No," Todd said. "She drinks a lot and did a lot of drinking four hours earlier."

When she asked him who was in the house at the time,

he told her that only his dad and his stepmother were at home.

Ben Maynor stumbled out of the house. He reeked of alcohol and his speech was slurred alerting police that he was too intoxicated to be moving vehicles out of the way as he planned. He was sent back inside. The presence of Todd's drunken friend added a layer of chaos to a complicated scene filled with dozens of officers and first responders who were trying to do their jobs.

Sergeant Terry Wilkins arrived and took charge of the scene. He spotted the lower half of a body at the foot of the back stairs. He continued foward until he saw the large area of blood outside the staircase in the hallway. He stopped moving—he realized the scene needed to be secured with more crime-scene tape.

Wilkins noted a large spot of blood outside the staircase in the hallway near the front of the door. It had a glazed surface with no sheen of wetness. It was then that he got his first look at Michael Peterson—he was covered with blood and in an apparent state of shock. Wilkins said nothing to Peterson at the time. He was too focused on analyzing and securing the scene.

Peterson went into the kitchen and stood in front of the sink. He turned on the water and put his hands under its flow. Wilkins ordered Peterson to stop and he complied. Mike and Todd Peterson and Ben Maynor were then sent out onto the patio with an officer. Between the door and a table, they walked past a splash of spilled liquid and a silver tea kettle—an odd location for an item that seldom escaped the kitchen.

Wilkins sent home the neighbors who had been drawn

to the house by the flashing lights. A few minutes later, Wilkins saw Christina Tomasetti again. She had attended a party with Todd earlier that evening and was now in the foyer area by the foot of the spiral stairs with Heather Whitson. He directed them into the den. He advised them not to talk to each other so that the perceptions each one had were not tainted by the memory of the other one.

At 3:09, Investigator Art Holland stirred from his sleep at the sound of the page from CID Sergeant Fran Borden, who was on the scene but had not yet entered the house. With his many years of experience in criminal investigation, it was not unusual for him to receive a call in the middle of the night. He was a committed officer and loved working homicide. Some cases were hard to believe, some were hard to solve, but he welcomed the challenge and relished the added knowledge that every case brought to him.

He thought this call to the wealthy, older community of Forest Hills would be a routine matter. To the best of his knowledge, an elderly woman fell down a flight of stairs in a wheelchair—a tragic accident, but nothing more. He figured he'd make a brief appearance, assess the situation and return home to his bed. He told his wife that he'd probably be back in an hour. It would be twenty hours before he saw her again.

When Sergeant Borden entered the residence, he observed smeared blood on a kitchen drawer and on the glass-front cabinet above. That was the first red flag for this seasoned investigator—the first indication that things were not as they seemed.

When he observed Kathleen's body, he was surprised by its position—it was in a straight line, her neck in complete alignment with her spinal cord. That was the second red flag.

Then he noticed that the blood coating her body—the massive amount around her waist area, in particular— had a discoloration that indicated it had begun to dry. That was the third red flag.

He was now convinced that the scene was not consistent with any other accident, in his experience, where a victim had fallen down the stairs. This was a suspicious death. This stairway was a crime scene. He exited the house to await the arrival of detectives. Borden made the official crime scene declaration at 3:40 A.M.

Outside, the cool, damp night air grew chillier. Michael Peterson complained about the cold and attempted to enter the home several times to get a change of clothing. Wilkins tried to locate the sweatshirt and pants Peterson requested, but could not find them. He allowed Mike to go into the house and get them from a linen room off the kitchen. When Mike returned to the patio, he did not change clothes, but continued to complain.

Just before 4 A.M., Detective Holland of homicide and a domestic violence detective arrived at the house. Something clicked in Holland's head at first sight—too much blood. It did not look like a fall. He and Borden conferred outside and decided a search warrant was needed before they re-entered the premises. Holland

went to headquarters to draw up the necessary paperwork
and obtain the signature of a magistrate.

Canine Officer Trent Hall was on Durham Freeway near
route 15/501 at a traffic stop when he heard the call over
the radio. Half-listening, he heard something about
officers responding to 1810 Cedar Street. Immediately, he
thought of someone he knew and liked, Mike Peterson,
but could not recall his exact address. From the number of
officers being called to the scene, he knew this was not
routine and he was worried about his friend.

When he could not get details over the radio, Hall
went to the scene to make sure it wasn't the Peterson
house and that Mike was okay. He parked in front of the
gate, blocking the entry of other cars. He was told about
Kathleen's death and asked if he could be of any assistance. When he was told he was not needed at this time,
he strung crime-scene tape across the entrance to the
driveway and left the scene.

4

The chill night air drove the men inside, where they joined the two women in the den. Heather requested to use the bathroom. None of the officers knew where to find one, so Heather led them to the upper floor via the foyer stairs. They checked the room before she entered. They waited outside until she was done. Then they checked the room again and escorted her downstairs.

Christina requested a trip upstairs, and the process was repeated. Christina told the officers that she had brought Todd Peterson to the house and that they had arrived right after the fire department had.

When Christina returned, Todd told the officers that Michael and Kathleen were the only ones in the house at the time of the accident. "They both drink heavily. If you want my opinion, they were probably shit-faced and she fell," he said.

The police had their hands full in the den. Three of their charges were not a problem at all—the two women sat side by side on the sofa and Michael Peterson paced the floor. But Todd Peterson kept trying to leave the room, was asking to talk to his lawyers, asking for a time frame for when they could leave, asking for a grief counselor—asking for anything and everything that crossed his mind—and talking to the drunk Ben Maynor at every opportunity. Wilkins was paged to the den, where he explained again the need to refrain from verbal communication, and requested that they remain in one locale. Mike said, "What is this? Do I need to call a lawyer?"

When Ben and Todd would not stop their whispered conversations, the two women were taken into the living room, where each sat on a separate couch and were told there was to be "one hundred percent no talking." Both complied without a word—stretching out on the sofas to take naps with blankets the officers supplied.

In the den, Ben, Michael and Todd got the same message: "In order for you to stay together in this room, there is one hundred percent no talking. If you talk, you will be separated."

The officers felt some discomfort with what they had to do. It *was* a suspicious death. But what if the suspicions were unfounded? If so, Michael Peterson was nothing more than a grieving widower and they were preventing his son from comforting him.

Michael Peterson removed his bloodstained clothing, dropped it all to the floor and pulled on the sweatpants and sweatshirt. Ben Maynor picked up the discarded clothing and tried to turn them over to a uniformed officer. He would not accept them, because chain of custody procedures required that an ID tech remove the clothing from the scene.

Ben placed the garments on the windowsill near Mike's desk as requested. They were instructed not to go near the clothing. The two dogs were not eager to follow these orders, but someone shooed them away every time their twitching noses approached the window.

In the den, Mike settled down at his computer. He surfed the Internet and checked his email. He had stopped crying, but mumbled a lot—at times, mentioning the email his wife received about a meeting she was supposed to attend.

Todd Peterson picked up a phone and called his father's brother, a civil attorney in Reno, Nevada. "Uncle Bill, Kathleen is dead."

Bill Peterson dropped the phone to the floor. When he retrieved it, his shock was obvious to his nephew. "I need you to calm down," Todd said, "and I need to ask you some questions."

Todd went on to describe his view of the situation at the house to his uncle: The family was sequestered, two women were not being allowed to use the bathroom, crime-scene tape was all over the place, one police officer was being abusive, and they were being treated as suspects. Then he asked, "Is this normal?"

A cold dread spread through Bill's chest. He knew without being told that this was a custodial investigation and it appeared the police had fixated on his brother as a probable murder suspect. "It's absolutely not normal," he said.

"What should I do?" Todd asked.

"First thing, go up to your dad and instruct him not to say anything."

Todd said that a police officer was talking to him. In fact, he said, the cop had his arm around Mike's shoulders.

"Go up to that police officer," Bill ordered, "and tell

him that your dad is represented and his attorney is on the phone and has instructed him not to talk anymore. And I want to talk to the chief detective on the scene."

Bill Peterson was cool and calm in the courtroom. He was bright and articulate, and he represented his clients well. But this wasn't just any client—it was his brother. And it wasn't a civil squabble over money—it was a criminal matter, and the most serious felony of all.

After a moment, Todd returned to the phone. "Dad will follow your instructions, but there is no detective in the house to talk to you."

Bill uttered a few hollow words of assurance, hung up and dialed the downtown Durham police station. "This is Bill Peterson. I understand that you are doing a crime scene investigation at my brother's house at 1810 Cedar Street. I am his attorney, and I do not want him spoken to until such time as I have gotten to Durham."

"Why are you telling me this?" the desk officer asked.

"The reason I am telling you this is because no one at the scene will talk to me."

"Wait a minute and I'll get back to you."

Bill clutched the receiver, his thoughts getting darker with every passing second. The officer called investigator Holland's desk and asked him if he would talk to Bill. Holland was busy typing the paperwork for a search warrant and had nothing to say to Bill—or any attorney— at that time.

The desk officer then told Bill, "Your instructions are understood."

And that was the end of their conversation. Bill made arrangements to leave for Durham first thing the next morning.

• • •

Exasperated officers switched positions hoping to get Todd to pay minimal attention to someone. But no matter who spoke to him, Todd continued to make phone calls, whisper consoling words to his dad and talk to Ben.

Outside, the Mobile Police Station—a retrofitted recreation vehicle—arrived on the scene. It would give officers a place to make reports, use communications equipment and take a break. Beside it, investigators waited for Holland to return with the search warrant.

In the den, to everyone's relief, Todd finally fell asleep on the floor with the dogs—at last, he was not talking. Michael was writing on a notepad.

When Borden told Corporal Kim Gregory that the victim reportedly died from a fall down the stairs, she laughed—the first light moment in the house in hours. She thought Borden was making fun of her for the fall she took down the stairs the day before. He called her clumsy then—she thought he was ribbing her now. The seriousness of his demeanor penetrated and wiped away all traces of amusement.

At 6:05, District Attorney Jim Hardin's home telephone rang. He listened to a briefing about the events of the night at 1810 Cedar Street. He was grateful for the call. There was nothing worse in his profession than being caught unaware when the reporters started to phone.

Lieutenant Art Holland returned with a search warrant. He was now the lead investigator. The document granted the Durham Police Department the authority to seize any forensic evidence, possible weapons, documents and a measurement of the premise. It also granted permission for taking video footage and still photographs. In short, they were entitled to take possession of "[. . .] any and all evidence that may relate to the Death Investigation."

Holland pulled on protective gloves and booties and entered the house. Dan George donned a head-to-toe Tyvek suit and followed him in. When Holland served the warrant, Mike was speechless and the washed-out expression on his face seemed frozen in place. As Holland read the warrant aloud, Todd snatched the copy from his father's flaccid fingers and read along. Then he turned a face of stunned silence to the investigator. As clearly as if spoken, two questions scratched across his face: "What are you doing? Why are you doing this?"

Holland and George did a walk-through to get a feel for the scene and then the evidence gathering began. George, armed with a video camera, taped a 360-degree view from the entrance. Then, he proceeded through the foyer, through the dining room and into the kitchen. Finally, he shot the body at the foot of the stairs. ID Tech Angie Powell followed him every step of the way, shooting the same scenes he did with a still camera.

Dr. Kenneth Snell of the medical examiner's office responded to the scene, suited up and went inside. A quick assessment of the body *in situ* revealed a four-inch laceration to the back of Kathleen's head. Snell said the injury was possible with a fall, but an autopsy was needed to be certain.

Snell and George lifted Kathleen's body from the stairs and placed her in a body bag. The pooled blood dropped from the seat of her pants as they moved her. The blood elsewhere on her clothing was damp.

Snell continued to manipulate the body and discovered three more major injuries to the head, as well as other minor lacerations, bruises and abrasions. After ten minutes, he ended his examination knowing he could not make any definitive determinations at the scene.

He told Lieutenant Holland, "If it is not a fall in the stairs, it was a rod-like instrument. You should be looking for something like that."

George removed the bloody Rolex watch from Kathleen's wrist and bagged it as evidence. The body bag was zipped shut.

George retrieved Mike Peterson's clothing from the windowsill in the den. He placed the shorts and shirt in one paper bag and his watch in another. He did not use plastic bags because their moisture-retaining properties would cause the blood to degrade. The shorts and shirt were still damp, but no blood transferred to his gloves. From the area by the stairwell, he picked up the shoes and placed them in one bag, the socks in yet another. He labeled each bag with the location where he found each item, sealed it with evidence tape and added his initials.

He then requested Todd Peterson's clothing. Accompanied by an officer, Todd went upstairs to change. He returned and handed his jeans, a knit shirt, a dress shirt, shoes and socks to George. Those items, too, were encased in paper bags, marked, sealed and placed in the designated area near the door.

The mortuary services arrived at 8:30 A.M. to remove Kathleen Peterson's body and deliver her to the medical examiner's office in Chapel Hill. Now that she had completed photographing the scene, Angie Powell was free to travel with the body to ensure the chain of custody for any evidence taken at the autopsy.

When Todd Peterson stepped out of the house, a police lieutenant asked, "Has anyone asked you for a statement?"

"No," Todd replied.

"Would you be willing to make a statement?"

"No," he said again.

Michael Peterson followed his son out the door, but did not say a word to anyone.

Mike was the guardian of two daughters of deceased friends, George and Liz Ratliff. He called Tulane University in New Orleans and summoned Margaret Ratliff home. He placed a call to Martha at the University of San Francisco to let her know she was needed there, too.

Late morning, the telephone rang at the northern Virginia home of Kathleen's sister Candace Zamperini. Candace answered the call. It was Mike Peterson. "I want to speak to your husband," he said.

Her husband, Mark, was not at home. Candace gave him Mark's cell phone number. Michael would tell her nothing, but she knew from the tone of his voice that something was amiss. Her imagination ran through the possibilities. Perhaps Kathleen lost her job. Maybe her employer was going bankrupt or the stock plummeted down so far it was close to valueless. Neither sickness nor death crossed Candace's mind.

An hour later, Mark arrived at the house. Candace took one look at his horror-stricken face and her first fearful thought was that something had happened to one of her daughters. Her eyes scanned her husband's face for hidden answers.

Mark led her to the porch outside of the kitchen. "I have some really, really bad news," he said. "Kathleen fell," he continued. "And she's dead."

Candace fell to the floor, and fell apart. When she regained a modicum of composure, she wanted to know what happened. "How?" she asked him. "Did she fall off a ladder while decorating the tree?"

Mark could not give her any answers—Michael told him no more than that. When they called him back, the only additional detail he provided was that Kathleen had fallen down the stairs.

Mark phoned the northern Virginia home of Kathleen's other sister Lori, and talked to her husband, Bruce Campell—he, in turn, informed his wife. Candace called a good friend of her mother's. That friend and another woman delivered the news to Veronica Hunt at her home in Florida. They stayed with her to offer any comfort they could. Veronica crumbled—no mother should live to bury her daughter.

At the Tennessee home of Kathleen's brother, Steven Hunt, the phone rang, then flashed off. The caller ID readout told Steve's wife, Cynthia, that it was Kathleen's number. The phone rang again. It was Michael. He was sobbing and incoherent.

"What's wrong? What's wrong?" Cynthia asked.

Michael's caterwauling turned off as if he had flipped a switch. "Kathleen's dead."

"What happened?"

"She fell down the stairs."

"Are you alone?" Cynthia asked.

He told her that his boys were there and his brother, Bill, was on the way. "I cannot talk to the Hunts. You have to tell your husband."

Steve was in Puerto Rico working on an engineering project for the government. Cynthia reached him there. "There's no way she fell down those stairs," Steve said. "He must have had something to do with it." He flew home to Tennessee the next day.

At Cornell University in Ithaca, New York, sophomore Caitlin Atwater, Kathleen's only biological child, was out to brunch with a friend when the call came from Durham. She returned to her sorority house and found a note from the sorority president asking her to come see her right away.

When Caitlin entered the president's room, Becca, Caitlin's roommate and best friend, was there, too. Becca's tear-stained face alarmed her. She was certain her friend was in trouble and asked what was wrong.

Becca said, "Caitlin, it's fine. It's fine. Someone is coming to talk to you in a minute."

Caitlin was not letting Becca off the hook. She looked her in the eye and said, "Becca, you can't do this to me. You've got to tell me what happened."

"Caitlin, it's your mother," Becca said. "She's dead." Becca had spent time with Kathleen on four different occasions. She had some sense of the devastating loss Caitlin felt.

Caitlin found it difficult to comprehend those simple tragic words. The only other loss she had experienced in her life was the death of her great-grandfather. And he lived to the respectable age of 104. Her mother was only in her 40s. It was impossible that she was gone.

Grief counselors arrived to minister to Caitlin. The grieving girl was too numb to feel their words of compassion. All night long, a procession of sorority sisters paraded in and out of Caitlin's room. They brought offerings of stuffed animals and ice cream, both to comfort Caitlin and to stave off their own feelings of helplessness.

Fred Atwater, Kathleen's ex-husband and Caitlin's father, was consulting on a job in Philadelphia. He spent the weekend at home in North Carolina and just arrived back for the work week when he got the news.

He drove to Ithaca to be with his daughter. The next day, they would drive back to Philly and then fly together to face the horror of Durham.

5

Dan George looked over the stairway for any other evidence. Using tweezers, he extracted hair, fibers, Christmas tree needles and samples of wood. While he gathered the minute traces of evidence, Lieutenant Holland and his team spread out over the house looking for any possible weapon. They searched upstairs, downstairs, in the garage and up in the attic, and performed a cursory search around the perimeter of the house.

George loaded the accumulated evidence into his car and took it to the station. For some reason even he cannot explain, he did not seize the towels that rested beneath Kathleen's head, the eyeglasses in the stairway or the telephone with its telltale spot of red.

In the locked, secured evidence room, he rolled out a clean white sheet of paper and laid out all the clothing. He hung each article on a separate hanger and put it in the evidence drying cabinet.

It was now 2 P.M. Dan George had been on duty since 5 P.M. the previous day. After twenty-one hours, he was exhausted. He went home and slept for four hours before returning to Cedar Street.

. . .

At the medical examiner's office, Dr. Deborah Radisch, forensic pathologist, received a call from Dr. Kenneth Snell early Sunday morning informing her that he was on the way to a scene that would probably require an autopsy. She prepared to perform another one of the 3,200 autopsies she had conducted in her career.

Snell arrived at the office before the body did. He ran down the details of the death scene and showed Radisch the Polaroids he had taken.

When Kathleen's body arrived, Radisch removed the clothing and submitted it as evidence. She weighed her—120 pounds—and measured her: 5'2". She scanned the body for scars, marks and injuries that could have been involved in the death.

On Kathleen's face, the pathologist found three small bruises in a line pattern over the right eyelid and three scratches on a diagonal over the right eyebrow. Those injuries could not be the result of impact with a flat surface—like a stair step—since they were in locations on the face protected by surrounding bone. Only prominent areas of the face—like the nose, the cheekbones and the chin—would be injured in a fall.

She noted a small area of damaged skin and a faint bruise on the forehead. There were other marks on Kathleen's face most likely caused by fingernails. Radisch located bruises on the earlobe and nose caused by blunt trauma—either by falling against a step or by being impacted with force into a step.

She found no damage inside the mouth. There was a

chip off of one tooth, but it was not possible to determine if it was recent in origin.

Radisch shaved Kathleen's head to better view the injuries there. She discovered seven areas of wounds on the head—many spanned the full thickness from the scalp through to the skull. There was a lot of bleeding into scalp tissue around these wounds. One of them created a flap of skin—or avulsion—that could be lifted up, enabling Radisch to see the skull beneath. Another was a tri-pronged cut—looking as if a small, sharp rake had dug three inches along the scalp. Each cut was caused by at least one individual impact. In Radisch's opinion, the injuries were the result of being struck by an object or against an object and were inconsistent with a fall.

Turning to Kathleen's hands, Radisch found hairs grasped in each one. She removed them and packaged the samples as evidence. She scraped dried blood from beneath the fingernails, but found no tissue. Frazier fir needles were stuck in the blood on the hands. On the left hand, there were two injuries and some bruising. Another bruise was on the back of the right hand. Around the wrists and elbows were more bruises.

In the doctor's opinion, these external injuries on the arms and hands were most consistent with those received when someone is trying to fend off attack. They appeared to be defensive injuries caused by separate impacts.

After she was certain she had observed and documented all relevant characteristics on the outside of the body, the doctor made a Y-incision to the trunk and began the internal examination. First, she viewed all of the organs in place. She looked closely for any disease process in the body cavity and found none.

She drew an aorta blood sample and took toxicology samples. She then cut the scalp with a Stryker saw and found a large amount of hemorrhage, but no fractures to the skull. She removed the top of the skull and turned her attention to the brain, where she found a small amount of sub-arachnoid hemorrhage. She removed the brain, weighed it and fixed it in formalin for future neuropathology review.

She moved her examination to the internal neck area, and discovered a bloodied fracture with hemorrhage on the small extension off of the left thyroid cartilage. It was an injury unlikely to occur in a fall. Usually it was the result of direct trauma to the bone and was common in strangulation or attempted strangulation.

She encountered no visible blood in the airway. She found no evidence that Kathleen had aspirated—breathed—blood into her lungs. She also did not find any evidence of expelled blood. The blood alcohol level was .07—three-tenths of a point below the legal definition of intoxication in North Carolina at the time.

When she submitted the final report, Dr. Radisch determined that the cause of death was blunt force trauma to the head. The manner of death was homicide.

Angela Powell left the medical examiner's office and returned to headquarters at 2:10 P.M. She turned in the evidence obtained during autopsy: a tube with blood; fingerprints; footprints; hair samples—some from Kathleen's scalp as well as the hair found in both of her hands; a small wood/metal chip found on the back of her head; a DNA card; and the sweatpants and sweatshirt Kathleen had been wearing when she died.

When Durham Police Department blood spatter expert Rebecca Reed saw the large quantity of blood and the multiplicity of stain types, she determined that the scene exceeded her ability to analyze. Someone with more knowledge and experience was needed. A call was made to the North Carolina Bureau of Investigation. In one hour, Agent Duane Deaver from the environmental crimes unit was on the scene.

Deaver was not just any blood spatter analyst; he was the SBI's lead instructor on bloodstain evidence, teaching police officers, prosecutors and pathologists all over the state. He had testified as an expert in the courtroom for more than sixty trials.

He walked through the scene observing the blood transfer stain on the inside of the door, the barefoot print transfer close to the door and the stain on the sofa where Todd directed Mike to sit after he removed him from the stairwell.

Deaver went back to his car for the equipment he would need. He returned in a Tyvek suit and booties to begin his general examination of the stairway. Although the blood was dried by now, the musty, acrid scent lingered and filled the air with an olfactory scream of death.

Deaver sketched a diagram of the area, including the stains on the walls, on the steps, on the risers, at the base of the stairs, on and behind the chair lift and on the trim and header panel above the entrance to the kitchen area. He noted impact spatter, cast-off patterns, transfer patterns and blood smears—some the result of attempted cleanup.

It was this cleanup that surprised the SBI agent the most. Many times, there are no indications that anyone tried to sanitize the scene. In most cases, when they do, the cleanup by the perpetrator is thorough. He expected this typical all-or-nothing scenario—instead he found an irrational, partial job.

After completing his diagram, Deaver measured the length and width of the drops on the wall to determine the velocity and direction of the blood. To quantify the size and angles of the spatter, he used a comparator, a magnifying device with a lens that is accurate to one-tenth of a millimeter.

Then he began the stringing process. Stringing is a method of configuring the movement of blood from its source to its final destination. Because this activity always follows the basic laws of physics, trigonometric calculations can ascertain the path of the blood and a point of origin can be determined. Some analysts use a computer program to do the calculation for them. Others stick with the tried-and-true manual method. Believing nothing is better than being at the crime scene where you can check and double-check the process every step of the way, Deaver preferred the latter.

He used a special white tape designed not to damage the bloodstains to attach a very thin nylon twine to the forty-two droplets of blood he selected. Each string was pulled with a protractor held on the wall to get an accurate angle. Then the other end of the string was taped to a ring-stand rod on the steps. The strings from the drops came to two very sharp points of origin. One was eighteen inches above a step. The other was eleven inches up from another step. Both points were in space—not on any surface. Neither one was consistent with a fall.

At 11:30 P.M., the scene was sealed and all of the officers were sent home. It had been a long and trying day, and everyone needed some rest.

Instead of heading to the much-desired comfort of their beds, Agent Deaver, Investigator Holland and the ID techs went over to the evidence room at Durham Police Department headquarters to view the items worn by Michael, Todd and Kathleen Peterson.

Each article of clothing was laid out on brown paper on a table. One by one, with gloved hands, Deaver examined them and sketched what he saw.

On Michael Peterson's shorts, he noted a large diluted stain in the front as if something had been applied to the top of the pants and washed the blood down. The blood inside the pocket was darker than it was on the outside. If the silver tea kettle on the patio had been seized, Deaver thought he might have surmised that it was the source of the water poured on the shorts.

There was spatter and bloodstain on the back of the shorts. But most curious of all were the blood spatter in the crotch area and the spatter inside the right leg. No one had mentioned the possibility to Deaver, but the evidence indicated only one scenario to him—a situation he had seen over and over again in other cases:

Peterson had to have been standing over Kathleen as he beat her.

On Mike's right shoe, Deaver saw 90-degree drops of blood on the toe, indicating that his foot was directly beneath dripping blood. On the outside edge of the shoe were small droplets with noticeable directionality showing that the blood had fallen while the foot was in motion. On the sole of that shoe were smears of blood. On the left shoe, there was similar staining.

The front of Kathleen's pants showed heavy staining in the waist area, fan-shaped blood spatter and a curious shoeprint-shaped transfer stain on the thigh. The back of the pants had soaking blood from the waistband with a dilution stain below it. The back of the leg also had contact and transfer stains.

All of this evidence was to be expected. What surprised Agent Deaver was the clear, sharp impression of the sole of a foot on the top of the back of Kathleen's leg, as if someone had stepped on her as she lay there.

On Todd Peterson's clothing, most of the blood was transfer stains and smears. But on the bottom right leg was one large drop of blood. To Deaver's trained eye, the totality of the stains was consistent with Todd carrying a large heavy object over his shoulder. That object must have had sufficient blood on it to drip down on his jeans.

That same evening, Margaret Ratliff called her Aunt Margaret in Rhode Island and left a message on her machine saying that she was at Washington Duke Inn and asking her to please call as soon as she could.

When Margaret Blair returned home and listened to her messages, she was worried and confused. Her niece had spent a pleasant Thanksgiving holiday weekend with her and then returned to school in New Orleans. Now, two weeks later, while school was still in session, she was calling from Durham?

Margaret Ratliff's first words to her aunt were: "I'm okay. Everybody's here with me."

"Margaret, what *is* wrong?" Margaret Blair asked.

Two words choked out of the young woman's mouth: "Kathleen's dead."

After a moment of silence, Margaret Blair asked, "How did it happen?"

"She had an accident and fell down the stairs and Dad found her."

Margaret Blair was stunned. It required conscious thought for her to continue breathing. "Do you know what you are saying? That's what happened . . ."

"I know," Margaret Ratliff interrupted.

Her aunt heard the voice of Michael Peterson rise up from the past. She heard the call she received in 1985. "She's had an accident and fell down the stairs."

6

At 6 A.M. on December 10, detectives filed back into the Forest Hills home. The stars of the exterior search were Master Officer Trent Hall and his canine partner, Bosco, whose specialty was article searches. When Hall drove out to the Peterson home the night before, he hed not anticipated this turn of events. He had to set aside all of his personal concerns this morning and—he and his partner had a job to do.

Deployed with one word from Hall, Bosco was off and searching. He sniffed through grasses and massive mountains of kudzu, down a hill covered with a dense grove of bamboo leading to the unpaved section of Cedar Street, to the outside shed and around it. Bosco searched the whole property in a back-and-forth circular pattern for about one hour and forty-five minutes. He did not find a weapon.

Lieutenant Connie Bullock then deployed five teams into different areas marked with flags. When a team finished their designated area, they reported back to the mobile unit, where the completed section was marked on the map, and were assigned a new area to search. The contents of the trash can and a recycling bin got intense scrutiny. When all the areas of the grounds had been covered, Bullock sent some of the officers inside to help with that search. He sent the rest of them home.

Holland and his homicide team scoured the inside of the home and the four vehicles at the residence: a Volkswagen Cabriolet, a Mitsubishi Montero, a Mitsubishi 3000 GT and an aged Jaguar.

While the search of the home and property were under way, Candace Zamperini and Lori Campell drove down from Northern Virginia to Durham. On the way, they talked about what happened to their sister and how it could have occurred. In their minds, they envisioned the front stairs, where four and a half years earlier, a radiant Kathleen had descended to take her marriage vows. Did she tumble over the railing and fall to the floor? Did she trip and cascade down the steps? They talked about Duke Chapel and how nice it would be to hold the service there. They hoped it would be available and wondered about the process for securing it.

At one point during the ride, Lori blurted out her darkest thought: "He did this to her. He didn't love her."

The sisters went straight to 1810 Cedar Street, arriving at about 4:30 in the afternoon. They pulled up to an unexpected sight. Up to that moment, they thought the police went to the house to have a cursory and casual look—just a routine check to confirm that the death was an accident. They did not think they would find yellow crime-scene tape all around the perimeter. They did not anticipate the legions of television trucks, cameramen and other members of the press corps lying in wait. Their minds went blank trying to absorb it all.

A police officer was at their side in an instant to tell them that they could not enter the house. He pointed out the mobile unit. Candace and Lori gaped at it in disbelief.

Across the street, in the driveway of Maureen "Mo" Berry's house at 1819 Cedar, Candace and Lori saw Todd waiting for their arrival. He waved them over. Todd told them that since his dad was just too upset to talk about what happened, he would fill them in. He said that he had gone to the house earlier in the evening with Christina Tomasetti. Mike and Kathleen were watching *America's Sweethearts* with Julia Roberts—he repeated that assertion several times throughout the conversation as if it were a vital piece of information.

He said that Kathleen had been "drunk, drunk, drunk" and stumbling through the house when he was there. He told them that he and Christina left for a party in the neighborhood. He'd returned to the house with the intention of getting Christina into his bed. When he arrived, however, emergency vehicles were at the house and he jumped out of the car and ran inside. He complained about the actions and insensitivity of the police.

After talking to Todd, the two went inside. They spent an awkward hour and a half in the home of a stranger. It was a long time in the presence of the stilted social interaction that is natural in the aftermath of unexpected death.

Most of the members of the Peterson family were at

the home of Kerry Sutton, who was now serving as
Mike's criminal attorney. Before heading over to join
them, Candace wanted to make a stop at the Mobile
Police Station. Lori waited for her in the car. Candace
introduced herself to Lieutenant Connie Bullock and said,
"I'm here for my sister. She died. When can I get into the
house?"

"I'm not sure. But I think maybe later tonight."

Candace left the unit dissatisfied and followed Todd
over to Kerry Sutton's house. The place was full of
people, among them Mike Peterson; his brothers, Bill and
Jack; his sister, Ann Christensen; Margaret and Martha
Ratliff; Mike's friend and webmaster, Guy Seaberg; and,
of course, Kerry Sutton.

After an exchange of greetings, Mike said, "Candace,
now that you're here, I'd like you to take care of all the
funeral arrangements."

"Yes, I will. I will take care of everything for the
funeral." She then asked Mike where Kathleen's body
was and other details she would need to know. Mike did
not volunteer any information about Kathleen's death.
Candace went off by herself to think about the best way
to honor her sister and to make a mental to-do list.

Mike turned to Lori and asked, "What music do you
think we should play at the service?"

Her thoughts flew at once to a group loved by all
the family, the Mills Brothers. She realized that the tune
running through her head was "You Always Hurt the One
You Love." Her mouth opened as if to speak. She snapped
it closed and shook her head.

After an hour or so, the mourning family left the

Sutton home to return to Maureen's house, where Caitlin Atwater was expected to arrive. Kerry, Mike and Bill urged Candace to try to get the police to allow them into the house. On the way back, Candace stopped by the mobile unit to speak to Lieutenant Bullock again.

"Now I am concerned about when I can get into the house, because I want to get clothing and things for my sister's funeral. If nothing else, could a police officer escort me up to her bedroom so I can at least get some clothing?"

"No. You're probably going to be able to get into the house tonight. No problem. It might not be till nine or ten. I'll let you know." Bullock warned her about the cleanup that was needed in the house. "There's blood," he said.

"That's no problem. I am here to take care of things for the family. I will clean up the blood. It won't bother me."

Having seen the blood covering the floor and the landing and reaching high up on the walls, Bullock raised his eyebrows.

Candace noticed the surprised expression he gave her and reassured him, "I can do this. I can clean up the blood."

"Well, there's a lot of it."

"That's okay. I can do this."

She then gave him her name and a phone number and joined the others at the Berrys' house, where Maureen served dinner. Then, a candle-covered cake was placed on the table in front of Margaret. It was her 20th birthday. Family gathered round and sang a lusty refrain of "Happy Birthday." It was a *Twilight Zone* moment for Candace. She walked out of the room shaking her head. She could not believe anyone could think about a birthday with the horror of Kathleen's death still choking the air.

Fred pulled up to Maureen's home a little while later. He dropped Caitlin off and went on his way. Although he wanted to be with his daughter, he did not want to insert any conflict into an already difficult situation. He checked in at the Washington Duke Inn, where Kathleen's family had rooms.

When Caitlin entered the house, Mike whisked her upstairs to talk in private. He went through his story about what happened to her mother. He told her that he was a suspect in Kathleen's death. At that moment, Caitlin did not care who or what was responsible. All she wanted to do was grieve and adjust to her loss. Everything else was insignificant and irrelevant.

Candace's frame of mind was very similar. At some point that evening, she told police that ". . . the happiest day of Kathleen's life was the day she married Michael." ". . . [S]he had found her soulmate." "I thought they were happy people." And that she knew of no financial problems the couple faced.

Candace did not want to talk to the police that night. She did not want to dishonor Kathleen by discussing personal matters. She wanted to be left alone to absorb the cold fact of her sister's death.

As the families played musical houses, investigators worked in the dark at Cedar Street. Dan George prepared the solution to spray luminol a short distance from the stairwell toward the kitchen. As he sprayed the floor, officers followed behind him looking for any signs of the faint glow that heralded the presence of blood. Their eyes could not wander—the luminescence would only last ten to twenty seconds before it faded away.

A briny smell reminiscent of the seashore wafted through the air with every squirt of the chemical. The observers were rewarded with a footprint, shining and bright with five clearly defined toes, the ball of a foot and a heel. George crawled forward spraying a path where prints appeared like ectoplasmic markings of a ghost as they led the team footstep by footstep to the laundry sink. The feet turned toward the sink, then walked off to the washing machine. Again they turned, marking the spot. There was no way to tell how long the feet stayed at those stopping points or what they were doing while they were there.

George kept spraying and the three men followed, watching the trail of feet travel to the kitchen sink and turn directly in front of it. Then the apparitions of feet pattered over to the kitchen cabinet to the spot where blood was found and turned forward yet again.

At 8:30 that night, the police released the house. They seized a walking stick beside the fireplace and other possible candidates for the implement that applied blunt force to Kathleen's head, but no obvious weapon was found anywhere in the home.

Investigator Holland had discovered something significant in the last two days. By the time he left 1810 Cedar Street that night, he had a strong conviction about Michael Peterson's guilt. He knew without a doubt that Kathleen Peterson was murdered. Now, all he had to do was prove it.

7

Michael; his brother Bill; his sons, Clayton and Todd; and his good friend Guy Seaberg slipped out of Maureen Berry's home and scurried across the street and into the house. Not one of them told Kathleen's sisters or her daughter that they could now go back inside.

They cleaned up all the blood from the hallway, off the back of the door and any other place they could find outside the stairwell. When they realized that the men were over at the house, Candace and Lori crossed the street to join them. They walked together through the side door and down the hall.

There on the staircase, they saw the blood. Their sister's blood. It chased any possibility of denial out of their hearts and minds. Lori climbed into the stairwell pointing at blood here. Blood there. Blood everywhere. Her sister's blood surrounded her and beat a panicked rhythm into her head. Candace hung back, unwilling, at first, to enter Kathleen's altar of death.

They were incredulous at the volume of blood they saw there. No one told them that some of the scene was already sanitized. In fact, they did not know about the pool of blood at the foot of the stairs until they saw the crime-scene photos weeks later.

Mike came up behind the women and the three ascended the stairs with deliberate slow steps. When they reached the top, Mike said, "I came up the stairs, I think, to get some towels." He turned and looked down the steep angle to the landing. "She fell down the whole staircase."

Candace was shaking and wildness ran loose in her mind. She knew she needed to calm down, and stepped off to a corner by herself. She remembered the example set for her all her life by her older sister—when you're at wit's end, get busy. And so she did.

She went into her sister's bedroom and slid clothing up and down the rack until she found a suitable outfit. She took it, and Kathleen's jewelry box, wallet and passport, and carried the bundle downstairs and set it by the front door. She felt a bit better having done something useful.

She looked again at the red, forbidding spot where her sister breathed her last breath. She knew she had to clean up that blood. Her mother was coming in another day. Candace did not want her to see this. She did not want her mother to be haunted by the image of her daughter's blood spattered all over the walls and steps. Candace could hear the blood screaming at her as if it held the essence of Kathleen's last moments buried in its dried, browning surface.

Todd and Clayton attempted to conceal the stairway from view. They held up a big, cream-colored blanket and tried to staple it to the wall. But the staples buckled as they emerged from the gun, the old hard plaster denying them penetration. They whisked duct tape up on the corners, pressed it hard onto the plaster, but to no avail—it would hold for a hope-birthing second and then give way. The blanket was not big enough to cover the whole doorway anyway.

Cleaning, Candace knew, was the only answer. She looked under the kitchen sink and in the laundry area for supplies. She emerged with a bucket of water, a can of Ajax, a bottle of spray cleaner, rags and paper towels.

As Candace tackled the cleaning, Lori sat in the living room with Clayton. "Poor Margaret and Martha—losing both of their mothers," Clayton said.

Lori sighed and shook her head.

"You know how their first mother died?" Clayton asked.

"No."

"She fell down the stairs, too."

Lori fought back an attack of nausea. It was the first time she had heard about Liz Ratliff's death. Clayton's words echoed in her mind, pounding out a painful dirge of doom.

In the stairwell, Candace sprayed a piece of the landing and wiped. All she did was smear the blood. She moved to the woodwork and tried there. More smears—there was just so much blood.

She wiped in the lower corner, but working there made her feel uncomfortable, trapped, surrounded by blood. At last, she decided on a logical method. She would start at the top and work her way down. She pointed the spray bottle at the wall at the end of the landing. She pushed in the button and got cleaner on the wall and on the print of

"Toulouse-Lautrec's *Chat Noir—Black Cat*—hanging there. She wiped across the cat picture and a stream of cleaner mixed with blood formed a trail down her arm. She looked at it in horror. Her sister's blood. Trailing down her arm. She couldn't take it. Not tonight. She'd worry about it tomorrow. She had to get out of this house. Out of the house that stole her sister's life. She had to get out now.

She fled the stairway and stuffed the used rags and paper towels deep into the waste can—burying them under other trash so that no one else would have to see them. She grabbed Lori and rushed out of the house. They took refuge at the Washington Duke Inn. They will never forget the warmth and solicitousness of the staff. The hotel became their shelter from the storm.

Someone stayed up all night at 1810 Cedar Street. He sat at Michael's computer deleting files, emails and Web pages. It would take experts to retrieve the data buried deep in the hard drive.

In the morning, Candace went to the Howerton–Bryan Funeral Home with Kathleen's clothing, jewelry and identification. She handed Kathleen's passport to the director. She clung to a desperate hope that it was all a mistake. A misunderstanding. She asked him to make sure it really was her sister. With a sorrowful nod, the director dashed that hope on the rocks of Candace's broken heart.

Next, Candace dragged herself over to Maplewood Cemetery, an old, peaceful graveyard only a short distance from 1810 Cedar. A staff member drove her around and pointed out the single plots available. With listless dread, she selected a $700 plot on a hillside and agreed to purchase it. The spot she selected had room for a footplate, but could not accommodate a headstone.

Candace sat down in front of Michael's computer and opened Microsoft Word to type the obituary notices to send to the newspapers. While she worked, Michael wandered in and out of the room. At one point, he stood by the French doors and looked out on the patio. He said something Candace could not comprehend. She got up and stood beside him and looked out at the swimming pool. She noticed that there was no furniture around it. She thought that was odd. It bothered her in a way she did not understand. She tried to put the puzzle pieces together, but a coherent image did not develop. She returned to the computer and finished Kathleen's obituary.

That same day, a search warrant was served at the funeral home. Because of the discovery of a discarded, used condom in the master bedroom, the investigators needed to conduct a search on Kathleen's body. They obtained samples of her head hair, pubic hair and bodily fluids—the same sampling often referred to as a "rape kit."

Kathleen's brother, Steve Hunt, his wife, Cynthia, and their three children drove to Durham and arrived late Tuesday. They had been to the Cedar Street home on a number of occasions, but tonight they got lost. They called the home and talked to a woman who answered the phone. She told them to look for the TV satellite trucks—they couldn't miss it. The revelation jolted the Hunts.

Candace took the phone and told her brother not to come to the house. She did not want his family seeing the blood. She sent them to the Washington Duke Inn.

Kathleen haunted Candace's sleep that night. Candace dreamed her sister approached her, grabbed her and shook her hard. All the while, Kathleen pleaded, "Don't put me in there. Don't put me in there."

On the morning of December 12, Candace woke up in a cold sweat, knowing that her sister wanted a headstone. She called the cemetery office and said that she was unhappy with the lot she purchased. She really wanted to honor her sister with a headstone. How could she do that?

She was told she would have to purchase four contiguous plots to have the space needed. But she needed to select a new location that day.

Candace's to-do list was growing to an alarming length. This was a job she needed to delegate. She went to see Caitlin, Margaret and Martha. She told them, "I know your mother wants a headstone. Please go pick a place where we can do that."

The girls agreed to assume that responsibility and set out for Maplewood. It was a difficult task for these young women, but they had each other. They found a lovely spot shaded by a large, ancient tree.

After talking to the girls, Candace went over to Cedar Street to tell Michael about what she had done. She sat down at the computer and opened Microsoft Word again. This time, she wrote notices about the viewing and the funeral services to hang on the outside doors of the home. An endless line of friends, neighbors and members of the press corps had been rapping on the doors asking for this information. If she posted it, she felt the family would be left in peace.

Sitting still at the computer, she soon got cold in the chilly old house. She asked Michael if he could turn up the heat or build a fire.

He snapped back, "I can either turn the heat on or buy four plots. I can't afford to do both."

Candace felt as if she had been slapped. She turned back to the work at hand, printing out the notices and posting them on the doors. That chore scratched off her list, she moved on to the most dreaded task of all, cleaning the back staircase. She could not put it off any longer. Her mother was coming that day, and Candace could not let her see it.

A tiny smile flitted across Candace's face as she remembered Kathleen—the queen of clean—telling her that bleach was the best thing. She recalled the intense pleasure Kathleen got when she power-washed the exterior of the house, and grinned. What a woman! For a brief moment, she felt as though her sister was still there by her side. Her burden lifted as memories of Kathleen's voice teased her ears.

She found the bleach, a mop and a scrub brush and was ready to take on the challenge. Before she could enter the stairwell, a photographer walked into the house. He set up extensive photographic equipment and lights.

"What is this all about?" she asked him. "Are you with the police?"

He told her he was not with the police, but would not tell her anything more. After an hour and a half, he packed up and was on his way. Candace again prepared to enter the stairway. This time, Michael stopped her. He told her not to clean the stairway; he was going to take care of it.

Michael had lawyered up with Kerry Sutton and Barry Winston within hours of Kathleen's death. Now, he raised the stakes. David Rudolf, a flamboyant, high-priced Chapel Hill attorney, was called onto the case. Rudolf placed a call to private investigator Ron Guerette, who asked that the scene be secured until his arrival on Friday. This information was relayed to Michael, but he did not share it with Candace. She had no knowledge that this was what he meant when he told her he would take care of the remnants of his wife in the stairwell.

Before she could insist to him that she could do the cleanup, two men dressed for work came into the home. At first glance, they looked like painters. Candace thought, "Good. A few coats of paint will cover it all up."

Until this moment, she had planned to have people back at the house for refreshments. What happened next made that impossible.

The workmen drilled holes into the doorframe and screwed a piece of plywood over the opening to the staircase. Candace was aghast. She ran to Bill. "Don't do this. Don't do this. Please, don't do this."

But her desperate pleas were ignored. No one commiserated with her. No one explained why. It was as if her sister was being entombed in a dark and lonely place and Candace was the only one who cared. Sickened, she left her sister's home and fled to the comfort of the Washington Duke.

8

The viewing for Kathleen was scheduled from 5 until 8 P.M. at the Howerton–Bryan Funeral Home on the evening of December 12. Fred Atwater was there, standing in the background, ready to help Caitlin in any way he could.

Kathleen lay in her coffin wearing a black dress and pearls—an elegant woman even in death. On her pillow was a simple gold cross on a chain. Clayton, at Candace's request, had purchased it at a jewelry store for his stepmother.

Next to Kathleen was a visitors' book waiting for entries. Earlier that day, Candace asked Michael to write a note on the front page. He inscribed: "The next book will be about love—requited love—and will be about you, of course. Love, Mike."

Standing on an easel, a collage of photographs of Kathleen—with Mike, with the five children and posing alone—greeted those who came to pay their last respects.

Mike was supposed to meet Candace at the viewing at 4:30 that afternoon. Steve and Cynthia were picking up Kathleen's mother, Veronica, along with the friend who traveled with her, at the airport. Mike had told Candace he would be at the funeral home to greet his mother-in-law.

Candace felt lost when people started to arrive. They were Kathleen and Michael's friends and she did not know them at all. Michael had promised her that he would be there.

But Michael Peterson apparently did not plan to attend his wife's viewing. He was at home in his underwear at 6 P.M. when seven members of the Durham Police Department arrived on his doorstep.

After discussions with the medical examiner and the district attorney, Investigator Art Holland reached the conclusion that there was more evidence in the house that needed to be seized. Bill Peterson answered his knock. Holland read the warrant to him.

Officers went upstairs to round up any people on the second floor. Michael Peterson was in his bedroom. "Do you mind?" he asked. "I am getting dressed to go see my dead wife in a coffin." Martha Ratliff was retrieved from another room and escorted downstairs. She left the house and went to the funeral home.

When the viewing was over, Candace clipped locks of Kathleen's hair and placed them in envelopes to preserve them for family members. She removed her pearls to give to Caitlin. She put the gold cross and a rose in her sister's cold hands. The lid of the casket was lowered.

By telephone, attorney Kerry Sutton advised her client, Michael Peterson, to remain in any room they were searching if he could. She attempted to enter the house herself, but was rebuffed by the police.

The search was completed at 8 P.M. Among the items seized were three computers, blood swabs from the kitchen couch, a copy of the *O. J. Simpson Notebook*, a hand grenade now serving as a paperweight—Mike's souvenir from Vietnam—and a document granting power of attorney to Todd and Clayton and allowing them to appoint another in their stead.

At 9:30 that night, Michael, Bill, Todd, Clayton, Margaret, Martha and Caitlin made a short pilgrimage to the funeral home. Michael told Caitlin that the Durham Police Department had it in for him. He warned her that things might get very ugly. The police, he told her, would concoct a story as outlandish as possible. He also made Caitlin aware of the condom found in his bedroom. He said that he thought the police might use it to say he and Kathleen had a perverted sex life and were having orgies in the house. Later, Todd told police that the condom belonged to one of his friends who had sex with a girl in Kathleen and Mike's bed.

The next day, Candace and Steven both had to be at the funeral home early. Cynthia stayed with her mother-in-law and her friend to wait in the lobby for Michael to arrive in the limo. When the car pulled up, Michael leaped out. Although he had made no attempt to contact Steve or Cynthia in the last two days, he now grabbed Cynthia's arm and spoke to her for the first time. "Where's Ronnie?" he asked, referring to his mother-in-law by her nickname.

Cynthia pointed to Veronica. Michael threw himself at her feet, laid his head in her lap and sobbed.

• • •

At 11 A.M. on Thursday, December 13, three hundred family members and friends of Kathleen Peterson walked the sidewalks, dampened from an overnight downpour, and entered the Duke University Chapel. They came to mourn the death of one taken so young, and to celebrate the life of one who had given so much. Kathleen's casket was flanked by an army of poinsettias placed in the chapel for the holiday season and buried in a mass of red, pink, yellow and white roses. Later, when Michael received the bill from the florist, he fired off a nasty email to Lori complaining about her extravagance.

Throughout the service, the Hunt and Peterson families sat at the front of the chapel. Fred Atwater sat in the back with his wife—inconspicuous, but available for Caitlin.

Candace distributed copies of "Ascension," a stirring poem she had first seen at the funeral of a neighbor's child who died of cancer. Candace believed, and the media reported, that Emily Dickinson was the author of the piece. This myth had followed the much-loved poem from funeral home to cemetery across the country. In actuality, Colleen Hitchcock, a suspense novelist, wrote it after her mother died of cancer.

Maureen Berry read a thank-you note written by her and four other friends of Kathleen. She called her the "48-hour-a-day" woman. "We love you," she said. "You will be missed. You lit up our lives. Now, Michael has lost a soulmate and we have gained an angel."

Flanked by Todd and Clayton Peterson and Margaret and Martha Ratliff, Caitlin Atwater remembered the lullabies her mother sang to her, and shared the advice her mother gave her: "Life is too important to waste a single moment." Fred's heart broke as he watched his child deliver the eulogy she should not have had to give for at least another thirty years.

After the service, as the pallbearers carried Kathleen's coffin from the chapel, Michael Peterson stood at the top of the steps holding the hand of his departed wife's mother, 81-year-old Veronica Hunt. He turned to her with tears in his eyes and wrapped an arm around her. "I've always called you by your first name, Veronica," he said. "But now may I call you Mom?"

By peculiar coincidence, Todd Peterson, who always called his stepmother Kathleen or nothing at all while she was alive, now referred to her exclusively as "Mom."

That same week, Ron Guerette, at David Rudolf's behest, arrived at 1810 Cedar Street to inspect and secure the scene. He unscrewed the plywood and examined the blood-spattered staircase. He installed a hinge and padlock at the top of the stairs. He screwed the plywood back in place and used a saw to cut three louvers at the top and bottom to allow airflow into and out of the cloistered space.

At the medical examiner's office, the neurological examination of Kathleen Peterson's brain tissue began. Dr. Thomas Bouldin first examined the *dura meninges*—the layer that provides direct support to the brain. It is located beneath the strong fibrous covering that connects to the skull.

Multiple sections of the brain were stained to enhance abnormalities. A microscopic examination revealed the presence of rare red neurons. This unusual condition was accompanied by early acute ischemic necrosis—or cell death—in both the cerebrum and the cerebellum.

These red neurons revealed an ugly truth about the death of Kathleen. Because of their existence, it was apparent that she did not die quickly—it took her two to four hours. She lay on the stairs all that time with the blood draining from her body. As she bled out, the blood flow to her brain decreased, depriving it of oxygen. Without this vital nutrient, a gradual process of death began. As her brain cells died, the red neurons were born. The process was slow. And it was widespread. The time it took the red neurons to develop provided plenty of opportunity for Michael Peterson to get help for his injured wife. Two to four hours was more than enough time for premeditation to exist.

9

On the sixth floor of the Durham County Courthouse, the results of the neurological analysis spurred Jim Hardin to make preparations to call a special grand jury. Superior Court Judge Ronald L. Stephens approved his request.

The grand jury convened at 9:48 A.M. on December 20, 2001. They heard testimony from three witnesses: Dr. Deborah Radisch, Agent Duane Deaver and Investigator Art Holland. At 2 P.M., they returned a true bill of indictment for first-degree murder against Michael Iver Peterson. "[. . .T]he defendant named above unlawfully, willfully and feloniously and of malice and aforethought, did kill and murder Kathleen Hunt Peterson."

Fifty minutes later, Michael Peterson got into his tan Jaguar and led a caravan of four other vehicles from his house into downtown Durham. In the parking lot across from the jail, he gathered his entourage around him: Todd, Clayton and Bill Peterson, Martha and Margaret Ratliff and Thomas Maher, David Rudolf's co-counsel on this case. The circus-loving defense team had, of course, alerted the media, and a grand gaggle of reporters with cameras and thrusting microphones greeted the somber troupe as it crossed the street and entered center stage.

Peterson paused before the press and proclaimed his innocence with all the drama of a tragic Shakespearean figure: "Kathleen was my life. I have whispered her name in my heart a thousand times. She is there and I can't stop crying." They were beautiful words, but they were stolen from Colleen Hitchcock's poem, "Ascension," and altered to suit his purposes. They lay like lead on his lips.

As Michael exited stage left, Thomas Maher told the gathered media that his client was the victim of overzealous prosecutors. "We're very disappointed, obviously, that he's been charged—particularly disappointed that the D.A. decided to rush something we don't think is warranted."

Mike disappeared inside the jail and sat down in the waiting area with his legs crossed—a Bible and a pair of tennis shoes beside him. Investigator Holland greeted the speechless, dazed defendant. Mike mumbled answers when necessary, but otherwise did not speak as Holland jotted down the everyday identifying characteristics of Peterson on the arrest report.

Holland escorted his charge into the detention area. Mike emptied his pockets on the counter, leaving $100 in cash to be logged into the ledger. Sergeant Vicky Menser checked the felony warrant to ensure all was in order and then processed the prisoner.

She rolled his fingers on an inkless plate that sat by the computer. It performed a laser scan that unfolded the prints on the monitor of the live scan computer as she progressed. The computer assigned a booking number to Michael Peterson.

The next step in the process was taking Mike's palm prints. These were done the old-fashioned way. Menser pushed the fingers of his hand back and applied ink on his palm. She pressed it onto the back of his felony card, applying enough force to flatten his hand on its surface.

She rolled his right thumb with ink and mashed it down into the supplemental sheet four times. Mike's booking photos were taken next. Three poses were shot as Mike called out his full legal name.

The new prisoner's money, herringbone jacket and pants were put into property bags. Mike now wore a regulation orange jumpsuit. In this sartorial splendor, Holland escorted him to the magistrate's office. There, they read the charges to him.

Michael Peterson, decorated Vietnam War veteran, accomplished novelist and political aspirant was locked behind bars. All he had to keep him company were his Bible, his tennis shoes and his memories of December 9, 2001.

MICHAEL PETERSON

"Somewhere along the line, short going of 22 years, I've forgotten about individual responsibility—integrity. I'd like to think that I knew it once."

—Michael Peterson, 1965

10

Eugene Iver Peterson spent his early years in Golconda, Nevada, just sixteen miles east of Winnemucca. It is a desolate area where mining is the predominant industry. He was raised on a ranch that was both a resort for travelers seeking a true Western experience, and a working cattle business. He was home-schooled through his early grade school years, since there were no schools nearby.

Then the Depression crashed down on his family— they lost it all and moved to Reno when Eugene was in the third grade. The next move took them to a home in the Marina district of San Francisco. Eugene went to Galileo High School, where he excelled in tennis. He won the state championship and was ranked fourteenth among all high school players in the country.

After his graduation, the family moved back to Reno. Eugene continued to play tennis as a student at the University of Nevada, where he graduated with a degree in agriculture.

In Reno, his mother made friends with another woman, and the two conspired to bring their children together. This matchmaking resulted in the wedding of Eugene Peterson and Eleanor Bartalino.

Soon after the vows were spoken, Eugene joined the Army in the middle of World War II. His wife gave birth to their first child, Michael Iver Peterson, on October 23, 1943. It was a difficult childbirth. Eleanor developed an infection that kept her in the hospital for a week.

A month later, Eugene was shipped overseas. He landed on the beaches of northern France eight days after D-Day. While he was off defending his country and the world from Adolf Hitler and his Nazis, Eleanor packed up her baby and moved in with her sisters for the duration of the war.

Eugene returned from the war and re-enlisted in 1945. His career with the Army spanned thirty years before he retired.

He was stationed in Occupied Japan with his wife and child. It was during these years that the event occurred that gave birth to Mike's later claim that he was kidnapped and baptized in a Shinto shrine. The truth of the matter was a bit more pedestrian. With Japan under occupation and its economy in shambles, Army families were encouraged to hire as many locals as possible to work around the house. One of these maids took the young Michael to the shrine and had him blessed.

The family was stationed in Washington State when their next child, William Eugene "Bill" Peterson, was born on July 31, 1947. The foursome then spent another tour of duty in Japan.

When Eugene was transferred back to the States, he was stationed at Fort McPherson in Atlanta, Georgia. On May 11, 1951, their son John James "Jack" Peterson was born. Then on February 25, 1953, they finally had a daughter, Ann Ellen Peterson. After a decade of child-bearing, their family was complete.

Eleanor, half-Italian and half-Welsh, was staunchly Catholic. Eugene had converted to Catholicism when they married. The children were all raised in the Church. Michael spent part of his youth as an altar boy.

Throughout the years, the family lived the nomad existence so typical of military families. Eleanor created homes for her brood in Japan, Georgia, Kansas, San Francisco, Virginia, Pennsylvania, North Carolina and Copenhagen, Denmark.

As in most larger families, the siblings paired up. Mike and Bill formed close bonds and shared a bedroom in every place they lived. Jack and Ann, less than two years apart in age, developed a tight relationship despite their gender differences.

The two shared an adoration of their older brothers. Mike became a hero in their eyes when he was a student at rough-and-tumble Balboa High School in San Francisco and stood up to a bunch of bullies at a swimming pool.

His father was re-stationed on the East Coast and Mike graduated from Hampton High School in Virginia. Jack and Ann were excited and bereft when Mike left their home at Fort Monroe, Virginia, and went off to Duke University.

Michael Peterson was an active member of the student body at Duke. In his freshman and sophomore years, he joined the Air Force ROTC and a legal group called Bench and Bar. He was a representative of the Student

Union and on the staff of *The Chronicle*, the university newspaper. In his sophomore year, he became involved in the campus YMCA.

He continued his service with student politics and the newspaper in his junior year and added other activities— the debate team and the Publication Board, a group with oversight responsibilities for the newspaper, the annual yearbook and *The Archive*, a campus magazine.

In his senior year, he was the editor of *The Chronicle* and the president of Sigma Nu, and sat on the Inter-Fraternity Council and the Council of Presidents. He also was chosen for a much-coveted membership in the Order of the Red Friars.

This organization was a secret men's society founded in 1913 by senior class members of Trinity College. In 1924, Trinity became the undergraduate school of Duke University.

The original mission of the order was to promote the social spirit at the school. That purpose evolved through the years to one of fostering loyalty to and interest in the university through anonymous service in student organizations.

Each year's group consisted of seven men. These students were responsible for selecting the juniors who would take their places. Character, scholarship, qualities of and potential for leadership and outstanding service to the university were the criteria for selection.

The new seven were announced at a tapping ceremony in the late spring. A red-hooded figure stood on the steps of Duke Chapel and tapped the backs of the new initiates while the gathered crowd of hoi polloi and hopefuls looked on.

The seven, on occasion, selected honorary members of their secret society. Richard M. Nixon is reported to have been one of these when he attended law school at Duke.

Most of the activities of the club were closely held secrets. It was known, however, that they founded the Order of the White Duchy, the female counterpart of their organization. In the early years, the Red Friars selected the seven women each spring. Soon, the organizations split this connection and the co-eds selected their own members for the order. Elizabeth Dole is one of the best known members of this group.

Both organizations shared a similar tradition. Once a month, members of the Red Friars wore a red carnation. Those in the White Duchy wore a white carnation.

Although both organizations voluntarily disbanded in the early 1970s, the alumni quietly continued their connections and traditions. Elizabeth Dole received a gift of six white carnations when she was named the Secretary of Transportation in 1983. One day during his trial, Michael Peterson sat in the Durham County Courthouse with a red carnation in his lapel. He would offer no explanation to anyone for this affectation that day.

Michael graduated in 1965 with a major in Political Science. He would return to Duke in a few years, but the events of the intervening hiatus would leave an indelible mark.

11

While still in school, Mike paid an important visit to his family, who were then based at the U.S. Army War College at historic Carlisle Barracks about thirty miles west of Harrisburg, Pennsylvania. It was there, at a social gathering, that he encountered another Army brat, Patricia Bateman. She, too, was visiting her parents on a break from her school, the University of Texas in Austin. A romantic attachment developed and a long-distance relationship began.

After graduation from Duke, Michael Peterson entered law school at the University of North Carolina at Chapel Hill. It was an unpleasant and disruptive sojourn. He railed against the university's ban on speakers who had claimed their Fifth Amendment rights as protection in congressional hearings.

He created another flock of enemies when he assisted a law professor in his defense of a gay man charged with sodomy in a highly publicized case in Charlotte. He left school before completing the first year.

For a brief time, he returned to Reno, lived with his Uncle Jimmy Bartalino and earned a living doing roadwork. Then a job offer came from Washington, D.C.

A year earlier, the Pentagon had sent the first ground troops to Vietnam. The incursion provided new and profitable work for defense consultants and they were all in a hiring mode. One company hired Peterson as a systems science analyst.

Before that job started, he headed back east and made wedding arrangements with Patty Bateman. Mike's family was delighted. They had all fallen in love with the sweet girl Mike had chosen to be his wife. In 1966, the couple was married in a ceremony at Fort Belvoir Proving Ground, in Northern Virginia, just minutes from Mount Vernon, Old Town Alexandria and the nation's capital.

Soon after starting his new job with the defense consultant, Michael was sent to Vietnam. There, he was assigned to conduct a study to determine whether or not two or more mechanized divisions could win the war. The catch was that the truth was irrelevant. His superiors made it clear: They wanted him to return with convincing arguments to send in these divisions even if the evidence pointed to the contrary.

Peterson did what he was told, but the experience had added an extra edge of cynicism to his innate combative nature. There were other things about the experience that disgusted him. He witnessed illegal currency dealings by a colleague. He saw first-hand that the daily reports of those killed in action did not match up with the reports delivered to the public by the media back home.

His disgust, however, did not quench his desire to become a writer. Within the shadows of lies, the fever of battle and the corruption so common in this convoluted country, he saw rich fodder for fiction. He decided he wanted to write the great American novel about the war;

but first, like Hemingway before him, he needed to fight in the war.

It took some finesse and deception to make that happen. The Selective Service System had classified him as 4F—chronic pain in his leg made him unfit to serve. Somehow, Peterson managed to tamper with his records and eliminate that information. In 1968, he enlisted in the U.S. Marine Corps. After boot camp, the Marines granted his wish—he was deployed to Vietnam.

Patty moved in with Mike's family, who were now stationed in Copenhagen. Patty thought she would be able to get a job there, but it was not to be. She did, eventually, find a teaching position at Hahn Air Force Base in Hahn, West Germany, along the Mosel River and close to the border with Luxembourg. It was considered to have the worst weather of any air base in Europe, with long winters, short summers and lots of rain and snow. Hahn played a pivotal role in the cold war with the Soviet Union as the base for a tactical wing, the 50th Air Police K-9 section.

It was here that Patty met Pat Finn. Pat was on her first teaching assignment with the Department of Defense and knew no one. She was taken with Patty from the start because of Patty's friendly, welcoming manner and her very sweet personality.

Ironically, Mike Peterson was against the war and quite vocal about it. Patty was anti-war, too. She was out leading protests against the conflict while her husband submerged himself in the dark forbidding landscape of an alien country that reeked of death.

12

Early in 1969, Lieutenant Mike Peterson arrived in Vietnam with the eagerness and self-confidence only a man inexperienced in combat could possess. He was assigned to the First Amphibious Tractor Battalion headquartered on the Gulf of Tonkin at the mouth of the Cue Viet River.

In previous military action, these amphibious tractors, "amtracs," transported men and supplies from ship to shore. Marines in this war used them as patrol vehicles. The leathernecks attached to these vehicles called themselves "amgrunts."

Peterson headed north from the main headquarters past the small base of C-4, to Oceanview, the northernmost post in South Vietnam. This area of sand dunes circled by concertina wire was perched on the edge of the demilitarized zone and ripe for attacks by the North Vietnamese Army.

The inexperienced fighter was the ranking officer in command of about thirty men—the amtrac platoon, a mortar crew, spotters who called in missile strikes to the battleships out in the gulf, and a four-man Army team responsible for the dusters, the twin 40mm machine guns.

At first, the men saw Mike Peterson and his gung-ho 110-percent attitude as a joke. Humor was traded for resentment when he volunteered them for extra patrols—extra patrols meant extra risks. Lieutenant Peterson soon settled down in his command, earning more trust and respect from his subordinates than many other men in his position.

They found it difficult to sit down and have an ordinary conversation with him, though. He always seemed to have something going on in his head, as if he were analyzing every word they spoke.

On February 21, the amgrunts performed a public relations function with the local populace. They went into the nearest village and distributed toys to the children in honor of the Tet holiday, the annual New Year's celebration in Vietnam.

When darkness fell on February 22, a small patrol unit went across the wire to hunt for NVA sappers, men who attempted to slip inside the base loaded down with explosives. The group Peterson dispatched on that duty included Marlo Kinsey, Vernon Strickland, Winfield Page and his radio operator, Jack Peterson, a 19-year-old boy from Wisconsin—the two Petersons were not related.

The patrol beyond the wire assumed their positions in an L-shaped ambush position. Marines behind the line stared through starlight scopes, the night vision devices that used moonlight and other ambient illumination to enhance visibility in the dark of the night.

Enemy troops were spotted in the distance. On the radio, Peterson ordered the patrol to maintain their post. Then, ground radar indicated the movement of a larger number of NVA troops. Peterson ordered the men to retreat to a new position, just one hundred meters from the wire, and sit tight.

At 11 P.M., a Marine on a scope cried out a warning. Peterson peered through the green haze of the lens. What he saw created explosions of anxiety inside his head—twenty-five soldiers descending on his four-man patrol. "Run, now, as fast as you can. Run back to the wire."

They tried to retreat but were confused. They did not know which direction they should run. They lay on their backs staring at the sky, looking for a point of reference. When they saw a light on a tank flash, they determined the location of the other men and headed for it.

Sounds of movement encircled them—they were surrounded by NVA. Fortunately, the enemy soldiers were unaware of the Marines in their midst. Any noise the men made, the NVA attributed to their own troops.

Page and Kinsey paired up and moved toward the wire. Caught between NVA and Marines, they were hit in the crossfire. Kinsey, suffering from a concussion, lacerations and a nosebleed, lost consciousness. When he came to, Page had one arm wrapped around Kinsey's shoulder—but Page was dead.

Jack Peterson was wounded and moaning. Kinsey and Strickland dragged him through the wire. Jack complained about his legs, but seemed unaware of other more severe injuries. He died within a few minutes.

Kinsey was put on a stretcher and given a couple of shots. The medics wanted to send him to the rear, but a helicopter could not land in the midst of all the fire ringing out on both sides.

Lieutenant Michael Peterson approached Kinsey and asked, "What's going on?"

Kinsey jumped to his feet. "You dumb mother—you guys shot at us."

"Where's Page?"

"I'm two hundred percent sure Page is dead," Kinsey answered, "and your men shot him."

"I don't believe it."

"If you don't believe it, then go out there and see for yourself."

Peterson froze in place—his face expressionless—his mind numb. He needed to take charge of the situation, but he just stared into space.

"Winters!" Kinsey yelled. "Give Peterson a slap."

Dale Winters hauled back and delivered two hard hits to the lieutenant. Just like in the cartoons, the punches pulled Peterson back from the abyss. He yelled questions at his men, answered calls from division headquarters, called in air strikes and called for support. He rose to the challenge of leadership under pressure like an orchestra conductor pulling together the sounds of individual instruments into one harmonious whole.

Waves of enemy troops crashed down on the outpost. Between 100 and 300 North Vietnamese soldiers peppered the small contingent with rifle fire and mortar shells. When Kinsey heard the enemy inside the line, he got up from his stretcher for good. He was determined not to die flat on his back.

A sapper set off a trip flare when he slithered into the outpost. He was greeted with a shower of gunfire. Before he died, he heaved a grenade into the command bunker. But it was not Mike Peterson's day to die. The pin had not been pulled and the weapon fell impotent at his feet.

Peterson shrieked into the radio for reinforcements. His request was denied. At C-4 base, they wanted to help, but without a cessation of protective artillery fire, there was no safe way to get additional forces to the battlefield.

Six hours after it began, just before dawn, the enemy withdrew. Outnumbered and isolated, the men had defended their position throughout a terrifying night. The only American casualties that night were the Marines shot by their own men as they scrambled for the wire.

Kinsey, Strickland, and two others were medevaced out with the bodies of Jack Peterson and Winfield Page. Strickland and Kinsey returned to their platoon that night.

The base at Oceanview had not been singled out for this conflict. All across South Vietnam, bases were attacked on February 22, 1969. The second Tet offensive had begun.

Michael Peterson emerged from that night with a Silver Star for gallantry in battle, a souvenir grenade that failed to end his life and the haunting memory of his radio dispatcher dying before his eyes.

After leaving Vietnam, Mike was stationed at Atsugi Naval Air Base in Japan for his remaining time in the Marines. Patty joined him there. One evening, they invited Mike's friend Sergeant Beverly over for dinner. Afterwards, Mike drove him home.

On the way there, a truck slammed into the side of the

car killing Beverly. Mike was pinned in the vehicle, but was still alive. It took thirty minutes to extract him from the car as his friend lay by his side. Mike was rushed to Camp Zama where many Vietnam war injured were treated. He had a collapsed lung and a shattered leg. Despite the experience and expertise of the doctors who put his leg back together, Mike walked with a limp from that day on.

Mike and Patty left Japan and flew to Camp Pendleton, near San Diego. He and Patty looked up Marlo Kinsey. They invited him and another Marine to their house for Thanksgiving dinner.

It was during that visit that Kinsey first learned of Peterson's ambition to be an author. In the mezzanine area of their quarters, Mike had a study dedicated to his writing. On the walls were pictures from Vietnam. Kinsey found the photographs of the bodies of dead Viet Cong very disturbing.

After Mike received an honorable discharge and a permanent medical disability, Patty landed a teaching job at Giessen Elementary School in Germany, enabling the couple to move back overseas. It was a déjà vu time for Patty. She had lived in Giessen as a child when her father was stationed there right after World War II. She was impacted by the senseless destruction she saw first-hand in post-war Germany.

The couple made a trip to Hahn to visit Pat Finn. It was on this trip that Pat met Mike for the first time. Both Pat and Patty were enamored of the idyllic life in the small country villages—quiet, orderly places that moved at a much slower pace than life in the States—so much so that Pat, who had come to Germany for one year, ended up staying for thirty-two.

Each little village had its own flea market and every Saturday, they could stock up on fresh produce from the fruit and vegetable market.

In addition to a mutual love of the lifestyle small German towns offered, Pat and Patty shared an interest in cultural events and travel. Although Michael accompanied them to concerts and performances, he referred to the two woman as the "camp followers of the arts."

Mike and Patty then moved to Durham, North Carolina, where Mike enrolled again at Duke University for the 72–73 school year—this time under the GI Bill. While Mike prepared to step into the writing life, Patty taught school. They moved back and forth from Durham to Germany. Patty's next teaching position was at Rhein Main Elementary School near Frankfurt; Patty Peterson met the teacher across the hall, Liz McKee. The two became fast friends.

The Petersons had settled in Germany when their first son was born after thirty hours of labor on December 13, 1974. That night, a snowstorm caused an electrical outage. Clayton Sumner Peterson entered the world with the help of a doctor holding a flashlight to guide the way.

In half a year, Patty was pregnant again. This time she was in labor for eighteen hours before giving birth to their second son, Todd, on March 14, 1976. On a trip back to the States to visit Michael's parents, both boys were baptized in one service in Atlanta, Georgia. Richard White Adams, one of Mike's English professors at Duke, served as godfather to both Clayton and Todd. Liz

Ratliff was godmother to Clayton. Pat Finn was Todd's godmother.

Patty often tried Pat's patience. She always put the pre-departure care of her boys off until the last minute. This caused them to stumble in late to many events. After attempts to get her friend to change her habits failed, Pat told the couple that events started a half hour earlier than they actually did, and then they were all able to arrive on time to be seated and ready for the show to begin.

When Pat visited, Patty—who liked to go to bed early—would tuck in her children and then turn in herself. Pat sat up for hours talking with Michael. He often spoke of Patty's friend, Liz McKee. He said she was scatter-brained and nervous. He told Pat, "She is not like you—she has no sense when it comes to managing money."

Pat thought Michael was a very intellectual and interesting man, whose story-telling skills were extraordinary. Pat enjoyed seeing Michael with his boys. When they were young, he was very gentle with them. He was not, however, always gentle with his wife. As a house-husband, Mike had responsibility for a lot of chores around their home. He often neglected them and left the house in a perpetual state of chaos. If Patty spoke of it, he blew up.

Patty often hinted that Mike was not always nice to her. Nonetheless, she made never-ending apologies and excuses for his boorish behavior. Pat also noticed that her friend "walked on eggs" around her husband at all times.

Mike and Patty traveled to an extent that would make a

nomad ache with envy. They vacationed in the Azores, a jewel-like string of islands far off the coast of Portugal. Every Thanksgiving, the Petersons traveled to Copenhagen. Each Christmas, they attended the Christmas Fair in Nuremberg.

Pat Finn traveled with them on many excursions, including trips to Copenhagen, Vienna, Strasbourg, Venice and Lago di Garda—a beautiful lake area of natural, dramatic beauty, surrounded with medieval architecture and nestled in the Italian Alps. Pat and Patty were very close and enjoyed each other's company. In time, Michael Peterson would shred their relationship into tattered memories.

ELIZABETH McKEE RATLIFF

"The woods are lovely, dark and deep.
But I have promises to keep
And miles to go before I sleep."

—Robert Frost, "Stopping By Woods
On a Snowy Evening,"
One of Liz Ratliff's favorite poems

13

Elizabeth Ann McKee was born on November 3, 1942—the first child of Elizabeth and Harold McKee of Cumberland, Rhode Island. Her parents called her Betty Ann.

A Royal Decree in 1746 established the town of Cumberland, in the northeast corner of the state. Its early industrial growth was spurred by the abundant water power of the Blackstone and Abbot Run Rivers.

Betty Ann grew up in the lush green rural outskirts of this town, off a dirt road, in a home that was more than a hundred years old. From the house, she could see the Convent of the Religious Sisters of Mercy, an order of teachers and nurses, high on the hill. Every day at noon, their bells rang out through the community and all paused for a moment of prayer. In this idyllic setting, only one incident marred Betty Ann's early years: a serious bout of pneumonia that threatened to take her life.

By the time Betty Ann started her formal education at the Mercy Mount Country Day School, she had two sisters: Rosemary and Margaret. To Margaret, four years younger, Betty Ann was the object of endless hero worship.

Margaret looked up to her big sister in awe, anxious to be old enough to do all that she could do.

It was a loving and very Catholic family. They all went to confession on Saturday and services on Sunday at St. John Vianney, their parish church. It was housed in a historic building on Old Boston Post Road. In a previous life, the structure served as a tavern where travelers stopped for refreshment on their way to Boston.

Easter was a special day in the McKee home. Beforehand, the family dressed in nice clothes, as many did for shopping in that era, and traveled to Woonsocket to buy new dresses, hats, gloves and shoes for the special day. When the big morning arrived, Elizabeth prepared them for the service one girl at a time, starting with her youngest, Margaret. She tied each head of hair with rags to create the long, fat sausage curls so popular on little ones at the time, and dressed them in their new outfits.

One Easter, she had groomed her two youngest girls to perfection and waited on Betty Ann to finish her bath in the tub. Rosemary, the middle child, came into the bathroom to see her older sister. Somehow, she managed to tumble head first into the soapy water. She emerged with a wet dress, a soggy hat and her former curls hanging like dishrags on her head. Mom did double duty at top speed to make up for lost time. The family barely squeaked into church before the services began.

Christmas was celebrated with family togetherness, religious observance and exuberant glee. There were not a lot of presents, but each one was selected with care and deemed by the sisters to be perfect. And always, there were beautiful dolls from the nuns decked out in elaborate crocheted outfits.

All five members of the family made an excursion a couple of days before Christmas each year to shop for the tree. As soon as they were home, the decoration began. One year, the group trekked out into the woods, where Harold chopped down a tree and lugged it back home. It was a twisted, *Charlie Brown Christmas* kind of tree, but the girls loved it just the same.

Christmas morning, the first one to wake up would rouse her sisters. Betty Ann, Rosemary and Margaret tip-toed down to the tree and gazed at it and the packages beneath its branches. They tried to contain their excitement, but it bubbled out of them like soda from an agitated can. Full of unabated anticipation, they raced to their parents' bedroom, where they begged and pleaded until Elizabeth and Harold relented and got out of bed.

Later, the family would travel up a winding road on a steep hill to visit with the Provincial Sisters at their convent to thank them for their dolls. After a polite social interval, they would troop into the chapel and give their thanks to God. It was a pleasant annual ritual, but the young girls were always eager to complete the pilgrimage and go back home to play with their toys.

In addition to the fun of Christmas, the winter season brought massive quantities of snow to New England. The drifts were so high, the girls could burrow caves in their depths and build impregnable forts where they crawled and climbed for hours.

The girls all enjoyed ice-skating on the nearby pond. But best of all, they loved it when their dad pulled out the toboggan and took them all for a ride. They wedged on, one behind the other and soared down one hill, up another, then down the second hill and back to the house. Always the little voices demanded another hair-raising descent. They never wanted to go back inside.

When they were finally coaxed in from their winter wonderland, they piled their rubber boots by the door and laid their sopping wet mittens on the radiator. Soon, the air was filled with the peculiar earthy smell of wool overheating as it dried.

Unlike little Margaret, who was content to roam the hills with just her dog for company, Betty Ann craved the companionship of others. A constant stream of her friends flowed through the doors of the McKee home. Her younger sisters remembered many rides in the car to deliver Betty Ann to friends who lived twenty or thirty minutes away.

Betty Ann kicked off her teenage years in her typical gregarious fashion—with a Halloween party planned with elaborate care. In the dark basement of their old home, candles flickered in corners. The gaggle of giggling, screaming children grabbed hold of the ropes strung downstairs to guide them through the murky labyrinth. They stopped at stations set up along the way, where a gruesome story spilled out one body part at a time.

They felt the bowl of eyeballs—in actuality a bunch of peeled grapes. They held the severed hand—a rubber glove filled with Jell-O. And stuck their hands deep into the bowl of brains—a container of cold spaghetti. It was a delightful and spooky night filled with mock horror.

After the squeals subsided, Father John Randall, the priest at the Novitiate, judged the costumes. Margaret, disguised as a fairy princess, won first place.

When she entered her teens, Betty Ann developed a

real love for automobiles and the freedom they represented. Her father, who sold Ford cars for the National Motor Company in Woonsocket, often thrilled her by driving home new models. If he came to the house with a convertible, Betty Ann insisted on a photo session as she posed beside the car and behind the wheel.

A natural love for children led Betty Ann into a lucrative baby-sitting business—at fifty cents an hour, she was not getting rich, but it did provide the spending money a teenager always craved. She did so well caring for the kids that some of her clientele would cancel their plans for the evening if they found out she was not available.

Often, she baby-sat the two sons, Peter and Bob Farrelly, of a doctor and his wife. These two brothers grew up to write and direct hysterical Hollywood hits like *Kingpin*, *Dumb and Dumber* and *Something About Mary*.

Betty Ann's high level of creativity screamed for expression. Everyone who crossed her path became the subject of one of her charcoal sketches. Her musical talent was astonishing. She started piano lessons at an early age on the family's upright piano. For her 16th birthday, her parents gave her a baby grand. Any song she ever heard she could repeat with ease and grace.

But her musical skill did not stop with the piano. Throughout her life, she had the ability to master any instrument that came her way. She often played the organ for benediction on Monday nights at the parish church. She loved sitting on her stool, singing folk songs as she accompanied herself on her Martin guitar. Her favorite pieces were the ones she had heard Joan Baez sing. She played at many gigs on campuses and in coffee shops during and after college.

Throughout her teenage years, a yearning grew inside of Betty Ann. Like George Bailey of *It's a Wonderful Life*, she was consumed by a passion to travel to foreign lands, to learn the cultures of different people, to escape from "the sticks." Although many found contentment in such a peaceful, pastoral childhood in New England, to Betty Ann the tranquility was like a prison.

Nonetheless, she dutifully attended nearby Salve Regina College, the college by the sea, in Newport, Rhode Island. The school was chartered by the State of Rhode Island in 1934 and founded as an institution by the Sisters of Mercy. Established as an independent school in the Catholic tradition of education, this co-ed college did not begin to accept students until 1947 when it acquired Ochre Court, a limestone French Flamboyant Gothic palace. The first class of fifty-eight students attended all their classes in this mansion with its high roofs, turrets and whimsical gargoyles. The opulent building now houses the school's administrative offices.

When she entered the school in 1960, the enrollment at the college was less than five hundred. She had left "Betty Ann" at home. She introduced herself as Liz McKee to all of her new friends.

14

After college, Liz landed her first teaching job at Croton-on-Hudson in Westchester County, thirty miles north of New York City. This picturesque and historic village nestled on eight miles of Hudson River shoreline. It was a new and different place, a beautiful location with river gorge views that took her breath away. But still, for Liz, it was life in "the sticks." She yearned for someplace more exotic and was active in her pursuit of her dream to see the world.

Finally, she got her wish. The Department of Defense (DOD) hired her as a teacher in Sapporo, Japan's northernmost island. While there, she thrilled at the exotic musical instruments of the Far East. In no time, she mastered them as if they had always been a part of her life.

Another delight in this far-flung land was the Sapporo Snow and Ice Festival. This event began quite simply in 1950 when six statues were fashioned by a couple of high school students. By 1955, the U.S. military had joined in the festivities when members of Sapporo's defense force built the first megalithic snow statue.

By the time Liz arrived on the island, the festival had

evolved into an international event of carved and sculpted ice masterpieces that were lit up at night with colored lights. Today, hundreds of statues, some as large as a house, are showcased at the event, including ice renditions of the Statue of Liberty, the Great Wall of China and the pyramids of Egypt. The exhibition drew more than two million visitors to Sapporo every February.

In 1968, Liz was ready to travel on and the Department of Defense was prepared to accommodate her. Fluent in French and German, she was a valuable asset as a teacher of children in military families. They offered her a new teaching position in Germany.

Between her teaching, her folk singing, traveling and a growing battalion of friends, Liz's life in Europe was full. She became close friends with another teacher, Patty Peterson. Patty's family of four lived on her teacher's salary while Mike worked on building a career as a writer. Liz wrote home to her sister Margaret asking her to send hand-me-down clothing for the two Peterson boys. Margaret was delighted to help Liz's friends. Liz always remembered her children's birthdays with a card and a beautiful book. It was the least she could do.

There was only one thing missing and it came walking into her life in the form of a tall Texan. Liz met George Ratliff, an Air Force navigator, in a stereotypical rendezvous point for a DOD teacher, at the Officer's Club.

George Ratliff was All-state in football at Van Vleck High School in Texas. He graduated in 1968 and followed in his father's footsteps to Texas A&M University as a member of the Corps of Cadets. He majored in Industrial Technology and was a member of the G-2 company of Second Brigade.

A year later, another second generation Aggie, Randy Durham, joined the same company. He was the first one in the Corps to major in Philosophy. Despite their seemingly incompatible majors, George and Randy hit it off well—even selling encyclopedias together one summer.

Both cadets were in Army ROTC, but wanted to join the Air Force when they graduated. For Randy, that transition was easy. His dad was career Air Force and that gave him the option of transferring his commitment.

Transferring was not so easy for George. He had to bust his Army contract when he approached graduation. At times, the Army held tight to those agreements. But now, with the Vietnam War winding down, the Army was downsizing as quickly as it could. They let his contract slide and George enlisted in the Air Force.

By going this route, it took George longer to get where he wanted to go. He took basic training at technical school and followed that up with another basic training at Officers Training School. Then he was accepted to the Officers Commission program and sent off for navigator's training, where he reunited with Randy Durham, who had graduated a year after he did.

In the interim, George had married and divorced the sister of one of his classmates. The marriage lasted two years on paper, but in reality the couple was together only a handful of months.

George and Randy were both assigned to C-130s at Dyess Air Force Base in Abilene, Texas. After a couple of years there, an opportunity arose and George snatched it up.

Rhein Main Air Force base near Frankfurt, Germany,

had, until now, only temporary assignments or rotations for C-130 squadrons. The decision was made to station a permanent squadron there. George put in for the first cadre and resituated in Germany in 1978.

There he met Liz McKee, an artistic soul with a personality well suited for her job as an elementary school teacher. She was gentle with the children and the well of her patience was bottomless. George was enchanted.

By the time Randy came to Rhein Main in 1980, the two were an item. Liz was spending more time at George's loft apartment than she was at her own. They lived in Klein–Gerau, the same village as Randy and his wife, Carol Durham—they were the only two American couples living there.

Both men were members of the Blue Tail Flies, a squadron of C-130s with AWADS (Adverse Weather Aerial Delivery System) capability, which enabled their craft to operate in nasty weather. They delivered cargo and personnel and performed other missions all over Europe including down the Berlin Corridor. They were often gone for days at a time.

Before George and Liz married, they made a trip back to the States to meet each other's families. Liz's relatives were enchanted with George. Her nephew, Damon Blair, named all of his stuffed animals and superhero figures "George" after meeting his uncle-to-be.

Liz was getting close to the dreaded 40th birthday, and although George was seven years younger, time for starting a family was running out. The couple was ready to begin.

Liz selected her wedding site with care. She chose a
spot steeped in history, the Römer city hall, a complex
of three patrician buildings with an ornate balcony and a
crusty Gothic façade. The medieval surroundings lent
the civil ceremony a solemn air of gravity. The gods
must have smiled on their nuptials, because the early
May day was glorious.

This was one of the first warm days of the year—
unusually beautiful for Germany in the spring. Five
Americans were present when the couple made their
commitment: George and Liz, maid of honor Patty
Peterson, best man Randy Durham and George's mother,
Martha, who traveled to Germany from Cedar Lane,
Texas, for the occasion.

That evening, the newlyweds had a reception to
celebrate. All five members of the wedding party were
there. Randy's wife Carol, Patty's husband Michael, and
a few other close friends joined them.

Liz and George moved from the loft apartment—
which was little more than glorified attic space—down
to the second floor. This apartment had a balcony with a
breathtaking view across the fields to the neighboring
village of Gross–Gerau, one mile away.

Since Liz's first child was due in December, she took
a sabbatical from her teaching job. She opened a private
pre-school in her home. Her first student was Randy and
Carol's son, Jonathan.

Liz had a difficult pregnancy. So-called morning
sickness plagued her day and night throughout her
childbearing. A great fear lurked in the back of her mind.
Like her father and both of her sisters, Liz had von

Willebrand's disease, a blood disorder. It is believed to be the most common genetic disorder in the world—one hundred times more prevalent than hemophilia. It is thought to affect one in every forty people.

The main symptom is excessive bleeding—like recurrent nose bleeds or bleeding from the gums. The severity of the disease varies from person to person even within a family. People with milder cases experience nothing more than prolonged or easy bruising, a symptom that can be explained away or ignored. Moderate cases display unusual bleeding. In women, this is most noticeable in excessive menstrual flow, which is often misdiagnosed. It is unknown how many women have undergone unnecessary hysterectomies because of medical personnel overlooking the possibility of von Willebrand's disease.

Those with an extreme shortage or total lack of von Willebrand's factor in their blood have the most extreme form of the disease. They can experience spontaneous hemorrhages in major joints such as knees and shoulders. If undiagnosed and untreated, these severe cases pose a serious health risk as well as mental and emotional difficulties. Fortunately, Liz's fear of the worst case scenario was groundless—her condition was mild, and thus caused no complications during childbirth.

Like many military wives before her, Liz found herself alone when she went into labor. Her husband, George, was away on a mission. Cheryl Appel, who was living with the couple on a temporary basis, was at Rhein Main Elementary School teaching her class. Liz drove herself to the hospital in Wiesbaden, where the nurse on duty was

Randy's wife, Carol. On December 10, 1981, her first daughter, Margaret Elisabeth, was born.

George and Liz celebrated their first anniversary in grand style. They rounded up a group of friends and headed north of Frankfurt to the foothills of the Taunus Mountains and Schlosshotel in Kronberg.

The Empress Frederick, the oldest child of Queen Victoria of England, built this house from 1889–1894 following the death of her husband. She lived there for seven years after its completion. The castle still housed many of her books in English, including a fifty-year collection of bound *Pick's* magazines.

Magnificent grounds with rhododendron, an Italian rose garden and a romantic grotto surrounded the castle. Each of the fifty-eight antique-filled rooms has its own individual character and style. Some feature paintings executed by the Empress.

During World War II, the castle was commandeered by U.S. troops for senior officer headquarters. It was a favorite spot for General Dwight Eisenhower.

George, Liz and their friends celebrated with a champagne party and endless toasts to the blissful couple. Their friends returned to Frankfurt, but George and Liz stayed for the weekend. They slept in a royal bed in a corner suite with a romantic balcony overlooking the elegant, manicured back garden.

Thirteen months after their first daughter was born, along came Martha Katalin on January 3, 1982, named after George's mother. This time, George was on assignment in the States. Both Liz and George doted on the girls and made them the center of their lives.

. . .

George's tour of duty was about to end, but he and Liz wanted to stay in Germany. He extended his service in the 7405th Operations Squadron, a classified missions unit. Theirs was a happy, complete home until 1983.

MICHAEL PETERSON

"I think desire is not such a bad thing."

–Michael Peterson, *The Immortal Dragon*, 1983

15

In June 1981, Michael's sister, Ann, and her husband, John Christensen, flew off to Gräfenhausen, Germany, for a fourteen-month stay with Michael and Patty. From there, they made excursions all over Europe.

Ann had an opportunity to bond with her oldest brother in a way that had not seemed possible with their age difference as children. She also met and built a nice friendship with Liz. Ann liked and admired Liz and it surprised her that her brother never said anything good about her. In fact, he said she was crazy. He also said Patty was crazy, so Ann just let it slide.

The Christensens noticed that Mike spent time writing and working out at the gym every day. They also realized that the only discernible source of family income was Patty's salary as a teacher. And yet, the Petersons drove a Mercedes, dined on fine china and drank fine wine. It didn't make a lot of sense. John asked Mike if he was in the CIA. Mike would not answer. When asked, Patty would not reply. On another occasion, Mike told them that he did consulting work for countries on behalf of the government.

But Michael had told Amybeth Berner, another DOD

teacher who worked with his wife, that he did work for the CIA. In fact, he said that, on their orders, he had killed a man who was causing trouble in Vietnam.

To add to his mystique, Michael claimed to others that he had been "the next-to-the-last white man out of Ethiopia after Emperor Haile Selassie was overthrown" in 1974. He boasted that he drove through Yugoslavia, when it was a Soviet Bloc nation, twenty times and was in East Germany more times than he can remember.

With George and Liz Ratliff being friends to both the Durhams and the Petersons, Randy and Mike were often thrown together. Mike often implied in casual conversations that he was connected to the CIA, but never gave Randy any details he could use to pin him down. Where the truth ended and the fantasy began was never clear to anyone.

Pat Finn moved to Berlin and a strain developed in her relationship with Patty. The rift was caused by the difficulty that they had in communication. Pat never sent Patty a letter, because she knew it would be intercepted and read by Mike before—or if—it was passed along to Patty.

She could not call Patty because the Petersons did not have a home telephone—they always used one at a friend's or neighbor's house. It irritated Pat that she always had to wait for Patty's call. When it came, Mike hovered in the background supervising Patty's communication.

When Pat attempted to talk to Patty about her

frustration, Patty did not—or would not—understand her point of view. Patty thought that Pat should understand *her* position.

In May of 1983, Mike and Patty paid a visit to Pat and her husband, Joseph, in Berlin. Mike took the opportunity to steal Pat Finn's bank card, but he needed a PIN number to use it. While Pat took a shower, Mike crept into her bedroom and rummaged through her drawers in search of her personal code. He found it, and over four days, withdrew the maximum each day for a total of $1,000.

The Finns went back to the States for summer break days after that visit. All the mail addressed to them in Germany was held until their return. They received a letter at their U.S. address from Michael. He claimed that the baby-sitter who watched the children at the Finns' house stole money from his wallet. Pat thought his accusation was absurd—she knew the girl well. She was the daughter of the vice principal at the school where Pat worked.

Upon her return to Germany, Pat found a statement from her bank and noted that the balance was off by about $1,000. She assumed the bank had made an error and went to the office to straighten it out. They pointed to the four $250 drafts made in May. Pat insisted she never used that card. Someone had, they told her.

Then she realized that the dates of the transactions corresponded with the time that Patty and Mike visited. This revelation made her sick at heart. Yes, she had noticed that on every previous visit something had been missing from her home. It was never anything of value—a paperback book or small trinket—and she did not want to suspect her friends.

She even overlooked the time that German marks disappeared from her purse when she visited the Petersons in Durham. It wasn't a significant amount and it was not anything she could prove. This time was different.

On the advice of her bankers, she told Mike that since her card was stolen and he had lost money, too, there was going to be a thorough investigation of the theft. Mike, realizing the police would be involved, admitted what he had done and agreed to pay her back.

At first, neither of them shared this information with Patty. One day, Patty called Pat and said she would like to visit her.

Pat said, "Patty, you are always welcome in my home. But when you come, please leave your husband and children at home."

A stunned Patty asked, "What is this all about?"

"You need to talk to your husband about it."

Pat did not hear from Patty again for a long time. She received a payment from Michael and another from Patty, but they never paid the amount in full. More than the money, though, Pat was stung by the betrayal. It was the rudest awakening of her life.

Michael Peterson's dream of becoming a published writer had now come true. He longed to write about his experiences in the war, but his first published effort was set in nineteenth century France and Vietnam.

New American Library published *The Immortal Dragon*, a 527-page paperback, under their Signet imprint in July 1983. Mike dedicated the book to his wife Patty and his two sons, 9-year-old Clayton and 7-year-old Todd.

The novel traced the love and lust of three generations against the backdrop of the power struggle between France and Vietnam. Treachery abounded in the corrupt ruling court and the traders were bent on exploitation while priests labored to save the heathens' souls.

Sex played a major role—from the bliss of the marital bed to the rampant promiscuity of a sorceress, from the homosexual advances of powerful men to the humiliation and degradation of women. It was a thread that bound the book together. It was a challenging and monumental project for a first-time author. Michael handled it well, producing a cohesive and captivating tale.

George and Liz Ratliff were thrilled by Michael's book. A decorated war hero *and* a novelist? They thumbed through the pages looking for themselves—and they found characters who were loosely based on them.

Michael Peterson was borrowing from reality when he wrote of the birth of a child in *The Immortal Dragon*. The infant appeared to be dead and did not respond to normal stimuli. The grandmother ". . . held it by the feet and plunged it into a tub of cold water. She brought it out, then plunged it in again, and when she yanked it out the second time, the baby sucked in, filling its lungs. Then it screamed."

This tale was a re-enactment of the birth of Michael's mother. The woman who'd plunged her into water was Michael's Italian grandmother.

Michael Peterson's writing career was born, but it would be seven long years before his hands again held a new book bearing his name.

ELIZABETH McKEE RATLIFF

"A Book of Verses underneath the Bough,
A Jug of Wine, a Loaf of Bread—and Thou
Beside me singing in the Wilderness—
Oh, Wilderness were Paradise enow!"

—Edward FitzGerald
The Rubaiyat of Omar Khayyam

16

Captain George Ratliff's new squadron was nicknamed "the Berlin for Lunch Bunch" because of their frequent flights to Templehof Air Force Base in Berlin, where they would have lunch and fly back. It was assumed that they flew to other locations as well—but no one knew where.

They departed from Frankfurt and returned seldom spending the night away. They were not hauling cargo, but no one outside of the squadron knew what they were doing. Their C-130s were segregated from the rest—kept in a locked and heavily guarded hangar.

The men were assigned to a secret mission in October of 1983. Liz did not know where her husband was going. At first, she was comforted knowing that their friend, Bruce Berner, would be going, too. But when his wife Amybeth was rushed to the hospital with complications from her pregnancy, Bruce's plans changed. He was excused from participation and stayed in Germany.

According to rumor, George went to Panama, but no one outside of the squadron really knows—that information was still classified in 2004. It was oft-repeated that his group was part of Operation Urgent Fury, preparing to participate in the invasion of Grenada, but that rumor was groundless. Regardless of where George was stationed on this mission, something went wrong.

George lived in comfortable quarters with his roommate, Captain Kent Klein. The main living space had a kitchenette and a sitting area with a television. A moveable partition marked off the sleeping area with its two single beds and a bath.

George and Kent went jogging early in the day. That night, Kent went to bed early, since he had a flight at dawn the next morning. George stayed up, popped open a beer and plopped down on the sofa. He started to write a letter to his friend, Randy Durham, who was now stationed at Scott Air Force Base and attending Airlift Operations School. Like a true Aggie, the salutation read, "Howdy, Good Buddy." It was filled with cordial chit-chat: "I spent a week at home in Texas on leave. It was great. I really had a good time fishing and drinking Lone Star longnecks." He wrote three pages in this vein before he grew tired and went to bed.

It was still dark when Kent got up and turned on the light in the bathroom. It washed over his roommate's bed, where George was tossing and turning in his sleep. Kent thought nothing of it as he cleaned up to face a new day.

When he was done, Kent stepped into the bedroom to pull on his flight suit. George had stopped moving. The blankets were not even rising and falling with his breath. Kent looked closer. He tried to locate a pulse, but found nothing. He ran for help.

A couple of days later, Randy Durham was seated in class in the middle of a lecture. The commandant of the school poked his head into the room and motioned to

Randy to come take a phone call. Colonel Ron Peoples, head of operations for George's mission, was on the line. Randy learned that George was dead and that Liz wanted him to escort the body back to Texas.

It took a little luck, some fancy footwork and a high-ranking officer to get the security clearance to allow Randy to fly to the mission location. But by Sunday he was on his way. When he arrived, he found the letter George was writing to him still attached to the writing pad in the middle of the desk.

Randy was not allowed to contact George's family until he landed at Dover Air Force Base in Delaware. There he called George Ratliff, Sr., and gave him an estimated time of arrival.

Randy escorted George's casket by land to Philadelphia, where he boarded a commercial flight bound for Hobby Airport in Houston. Randy followed the hearse to Bay City in a rented car and helped carry his friend into the mortuary.

Michael Peterson escorted the grieving widow and her small daughters to the States for the funeral. Many thought it odd that Patty Peterson—Liz's best friend—was not there by her side. Again and again, Mike told anyone who would listen that George had died without a will. The finances were screwed up, and Liz couldn't handle it. He would have to straighten it all out for her.

George's casket was open for the viewing the night before the funeral. A distraught Liz refused to attend, claiming childhood trauma as her reason. When she was a young girl, she said, she was forced to kiss a dead grandmother in a coffin. She could not bear to see another dead person.

On October 27, 1983, the funeral began as an open-casket service, but when Liz arrived, that changed. Randy nodded to the honor guard from Lackland Air Force Base in San Antonio and they closed the coffin at his command. A devastated Liz went through the motions of the service with a numb mind and a shredded heart. Mourners accompanied the casket to Cedarvale Cemetery, a Bay City landmark since 1896.

Her mother and her sisters offered to join her in Texas for the funeral. Because of all the uncertainty about the timing of the arrival of George's body, the smallness of the rural Ratliff home and the lack of any nearby hotels, Liz discouraged them. She visited her family after the services and before her return to Germany.

At Margaret's house, Liz's sadness was so palpable, it weighed on everyone like a shroud of lead. Her sisters spent hours talking with her, comforting her and trying to bear some of her burden.

One evening, to distract her, they went out to a club for dinner. "If George were here tonight," she said, "he would order a beer." Then she ordered one and placed it by the empty space at the table.

After dinner, the group who was performing asked Liz to come up and play a song. Liz took Margaret with her and mounted the stage. Liz played the guitar and both women sang "Donna Donna," an old Joan Baez song. For that brief interlude, the veil lifted from Liz. And she smiled.

At first, everyone suspected that heart failure was the cause of George's death. In the preliminary autopsy report, however, the coronary workup did not indicate any blockage or other areas of concern.

Then, everyone was certain that the toxicology report would hold the answer to George's demise. When the final autopsy report was released, it contained the results of the toxicology testing. Every substance tested turned up negative. The military later told Liz that his death was caused when, in a condition similar to crib death, her husband's system shut down and he died in his sleep.

When Liz received the death certificate, it offered her no further information. Under "Location of death" was simply the word "Unknown." And under "Cause of death," there it was again, "Unknown." She never learned the whole truth.

17

The loss of her husband and best friend hung like an albatross around Liz's neck. She sunk into a bottomless pit of depression, overwhelmed by the responsibilities of caring for two small children and a household on her own. For a long time, George's uniform and boots remained laid out as if waiting for his imminent return.

Liz did have a strong network of support. The members of George's squadron and teachers from the school reached out to console her and help in any way they could.

At Patty and Michael's encouragement, Liz and her girls found a new home just up the street from the Peterson family. When it was time to move, all the men in George's squadron pitched in to help. Lieutenant Colonel Scott asked his new Scottish nanny, Barbara O'Hara, if she would come along and help Liz pack. She and Liz hit it off from the start.

Barbara offered to come over on Wednesday, her day off, and help Liz unpack. They did not get anything put away that day. Instead they sat drinking coffee, talking and playing with the babies.

Barbara told Liz that although she had only been at

the Scotts' house for three weeks, she just had to get out of there. She wanted to go back to Scotland. Liz offered to speak to the Scotts and make it possible for Barbara to stay with her until she could get the money to fly home.

After three days, Barbara had proven to be so valuable, and the two women had gotten along so well, that Liz asked her to stay on as nanny. Barbara accepted.

Liz's depression left her incapable of bearing much more responsibility than teaching her class at school. She was always exhausted and filled with the despairing thought that life was not worth living. There were days when she came home from work overwhelmed by it all and as soon as Barbara greeted her, she'd say, "I don't want to talk today, Barbara. I just want to go upstairs and lie down." That was the last Barbara or the girls saw of her until the next morning.

Like a white knight, Michael galloped into her life to handle finances and guide all the decision-making in the household. He made some of the decisions without consulting Liz at all.

He took charge of drafting a new will for Liz. The previous document she and George had signed—the one that Michael denied existed at George's funeral—stipulated that, should anything happen to both of them, George's parents would assume guardianship of their two girls. If they were unable to do so, Patty and Michael would assume that responsibility. Liz's new will stated: "I hereby nominate, constitute and appoint Michael I. and Patricia S. Peterson as Guardians, acting jointly or separately, of each of my minor children until he or she reaches majority or is otherwise legally emancipated." The will also granted either Mike or Patty the authority to dispose of her property for the support and education of the girls. The change seemed quite natural—the Petersons and Ratliffs were very close friends. Margaret and Martha called them Aunt Patty and Uncle Mike.

The all-female Ratliff household fell into a cozy routine. Barbara used the bedroom downstairs that also served as the girls' playroom by day. Upstairs, there were three bedrooms. Liz slept in the master bedroom and each girl had her own room across the hall. Only the living room was drawn in a dark shroud. Filled with furniture acquired by George, the room was never used.

Despite Liz's despondence, the home was filled with an exuberance that could not be denied in a house containing two small well-loved children. As a little girl, Margaret had a delightful and engaging personality, but she was clumsy and awkward. When she danced she exhibited all the grace of a toad. She had an odd little habit of screwing up one eye and looking at the ceiling whenever she was deep in thought. Liz doted on her— loved every little nuance of her character. Everything about Margaret reminded her of George.

Martha was a dainty, sensitive little girl, but she had a lot of spirit. From the age of one, she'd demonstrated a streak of rebellion. Liz, her patience often tried by Martha's defiance, was still amused and enchanted by her struggle for independence.

Many evenings, the girls popped into their pajamas and hunkered down on the carpet in the landing at the top of the stairs—Margaret with B Bunny and Martha with her Slim Bunny—to listen to stories. Barbara and Liz sat on the floor with them and took turns reading to them from their favorite books—the Beatrix Potter classics and Enid Blyton's Noddy books, an English children's series.

Barbara adored those two little girls and even took them with her when she visited her mother in northern Germany. Barbara lived in the house full-time at first. Then in the summer of 1985, Michael Peterson told Liz that it was not fair that Barbara did not have a life of her own. She should have an apartment where she could have some privacy, and Liz should pay for it.

Barbara found a flat in the neighboring village, but her room in Liz's home was still there, allowing her to spend the night whenever it was needed or desired. Margaret and Martha had occasional getaway weekends at her place. Mike visited Barbara there, too. She came to love and respect him as a friend and turned to him for advice and understanding. They did not always agree, but still, Mike was always there for her. She felt they had a very close friendship.

Barbara rode over on her bicycle to Liz's house most mornings, arriving between 7 and 7:30. Typically, Patty and Liz traveled to work together at 7:40. They taught classes across the hall from one another at Rhein Main Elementary School.

The glow of the lights from Liz's bedroom and the bath filtered down to the foyer each morning when Barbara arrived. At the door, she removed her footwear. Boots and shoes were always left standing by the door in this household—perhaps a vestige of the time Liz lived in Japan. The heating system, with warm water pipes running under a tile floor, made the home suitable to practice this habit with comfort.

In the kitchen, by the light of the "Goosy, Goosy Gander" lamp, Barbara could see the breakfast preparations that Liz had set out the night before—the oatmeal and pan by the stove and the plates set out on the children's table.

October 1985 rolled around with all its painful memories of George's death. It was a difficult month for Liz, but she was making progress toward her recovery. She was nowhere near as despondent as she had been on the first anniversary of her loss the previous year.

Liz's depression had lifted enough that she was making plans for the future. She talked to Barbara about wanting to go back to the States to teach if she could find a job in Texas. She wanted to get to know George's family. After a couple of years there, she hoped to move to Japan and settle down.

She wanted Barbara to come with her and care for the girls. They wondered about the difficulties of getting a visa for Barbara. Mike assured them that since Liz was the widow of a soldier killed in the line of duty, the military should make it easy for them.

The Ratliff crew saw the Peterson family almost daily. They dined together more often than not and developed a mutual dependency. When Patty's washing machine broke down, she lugged her baskets of dirty laundry over to Liz's house and cleaned them there.

That month, Liz's mother, Elizabeth, flew over for a three-week visit. During that time, her sister Margaret called and they made tentative plans for her to come to Germany. Throughout the years, Margaret had a strong desire to visit her sister in Europe, but financial constraints were always prohibitive. Now, the trip was affordable. The two sisters looked forward to their reunion and hoped to spend time skiing together.

Cheryl Appel, a DOD teacher who had lived with Liz and George when she first moved to Germany, married Tom Schumacher the previous June. In the fall, they moved from their small apartment to a bungalow in Buschlag. Tom had a Ph.D. in psychology and headed up the Family Advocacy Center on base.

Liz loved to entertain. Cheryl and Tom's marriage and move seemed a good reason to celebrate. She wanted it to be a surprise for the newlyweds. She led them to believe she was throwing a party for someone else that November. She even went so far in her ruse as to ask Cheryl to bring some dips.

The two arrived around 7 with dips in hand. They did not have a clue. Liz was delighted. The couple stayed to help Liz clean up after the party, leaving for home shortly after midnight.

The Ratliff home was plagued by repeated hang-up calls that year. Throughout October and November, the number of calls had increased. Their frequency had made Liz uneasy and frightened. She asked Barbara to stay over many times, including Friday and Saturday, November 22 and 23. Barbara slept there for those two nights and returned to her apartment mid-day Sunday to check on her place and get some clean clothes.

That afternoon, Liz took the two girls sledding on the freshly fallen snow. She and the girls had dinner with Patty and Michael and their two boys that evening at the Petersons' home. Mealtime conversation centered around the joint family trip to Copenhagen over the upcoming winter break.

After dinner, Michael walked Liz, Martha and Margaret down the street to their home. He helped Liz get the girls cleaned up and tucked into bed. After they were asleep, Liz drove her car to the neighboring village to leave it with a mechanic. Mike followed her there in his car and gave her a ride back home. Upon their return, he took out Liz's trash for pick-up the next morning.

About 10 o'clock that Sunday night, Liz's neighbor, Karin Hamm, looked out her window in time to see Michael Peterson, dressed in light-colored tennis shoes, dark blue jeans and a light-hued cardigan, emerge from Liz's home. He jumped down the three steps from the door and started to run away. He looked back over his shoulder in Karin's direction, stuck both his hands in the front pockets of his jeans and moved on at a quick pace.

18

Barbara O'Hara looked at the snowy vista outside her apartment on November 25 and decided it was not a good morning to ride her bike. She called for a taxi and Salvatore Malagnino picked her up.

The sun had not yet quenched all vestiges of darkness when Barbara arrived at 7:15. As soon as they turned onto the street, she knew something was wrong. Every light in the house was on—even the one in the living room that was never used. An ugly premonition clenched her stomach muscles tight as she slid her key into the lock.

Her eyes grazed over the kitchen. The oatmeal was not sitting by the stove. The plates were not on the children's table. She heard no sound of Liz stirring upstairs. An unpleasant, unrecognized odor hung heavy in the air.

Then she saw the body crumpled in a pool of blood at the foot of the stairs. Her heart thudded like an overworked piston in her chest. Her mind screamed out in denial and blinded her to what was before her eyes.

"Liz! Liz! Are you okay?" she shouted as she stepped over the body and lunged up the stairs.

Liz was not in the bathroom. Barbara opened the bedroom door. The room was empty. She checked on the two girls. Both were still asleep. That was unusual for Margaret, who was an early riser. Barbara went back to Liz's room. The phone was beside the bed, where Liz placed it every night. She grabbed the receiver. She would call Michael for help. He would know what to do. No dial tone. She stabbed the disconnect button. She pushed it again with more force. And again. Still, no dial tone. She dropped the receiver and, looking out the window, discovered that her cab driver was still sitting in front of the house. She raced back down the stairs.

Three steps from the landing, reality formed a tight fist that slammed into her head. The boots—yellow boots— Liz's snow boots. It was Liz at the foot of the stairs. It was Liz in the pool of blood. Was she wearing a red sweater? Or was there just that much blood? Her eyes registered the blood up and down the stairway. Too much blood.

She forced herself to go down the steps to Liz's body. Liz lay on her right side with her legs pulled slightly toward her chest. Barbara ran outside and asked the driver to call an ambulance and the police.

She hurried back into the house and took Liz in her arms. She felt warmth. Hope was still alive. Her fingers traced the open wounds on the back of Liz's head. Gently, she laid Liz down as she had found her. She fled the house to find more help.

She banged on the Petersons' door with the intensity of a jackhammer. Patty, half-dressed, flung the door open to a panting and wild-eyed Barbara.

"Something horrible has happened. Hurry," Barbara blurted.

Mike appeared at the top of the stairs in a pair of boxers and a tee shirt. Nothing Barbara said made any sense to Patty. She and Michael slapped on their clothes and followed a babbling Barbara over to Liz's house.

Once inside, Barbara raced upstairs to the bathroom—she thought she was going to be sick. Michael came to the door and, in denial, Barbara told him, "I touched her. She's warm."

"She's not warm, Barbara," Mike told her, placing his hands on her arms. "She's not warm—she's dead. The warmth you felt was from the floor heating."

The fear that the little girls would see their mother dead and covered with blood propelled Barbara into action. Wrapping a blanket around Margaret, she lifted her up and carried her down the fire escape stairs in the back of the house. She ran around the garden with her precious bundle and left her up the street at the Petersons' house with Todd and Clayton. She then returned for Martha.

She took the littlest one from the house by the same route, laid the sleeping baby down next to her drowsy sister and slipped back to Liz's house. When she reached the door, she could not bear the thought of stepping inside. Instead, she headed across the alley and six doors up to the home of DOD teacher Amybeth Berner.

She banged a desperate tattoo on the door. "Come quickly. Something's happened to Liz," Barbara pleaded.

Amybeth and her husband, Bruce, grabbed their coats and followed Barbara across the alleyway. Amybeth came through the front door and her eyes focused on the yellow boots. The rest of the body was covered, but she knew it was Liz.

Amybeth turned to Patty Peterson. "What happened?"

Patty said not a word. She just stared into space—a look of disbelief dragged on her face.

Amybeth turned back to the stairs. She absorbed the scene before her. Blood on the walls—a lot of blood. Blood on the floor—too much blood. Her eyes sought out Michael Peterson. She did not say a word, but he saw the question etched on her face.

He told her that Liz had a brain aneurysm and had fallen down the stairs. Something did not seem right to Amybeth, but in her shock she could not shape that vague feeling into a concrete conclusion.

Amybeth hurried back to her home. In the kitchen, she grabbed the green Christmas cookie tin that held her phone numbers. She rooted around until she found the slip for Tom and Cheryl Appel–Schumacher.

Her knees shook and her hands trembled as she dialed the number. Tom, who was home alone, answered her call.

"Tom, you need to sit down," she ordered. "You and Cheryl need to come right away. Liz had an accident."

After delivering the news, Amybeth went back to Liz's house. She approached Liz's body with the sensation that she was drowning in her own helplessness. She focused in on a bloody footprint on the third step. "Whose footprint is that?"

"That's my footprint. That's when I went to get Martha Baby and Gigi," Barbara admitted, referring to the little girls by their baby names.

"This is a crime scene," Amybeth insisted. "Someone needs to investigate this. Don't walk up the stairs."

"Yes," Barbara said. "There is an awful lot of blood here."

"Yes," Bruce echoed. "Something is wrong. Something is wrong."

At Amybeth's suggestion, Bruce went outside and checked the perimeter of the house for any signs of forced entry. Amybeth went down three steps to the lower level and checked the sliding glass garden door from the inside. It was locked. She went around to the washroom in the back of the kitchen. That door was locked, too.

She scanned the house, looking to see if anything was missing or disturbed. They found no evidence of a break-in—no clues pointing to a robbery.

19

Cheryl Appel–Schumacher was not at home when Amybeth talked to Tom, because she had already left to go to work at about the same time that Barbara O'Hara entered Liz's house. Cheryl taught a fourth-grade special education group at the same Department of Defense Overseas School where Liz and Patty were teachers.

When she arrived in the classroom, she posted all the week's assignments on the chalkboard. Her students filled in and took their seats at 8:10. It was a short week because of Thanksgiving, and the few days were crammed with work. She was explaining it all to her kids when the school counselor walked in and pulled her aside. She told Cheryl that Tom was waiting in the counseling office with some very bad news.

A puzzled Cheryl went to meet her husband, worrying about possible scenarios as she walked down the hall. "You have to sit down," he said as he led her to a chair. Gently, Tom broke the news. "It's hard to believe, but Liz is dead. She had a hemorrhage. She fell down the stairs. And she is dead."

They left the school and went to Liz's home. The

foyer was crowded with people—Amybeth and Bruce Berner, Barbara O'Hara, cab driver Salvatore Malagnino, Patty and Mike Peterson and the German emergency medical team—when they arrived at about 9 o'clock. Cheryl saw part of Liz at the foot of the stairway, her upper body covered with a coat and her legs and yellow boots sticking out. She turned away. Amy Beth greeted Cheryl with a mournful hug.

Barbara was near hysteria—crying, sobbing, shaking and talking in a loud voice. The cries and sobs of other voices joined in her chorus of grief.

The German police arrived on the scene soon after Cheryl and Tom. As the officials examined Liz's body, Amybeth noted the blood-soaked hair and a cut above her left eye. She translated for her gathered friends that the Germans were trying to decide if Liz died before she hit the floor. She watched as a doctor used a syringe to remove fluid from Liz's spine.

Although his German was spotty, Michael Peterson asserted himself as the man in charge of the situation. He communicated as best he could to both the German police and the medical professionals with a mix of English, German and hand signals.

Mike also called the American military to inform them that a Department of Defense employee was deceased. At noon, Steven Lyons, a special agent for the U.S. Army Command walked through the door with an interpreter in tow. Lyons' role was to assist the German police and report back to the Defense Department.

Lyons did not examine the body. He made a cursory exploration of the stairs, looking for anything that would contradict the story Michael Peterson had told him. He found nothing. Except for the pool of blood at the bottom, he did not notice any of the blood running along the length of the stairs. The only American he talked to was the one he described as "the dominating male on the scene," Michael Peterson.

Cheryl avoided the stairs as much as she could. Her first sight of Liz's body seared like a brand into her brain. She did not want the image to penetrate any deeper. She also did not want that image placed in the minds of others. She blocked the door and would not allow any other teachers or neighbors to enter. Patty Peterson spent the whole morning sitting in the kitchen. She heard nothing. She said nothing. She stared wide-eyed out into space.

Cheryl was appalled when she realized that the military were going to leave without Liz's body. She wanted to clean up the blood before Martha and Margaret returned home, but she knew she could not begin while Liz lay there abandoned in that crimson pool. She pleaded with Mike to do something.

When he questioned the departing men he was told they would have to wait for the mortuary people to come from Frankfurt. The military did, however, grant permission to move the body.

Amybeth laid garbage bags on the floor next to the body. Tom and Mike grabbed the rug beneath Liz and lifted it up and set it down on the bags, hoping to prevent the creation of a blood trail.

They placed Liz on the bed in Barbara's room. Tom placed the dripping, blood-soaked rug in a plastic bag and later took it to the cleaners.

In the house, the friends talked about what had happened. Mike said, "She had a cerebral hemorrhage and fell down the stairs. She was dead before she hit the bottom."

"I don't believe it," Barbara snapped.

And she was not alone in her skepticism. With the body moved, Amybeth took a hard look at the wall by the stairs. She was nearly six feet tall and yet, at the top of the steps, blood was higher on the wall than she could reach.

Barbara was antsy and could not wait to leave the house. When the decision was reached that Amybeth, in the middle of another high-risk pregnancy, should not be cleaning up, Barbara went with her and Bruce to their home.

Cheryl looked at the profusion of blood all the way down the wall by the staircase, the small spatter across the room and the endless lake of it on the floor. She wanted to flee. She wanted to forget. Instead she focused on the two baby girls. She did not want that blood—their mother's blood—to be part of their memory.

She got a bowl of water and the leather chamois that Liz used to wash dishes in lieu of a sponge. She trudged up to the top of the stairs.

The rough stucco-like texture of the walls made cleaning a challenge. Soon, she discovered that small circular motions were the most efficient method. Up above the light switch the spray of blood was so tiny, she had to peer at it to make sure she got every drop.

At times, she would think about what she was doing and her eyes would well with tears, making it impossible to see. She would take a break and regain her composure. She forced herself to think of this blood as just another mess and got back to work again.

Rubbing and rubbing. Rinsing the chamois in the
bowl until the water became too pink to clean the cloth.
Dump the water out. Refill the bowl. Rub and rinse
again. She emptied that bowl more times than she could
remember.

Tom cleaned the areas alongside the staircase that
Cheryl could not reach. He focused his energies,
though, at the foot of the stairs where Liz was discovered. Massive quantities of blood had leaked through
and around the rug underneath her body. By now, it had
thickened to a jelly-like consistency. The congealed
substance clung to the surface. When he wiped at it, the
blood moved around in smears. When he did absorb
some with the rag, dark blobs hung pregnant on the
edges.

The worst part for Tom was listening to the moans
that escaped unbidden through Cheryl's lips. When tears
rolled down his face in response, he wanted to wipe
them away, but his hands were covered in too much
blood.

Around 2 o'clock that afternoon, the mortuary
service arrived to take away the body of Elizabeth
Ratliff. Mike Peterson directed the removal of the
body. He did not help with the cleaning, but was busy
nonetheless. Then he worked the phones calling the
different military offices and government agencies that
handle the details surrounding the death of a government employee overseas.

Time and again, Cheryl and Tom thought they were
done with their onerous chore. They'd step back to
examine their work and one of them would notice more
blood. They got back to work cleaning stray spots on

the refrigerator, off the trunk beneath the stairs, off the steps. They hunted down every drop of blood, not wanting to leave the smallest bit of evidence for the girls to see.

At 5 o'clock that afternoon, Mike placed a call to Liz's sister, Margaret Blair, in Rhode Island. He told her there had been an accident—Liz had fallen down the stairs and died. When Margaret asked for a further description, he told her it was peaceful—that "there was only a little blood behind her ear."

After hanging up, Margaret called her other sister, Rosemary, and shared the news with her. Then she called a family friend who was a nurse. She asked the woman to meet her at her mother's house. Margaret had serious concerns about the physical impact on her mother when she and her husband, Jim, delivered the news of Liz's death. It was November 25, 1985. Their father had died on November 25, 1975. Margaret shuddered at the coincidence. This November 25 would be the most difficult day of her life.

When Cheryl and Tom were satisfied that every trace of blood was gone, they went up to the Petersons' house and retrieved Margaret and Martha. The week Liz died, Barbara O'Hara was too spooked to return to the house to care for them. The Schumachers stayed in the home and cared for the girls through Thanksgiving week.

The day after Liz died, second-grader Amy Carlson came home from Rhein Main Elementary School in tears. She sobbed as she told her mother, Donna, that her teacher was dead—Ms. Ratliff, the teacher whom Amy loved and talked about every day.

Amy said that Ms. Ratliff committed suicide. She was full of sorrowful questions. How could she do this? How could she leave us? How could this happen on stairs? How can you kill yourself by throwing yourself down stairs?

Amy knew something was wrong with the story she heard, but at her young age, could not understand what. The questions about Ms. Ratliff stayed with her for years. Donna had never met Amy's teacher. The school sent no information home. Down the street was another mother who hadn't known Liz. She, too, had heard it was a suicide.

Was the story about Liz killing herself merely an idle rumor that ran through the community, creating a life of its own? Or was it a story planted with malice? Or one circulated to protect someone from suspicion? No one knows the truth of its origin; nonetheless, the suicide story left a deep scar on Amy's heart—one that she carried with her to the end of her short, tragic life.

When Pat Finn heard the news of Liz's death, she flashed back to her friend Patty and her husband Michael. She had learned first-hand that Patty's fantasy image of Michael Peterson was divorced from any connection with reality. She remembered the constant negative comments Mike made about Liz. She remembered thinking that he was obsessed with talking about her.

She called the Criminal Investigation Division of the Military Police. She told them of her suspicions that Michael Peterson was involved in the death of Elizabeth Ratliff. They did not follow up on her call. To Pat, the military seemed determined to whitewash the incident and avoid scandal at all cost.

20

Liz's body was transported to the 97th General Hospital in Frankfurt for an autopsy under Army auspices. The base there had four staff pathologists in 1985—not one of them was a forensic pathologist.

Dr. Larry Barnes, a graduate of Kansas City College of Osteopathic Medicine, was assigned to perform Liz Ratliff's autopsy. He was in his third year of his tour of duty in Germany. Trained in pathology at an Army school at Fort Campbell, Kentucky, he was well equipped to handle the typical general pathology work like tissue pathology on a removed appendix or the clinical pathology of blood analysis.

He did not have much experience in autopsies, however. In fact, this was only his fifth one. The other four had all been on the victims of vehicular trauma. He had never conducted an autopsy on a person whose death was the result of foul play—he had never seen the results of blunt force trauma, gunshots or knife wounds. He had no significant training in forensic pathology.

He followed medical—not forensic—protocol during the two-hour procedure. He did not have equipment to weigh the organs or to take height measurements. He made eyeball estimates and noted them on the chart. No photographs were taken of the external examination. No diagram was made of Liz's wounds.

He found 100 ml of blood in her skull. There should not have been any there. He noted a hemorrhage at the junction of the brain and the brain stem with blood extending down into the spinal cord.

He did not take a skull x-ray. He conducted a visual search for signs of a depressed skull fracture, but did not find any. Barnes made one slide of an area of the brain he thought exhibited vascular malformation, which caused both the hemorrhage and tissue degeneration. He made one slide of a liver section.

The report Barnes submitted indicated Liz's death was caused by a "cerebellar hemorrhage." An initial view of the document by the Armed Forces Institute of Pathology stated that the slide of the brain tissue demonstrated a vascular malformation, a finding that supported Barnes' stated cause of death.

A neuropathology consultation by Dr. Andrew Parisi in April concluded that no final determination could be made. He did not find a vascular malformation. This finding contradicted Dr. Barnes' conclusion. On the back of the report, he left the following note: "There is nothing diagnostic of von Willebrand's disease in these actions. This is not a typical demise."

The final report from the director of the Armed Forces Institute of Pathology, however, stated that Elizabeth Ratliff's demise was a "sudden unsuspected death due to a spontaneous intercranial hemorrhage, complicating von Willebrand's disease; natural."

Barbara did not believe this was true. She told

everyone that she knew there was something more to Liz's death—there was too much blood. By the time she let it go, she was certain everyone thought she was crazy.

Michael Peterson accompanied Liz's body back to the States. Patty Peterson did not attend the funeral of her best friend. On December 2, 1985, Liz's sister, Margaret, delivered the eulogy for her sister in the service at Holy Cross Catholic Church. The funeral procession crawled through Bay City. On the side of the roads, men stopped, pulled off their hats and held them to their hearts. Others bowed their heads or flashed through the blessings of the cross. Margaret Blair was surprised at these signs of respect and found a warm place in her heart for the people of Texas. Liz was laid to rest beside her husband, George, in Cedarvale Cemetery—a pair of flat gray granite stones with bronze plaques marked the spot where they were reunited.

With calculating insight, Michael Peterson remembered to bring Liz's will with him to Texas. He filed the last will and testament of Elizabeth Ratliff at the Matagorda County Courthouse on December 4, 1985. The fate and future of Margaret and Martha Ratliff now rested in the hands of Patty and Michael Peterson. With this responsibility came an estate valued at $44,000 and a monthly check from the government for the two orphans.

There were questions, though, about the official evaluation of the estate. Liz's BMW was not on the personal property list. Nor was the court in Texas aware of the tapestry Liz and George purchased at a bargain for

$20,000 when they honeymooned. Also not listed were the Polish antiques from the mid– to late–eighteenth century or the hand-carved swan cradle, the French pots, and the rugs from Afghanistan. And what had happened to the money from George's life insurance policy that Liz had set aside for her girls' future? Years later, when the contents of the document were revealed, suspicion arose that someone had lied to the Texas courts.

In Texas, Margaret Blair learned about the provision in Liz's will for the guardianship of the two girls. She was not surprised. She knew her sister had a close relationship with Patty Peterson for some time.

After the Thanksgiving holiday weekend, Barbara moved back into Liz's house to care for Margaret and Martha. Mike took care of all the household financial affairs and gave Barbara a raise.

Barbara did not feel safe in the house. At night, she often heard sounds, as if someone were prowling around. She knew an unknown person had been in the house when she noticed items shuffled on George's desk as if someone were looking for something. On another morning, she awoke to find the living room door leading to the garden standing wide open. She spoke to Mike about it and he promised to check on things when he was out for his late evening rambles and every morning when he walked the dog.

Barbara got to know the Peterson family more intimately during these months. Their house, she said, was a disaster—very untidy and very dirty. Patty had no interest in housework and Michael had no clue. From time to time, Barbara cleaned their house for them. Barbara and the Petersons also worked out a mutual baby-sitting agreement that served both families well.

As a rule, Patty stayed late at school to do all her paperwork and preparation for the next day instead of bringing it home. That meant Mike had to feed Clayton and Todd. The evening meals for the little boys were TV dinners more often than not.

Barbara thought the two Peterson children were lovely boys, although they often wore unkempt clothing. Todd was an affectionate child. When she read to him or told him stories, he snuggled up as close as he could and looked up at her with big, gorgeous eyes. He could listen to her for hours.

Clayton, on the other hand, was more reserved. He could not sit still for anything. He preferred telling her what was wrong with a story rather than sitting down and enjoying it.

Barbara saw a change in Mike—a more violent, aggressive side of him emerged. He became mean and impatient. She had suspicions about the cause, but he was her employer and she kept her thoughts to herself.

Mike displayed a clear favoritism for Margaret, who was a friendly, outgoing and intelligent girl. Martha was more shy and sensitive. She developed a fear of Mike, hiding behind Barbara whenever he came to the house. Martha came home from the Peterson's on a number of occasions with black-and-blue marks on her body, but Barbara overlooked it—children often get bruised in play.

Then, Barbara went away for a week and left the girls with the Petersons. When she returned, Martha had two black eyes and blue marks behind her ears. This time, Barbara confronted Mike about what had happened. He said that Martha was a "bad, bad girl" and she needed "to learn manners." Barbara swore Mike's voice was filled with glee when he told her that he had rubbed Martha's nose in the carpet like a dog when she'd wet the floor.

Soon after that incident, Mike Peterson moved back to the States, taking Margaret and Martha with him. After six months of being a mother to the girls, Barbara missed them. It tore at her heart. But how much more, she wondered, did the little girls suffer?

Barbara helped the packers crate up Liz's things. Then she cleaned the house one last time, locked the door and walked away. Leaving that house of death brought her a strong sense of relief.

Margaret and Martha, having lost their mother and father, were now separated from their nanny. The path of their days was defined—a life that was a long litany of loss.

MICHAEL PETERSON

"Some people are simply not meant for one another. Though not wicked or evil by themselves, together they feed each other's weaknesses, turning petty faults into cruelties, and fuel the fires of vanity, jealousy and greed."

–Michael Peterson, *The Immortal Dragon*, 1983

21

In early 1986, shaken by Liz's death, Patty tried to contact her old friend, Pat Finn. When she dialed her number, she discovered that the phone was disconnected. In the silence of their falling-out, Patty was unaware that the Finns had moved to a new home in Berlin. She went to the DOD office, and asked for and received Pat's new telephone number.

When she called, Pat snapped, "How did you get my number?"

Patty was infuriated by the question and said, "Don't worry, I will never call you again." She slammed down the phone. It was the last time Pat and Patty ever spoke.

On June 6, 1986, Mike arrived in Rhode Island at Jim and Margaret Blair's home. He left Martha there and traveled to Texas to leave Margaret with George's family. These visits were explained to be temporary and were intended to allow Mike and Patty to get settled in a home in Durham, North Carolina.

Before Mike left Rhode Island for Texas, however, he made a proposition to the Blairs. Martha was too much for him to handle because of her frequent temper tantrums. He asked if they would keep her on a permanent basis.

Margaret and Jim were delighted at the thought of keeping Martha. But what about Margaret? The girls were so close. The only immediate family they had was each other.

Michael would not entertain the possibility of both girls staying in Rhode Island. With heavy hearts, the Blairs declined his offer. They believed it was too important for the girls to remain together.

In July, Margaret Blair received a phone call from the Ratliff family in Bay City. George Ratliff, Sr., had a heart attack. Could she please come to Texas and pick up her niece? Margaret flew down and brought her namesake home.

The girls had a carefree summer making cookies, planting in the garden and picking up seashells on the seashore. One night, they lay out on the cool grass and stared up at the black sky watching as meteors showered to earth.

On bad weather days, their older cousins, Jodie and Damon, entertained them with puppet shows at the foot of the double bed. A big favorite was the reenactment of the story of Pinocchio. And each evening before they climbed into bed, the two little girls said their night prayers: "God bless Mommy and Daddy in Heaven."

Margaret and Martha enjoyed their visit, but beneath the pleasures they experienced flowed a dark stream of sorrow. Great loss walked with them all their lives—loss that at this age they could feel, but could not comprehend.

Often they asked, "My mommy's dead. My daddy's dead. When are you going to die, too?"

After their Rhode Island summer, Margaret Blair drove the girls down to Durham and settled them into their new home with Michael, Patty, Todd and Clayton. One day during her stay there, Margaret heard screaming in the backyard and came running. It was so loud, she was certain it could be heard all over the neighborhood. When she reached the kitchen, she encountered a placid Patty.

Margaret asked her what was going on. Patty simply said, "Oh, that's just Michael."

Looking out the window, Margaret saw Mike's continued rant. The cause of his distress was a bicycle— Clayton had left his bike on the ground behind his father's car.

Worry about the safety of the girls surged through Margaret. She told herself she was overreacting. Patty was very nurturing and loving with her boys. And she was just as nurturing and loving with the girls. It was Patty who mattered to Liz. She stuffed her worries down deep in the back of her mind.

Michael and Patty continued their complaints about how difficult Martha was to raise. They told Mike's sister, Ann, that Martha had tantrums and was manipulative.

Ann was puzzled. A 3-year-old manipulative? What could Martha possibly do? When Ann asked Mike and Patty, they gave her an example.

When the family went out shopping, they said, Martha would stand stock-still all of a sudden, and wail, "Oh, my mommy died," and start crying. Patty insisted that she did this just to garner the attention of the other shoppers. Another demonstration that Martha was a grand manipulator, they said, was when she called all sorts of women "Mommy."

Ann, on the other hand, thought this kind of behavior was to be expected from a little girl who in three short years had lost her mother, her father and her nanny. When Mike and Patty asked if she would take Martha, Ann readily agreed. She was so excited about it, she told all her friends. And then, Michael changed his mind.

Some wondered why the Petersons were not more concerned about Clayton's behavior. He spent all his spare time up in the rafters of the garage tinkering with wires and mechanical objects. Once on a family trip to Hilton Head, he dismantled a Jacuzzi, then could not put it back together. Mike had to pay for a replacement.

A block away from the Peterson home was the house of Fred and Kathleen Atwater. Their daughter, Caitlin, was wedged between the two Ratliff sisters in age. The three girls met at a mutual friend's birthday party. After that, they often played together with Barbie dolls at each other's houses.

One day in 1988, Michael came home to discover two one-way flight tickets to Germany in the mailbox. The passengers named on the itinerary were Margaret and Martha Ratliff.

Michael was furious. He confronted Patty. She told

him that the Geislings, a wealthy older couple who had never been able to have children of their own, wanted to adopt the two girls.

At first, Michael refused to let them go. Patty persisted and eventually convinced him to allow the girls to go for a year and see if it worked out. Margaret and Martha were only told that they were going for a visit.

The 6- and 7-year-olds boarded the plane and flew off by themselves. The Geislings spoke very little English, making the transition more difficult. After a week, the girls were told to call them Mom and Dad. Margaret was confused.

No sooner had she accepted the reality of this change in her life than the rug was pulled out from under her feet again. The couple changed their mind about the adoption. The girls flew back to North Carolina. They cried all the way back across the Atlantic Ocean.

Michael was now working with a literary agent. Over a two-year period, the two men labored over changes to the manuscript about the Vietnam War that Michael began writing when he was stationed in Japan. They pounded and polished every chapter, every page, every word to prepare it for the marketplace.

It was sold to Simon & Schuster for an advance of $600,000. *A Time of War* was released in hardcover in 1990. Michael Peterson had made it.

The dedication in his masterpiece read:

> *To Patty, who suffered all my wounds.*
> *To Clayton and Todd, whose suffering, I pray, is*

only in my nightmares.
To the dead.
And to those whose suffering cannot be relieved.

Although he claimed to love Martha and Margaret as if they were his own, he neglected to mention them.

A Time of War was described as a cross between Tom Clancy and Graham Greene. The book was set in the midst of war in Vietnam and filled with high-level espionage, acts of personal bravery and both heterosexual and homosexual escapades. Noted authors praised it with enthusiasm. It was heady stuff for any writer and it propelled Michael onto the *New York Times* Best Seller List.

When the book was released in a paperback edition, *Publishers Weekly* added their praise, but with a caveat: "Peterson adroitly evokes embassy intrigue and his battle scenes are immediate and compelling. Some readers may be taken aback by the powerful, troubled current of sexuality, however."

One evening soon after Margaret and Martha had returned from their 1990 summer trip to Rhode Island, Margaret tattled on Martha. She told Michael that her younger sister did not say her good-night prayers. To him, the child sounded self-righteous. He thought her attitude was unhealthy and unwholesome. And Michael knew who to blame.

He fired off an angry letter to Margaret Blair on July 18, 1990. "The girls had a terrific time with you, and I thank you very much. My only concern is with the heavy dose of religion they—Margaret in particular—brought back. It borders slightly on fundamentalist fanaticism that Liz was utterly opposed to."

He informed her that Patty accepted a job offer to teach at the same school in Germany again. He and all four children were going back with her to live together as a family. He then lashed out at Margaret for wanting to adopt the two girls. It was, he said, out of the question. "They absolutely need me."

He rejected the importance of the girls' bond with the Blair family. "Believe me, if I thought that it would be better for Martha and Margaret to live with you, or that you could better raise them, then I would step aside, but deep in my heart I believe that I am the best person to mould and guide them—and love them too."

The Peterson clan moved back to Germany. It was a brief and bitter family experiment. Soon, Michael returned to Durham with Martha and Margaret. He left his two boys with their mother in Germany.

At the end of the school year in 1991, Patty came back to the States with her boys. She drove Margaret and Martha up to Rhode Island and told the Blairs they could adopt the girls. She said that she and Michael were separating, and Margaret and Martha needed a stable home environment. By this time, Michael had moved in with Kathleen Atwater and her daughter, Caitlin.

Margaret Blair had heard about their nanny, Barbara, from Liz and from her mother. Now, she heard from Barbara for the first time. Barbara was delighted about the impending adoption. She asked if she could send the girls mementoes and a tape of a German song she used to sing to them.

Margaret was pleased with Barbara's continued interest in the girls and encouraged it. Throughout the summer, Barbara called the girls, sent them short notes and arranged for the delivery of little posies to them from a flower shop.

One day in late August, Margaret Blair answered the phone. A hostile Mike Peterson was on the other end. He told her that he had no idea that Patty left the girls to be adopted. He said it was his decision—only his—and totally up to him.

He was coming to Rhode Island. He would take the Blairs out to dinner and announce his decision on whether or not they could keep the girls. Kathleen and Caitlin made the trip north with him and they stayed at the Biltmore in Providence.

Michael changed his story, telling Margaret and Jim that he would leave the decision up to the two girls. The Blairs knew how Margaret felt. She had complained to them that she had no privacy in the Peterson home—all of her mail was opened by Michael.

Michael, Kathleen and Caitlin sat down with Margaret and Martha to discuss the future. When Margaret suggested that she might want to live with her aunt and uncle, Michael said: "I leave this choice up to you. But I'm telling you that your mother never—never—wanted you to live with your Aunt Margaret. Never. But I'm leaving the decision up to you."

With that level of emotional pressure, 10-year-old Margaret and 9-year-old Martha succumbed. They said they *wanted* to live in Durham, but it looked as if they had been out-manipulated by Mike Peterson. From that day forward, Mike discouraged any visits to Rhode Island.

On September 11, 1991, Patty Peterson wrote a letter expressing her dismay to Margaret and Jim Blair. "Since learning of the removal of Margaret and Martha from your home, one week after the fact, I have been in a state of profound shock and physical unwellness. I offer to you both deeply felt apology, as I came to you in good faith. I sorrow that you and your children received the girls into your family with open hearts, and then were subject to their arbitrary departure."

She went on to emote her disdain for the actions of her estranged husband: "The present situation is anathema to my very soul." She reiterated her willingness for the Blairs to adopt the girls and concluded the letter on a solemn note: "I do not believe, however, that it was Elizabeth's will that her daughters be subject to frequent dislocation nor that the family of her friend and two sons be destroyed."

Now, Patty and Mike Peterson were separated. Kathleen Hunt Atwater was divorced from her husband, Fred. The three girls in the two households formed the link that launched the intriguing, successful novelist and the ambitious and beautiful dark-blonde engineer with gray-green eyes into orbit together. The stage was set for romance, extravagance and tragedy.

KATHLEEN HUNT
ATWATER PETERSON

"Life is too important to waste a single moment."

—Kathleen

22

Wanting a better life and believing the myth that the streets of America were paved with gold, the parents of John Franklin Hunt moved to Boston from Newfoundland, a maritime province of Canada, just before his birth in 1899. His father's death two years later left his mother in desperate straits. John was working to help support the family by the time he was 10 years old. The family soon moved to New York.

John learned the brick-laying trade in his new country and attended Cooper Union College. After completing his education, he started his own construction company.

In the 1940s, he was sub-contracting for another construction company. A young secretary there caught his eye. Veronica Ann Hogan, a New York native 21 years his junior, was responsive to his flirtation.

Veronica's father had died two days after Christmas when she was 16 years old. Her daughters thought she may have seen a substitute father figure in the older John Hunt, or perhaps she was looking for a way out of a hardscrabble existence. Whatever the motivation, Veronica fell in love. The couple married in 1946.

They did not stay in New York. They moved to

Kansas City, Missouri, where their first child, Steven Desmond Hunt, was born on January 23, 1951. The family then moved to Greensboro, North Carolina. There on February 21, 1953, Kathleen Morris "Kathy" Hunt first made her appearance.

The family settled in Lancaster, Pennsylvania, in 1955 and grew by the addition of another daughter, Candace Susan Hogan Hunt. A third girl, Lori Anne Hunt, was born five years later when John Hogan was 63 years old.

Both John and Veronica stressed the value of education to their children. John, unlike many men born in the nineteenth century, believed it was important for his daughters to go to college. He emphasized to his girls the need to have career objectives.

Although Veronica did not have a college education, she was a life-long learner. All of the children made their first trip to the library when they were 2 years old. Every evening, the family gathered at a dinner table stacked with books. A dictionary and encyclopedia were omnipresent. If any question was raised during mealtime conversation, Veronica had the resources at her fingertips to find the answers.

Steve was a protective and proud older brother. He was also ambitious at an early age, drawing his sisters into entrepreneurial schemes. In one instance, he supervised while his sisters wove fabric loops on a plastic loom to make potholders. Then he escorted them door-to-door as they peddled their wares to their neighbors.

All three girls were members of the Girls Club that met at their elementary school Tuesday and Thursday evenings. Each month, the most exemplary one in the group was named "Girl of the Month." Every year, one person was selected to be "Girl of the Year." In seventh grade, this honor fell to Kathy. She advanced to the next level of competition, vying with others who had won the same award in other clubs. Kathy came out on top, winning the coveted title of "Lancaster Lass."

Kathy carried her ambition to succeed into high school. She was president of the debating club and editor of the school magazine, *Generation*, at McCaskey High School. She played on the tennis team and volunteered at St. Joseph's Hospital.

She was the first student selected to take advanced Latin classes at the local college, Franklin & Marshall. She graduated first in her class of 473 and was selected for publication in *Who's Who in American High School Students*.

In 1971, Kathy Hunt earned a singular and historic honor—she was the first woman ever admitted to Duke University's School of Engineering. Her qualifications were so exceptional that admission was a breeze. When her brother Steve left for Virginia Military Institute to study engineering two years earlier, his badge of honor was his slide rule. Times had changed by the time Kathleen went off to school—she carried a $160 Texas Instruments calculator.

As an undergraduate, she was a contributing editor to *DukEngineer* magazine. She lived on the third floor of her dormitory. In a pair of wooden-soled Dr. Scholl's sandals, she raced up and down the stairs amazing everyone with her coordination and agility.

When she came home after the first semester, she

informed her family that she was no longer Kathy—she was now Kathleen. When Candy asked her to please pass the salt, Kathleen picked up both the salt and the pepper and instructed her younger sisters that passing them together was proper etiquette.

Kathleen took a Physics class in the summer of 1972. Her parents suspected that something more than academics drove this decision. They packed up the family and drove from Pennsylvania to Durham to find out what it was. When they met Fred Atwater, a graduate student and a teaching assistant in the Physics Department, the reason was clear.

Kathleen and Fred's relationship started with trips out for coffee after his evening office hours. Kathleen spent her spare time thinking up intelligent questions to ask in order to impress Fred. And it worked.

To Fred, she was an intelligent and thoughtful young woman eager to discuss points of philosophy and life itself. Besides being smart, she was very sweet. She was the kind of person who would do nice things for other people for no reason at all. And, Fred thought, she was very attractive.

After the summer session, Kathleen went home to Lancaster for a few weeks. When she returned to Duke for the fall semester, she and Fred started dating.

During the summer of 1973, Kathleen took her first career-oriented job as a junior engineer at Huth Engineers in Lancaster. The next summer, she was a junior engineer at W.M. Piatt & Company in Durham.

She graduated from Duke with a Bachelor of Science degree in Civil Engineering in 1975. She and Fred married on August 3 of that year in a civil ceremony at a magistrate's office in Durham. No family members from either side were present, but a handful of college friends were there to witness the exchange of vows.

The newlyweds took a trip to Kathleen's home later that month. Veronica and John welcomed them with open arms and threw a reception in their honor.

Kathleen and Fred returned to Duke to further their education. Fred continued his work on his doctorate in Physics, and Kathleen pursued a master's degree in Civil Engineering. She worked as a teaching assistant in the department in the first year of graduate school and as a research assistant both years.

In May 1976, she made her first professional presentation at the American Society of Civil Engineers conference at Waterloo in Canada. The subject was a futuristic look at magnetic power as a basis for transportation.

The Atwaters moved to Columbia, Maryland, when Fred finished his doctorate and accepted a position in research at Johns Hopkins Applied Physics Lab. They bought their first home there and Candace was a frequent visitor. She enjoyed hanging with the couple whenever she could.

In February 1977, Kathleen finished her master's thesis. She turned down an offer from Procter & Gamble because Fred did not want to relocate, and accepted a position as applications engineer at Baltimore Aircoil–Pritchard, a subsidiary of Merck & Co., specializing in the construction and repair of large-scale, field-erected cooling towers for use in industry and at power-generating facilities.

For more than two years, Kathleen tried to get

pregnant. She was becoming impatient and frustrated with her lack of success. Her long wait came to an end in the summer of 1981. She went to her doctor's office for a test on the morning of her husband's 35th birthday. The results were positive.

She greeted Fred that evening with ribbons wrapped all around her body. "Your birthday present is here," she told him. The couple was jubilant. Fred and Kathleen took birthing classes together—Kathleen practiced her breathing and Fred learned proper coaching techniques. They awaited the arrival of their first child with unbridled excitement.

1982 was a banner year for Kathleen. She moved into the executive stratosphere at BAC–Pritchard with a promotion to Product Manager for Engineered Products. Her responsibilities included goal setting, cost analysis, purchasing, developing marketing plans and writing catalogues.

The most fulfilling day of all, though, was April 27, when Kathleen gave birth to Caitlin Veronica Atwater. There was a small setback in their birthing plans when Caitlin was breech. It made a Caesarian section necessary, but Fred was there by her side just the same. He was overwhelmed with awe the moment he first saw his daughter and quite pleased that his secret preference for a girl was satisfied.

After ten years of bad health, Kathleen's father died before Caitlin was two years old. After forty years of marriage, Veronica Hunt was a widow. Her granddaughter was too young to understand the paroxysms of grief that swirled around her. Caitlin would be older before loss laid its lonely hand on her head.

While ambitious and purposeful in her career, Kathleen still made time to revel in the daughter she adored. Living in nearby Columbia, Maryland, the family often traveled to Washington, D.C. At a young age, Kathleen introduced Caitlin to the Smithsonian museums in the nation's capital.

Caitlin and her mother's favorites were the paintings of Mary Cassatt. Her frequent use of mother/daughter themes in her work evoked emotion in both of them. Caitlin developed an early love of standing in a room filled with artwork and absorbing its power.

Each trip to D.C. ended with a ride on the carousel. The Smithsonian National Zoological Park, however, was the major source of magic and wonder. On one occasion, Caitlin and Kathleen stood entranced watching as a baby giraffe was born. They went to the gift shop that day and bought a breakfast plate and mug to commemorate the event. Every Mother's Day, Caitlin would serve Kathleen's breakfast with these mementoes.

In 1986, Fred was on the hunt for a new job. He got offers from a number of companies, including ones in Long Island, Philadelphia and Raleigh–Durham. It was an easy choice. The couple enjoyed the area when they attended Duke, so they headed back south to North Carolina.

Fred began his new position at GTE Government Systems right away. Kathleen took a break from her career to set up their new home in the Forest Hills neighborhood of Durham, and get to know the neighbors. The Atwaters also bought a sailboat.

Kathleen shared Fred's love of sailing and loved to drive down to Washington, North Carolina, and set sail down the Pamlico River to the Pamlico Sound and on to the Outer Banks.

Caitlin loved when her grandmother, Veronica Hunt, came to visit their new home. Her attachment to this grandparent was magnified by the similarities between Veronica and Kathleen. Both were quick-witted and their banter rocked any room with laughter. They displayed similar mannerisms and possessed a deep well of nurture. Whether Veronica lived in Pennsylvania or Virginia or Florida, she showed up for every one of her granddaughter's birthday parties in addition to spending many weekends at Kathleen's home. Caitlin grew up knowing that, like her mother, her grandmother would always be there for her.

After a few month's hiatus in her career, Kathleen went back to work. June 8, 1987, was Kathleen's first day at Northern Telecom, later known as Nortel, in the Research Triangle Park, the commercial center for Raleigh, Durham and Chapel Hill. Her entry-level position was low on the totem pole. Kathleen's ambition and competence soon elevated her at Nortel as it had at BAC–Pritchard.

Her marriage to Fred Atwater did not fare as well. In fact, the foundation was crumbling beneath their feet. On her visits to their home, Candace noticed a young woman, a co-worker of Fred's, whose presence in the Atwater home seemed constant. She observed what she thought was an inappropriate level of intimacy between

Fred and this woman and spoke to her sister about it.

At first, Kathleen ignored the warning signs. At last, she could deny it no longer—her marriage was sinking fast. Fred moved in and out of the home for short periods of time.

Caitlin was aware of the fighting and unrest in the home, but she was having problems of her own. Second grade was proving to be a challenge. She had no difficulty with the academics, but the social interaction was a disaster. She didn't feel she fit in and she could not understand why the other children didn't like her. In the midst of her own turmoil, Kathleen took the time to listen to her daughter and help her cope.

She explained to Caitlin that her problem was only with one girl who was cruel to her, not with the whole class. "Don't let one little thing become a generalization," Kathleen told her. With every passing year, Caitlin developed a deeper appreciation for the consistency and constancy of her mother's advice and in her ability to break problems down to their bare essentials.

The last hurrah for the Atwater family was a trip to Disney World. Like millions of kids before her, Caitlin was enchanted. She did not like the teacups because her Dad—in a burst of enthusiasm—made them spin too fast for her taste. She was a bit leery of Space Mountain, too—a little too dark and a little too scary. But she was wild about Big Thunder Mountain Railroad in Frontierland. She squealed with delight as she zipped in and out of the deserted gold mine on the runaway mine train.

They picked up a set of four Disney placemats on that trip. Caitlin claimed the one with Cinderella on it as her own. When the table was set for dinner, that mat always marked her place.

After that trip, Fred moved out for good. The reality of the permanence of the situation sunk in for Caitlin when her mother gave her a Baby-Sitters Club book about divorced parents.

Kathleen worked hard to shield Caitlin from her marital problems. Her daughter, though, was a very bright girl, who noticed her mother's tear-stained cheeks and forced smile.

1987 was a difficult year for Kathleen. Still she took time away from her problems to help her younger sister, Candace, pick out her wedding gown and make other nuptial arrangements.

Candace Hunt married Mark Zamperini in a ballroom with a small, but traditional, ceremony. The bridal party consisted of a best man, a maid of honor and Caitlin Atwater as the flower girl. The family gathered round for the exchange of vows.

It was a bittersweet time for Kathleen. She had hope and joy for her sister and her future. For herself, she had despair. The service resurrected the memory of vows she had exchanged—vows that were broken—and a marriage that was shattered beyond repair.

As is natural in times of divorce, a bit of friction arose between mother and daughter. Caitlin wanted a "cool mom" like some of her friends had—a mom who would never say "no." But Kathleen did not succumb to Caitlin's childish attempts to manipulate her guilt. She simply told her, "Caitlin, I am not here to be your friend. I am here to be your mother. Whatever comes of that, does."

Although out of the home, Fred kept a constant connection with Caitlin. His efforts with his daughter enabled her to accept the divorce and not develop an unhealthy desire to salvage her parents' marriage.

At the same time, just a block away, Michael and Patty Peterson's relationship was deteriorating. Patty decided to go back to Germany to teach. She wanted Margaret and Martha Ratliff to go to Rhode Island and live with their family. She told Michael that she had not signed up for another family. She already had one and that was enough.

Michael refused to relinquish guardianship of the girls, and Patty and the boys went to Germany without him. Kathleen and Mike reached out to each other to fill the void in their lives. Caitlin, Margaret and Martha played together with increasing frequency.

One day, in 1989, Kathleen and Fred sat down with their daughter to ask her an important question. "How would you like it if Margaret and Martha came to live with you?"

Caitlin was delighted—Barbie playmates all the time! It would be like one big never-ending sleepover. In Caitlin's mind, Michael Peterson was just a tag-along.

When Margaret, Martha and Mike moved into their home, Kathleen took her daughter aside to reassure her. "Caitlin, you are my daughter. My love for you is not going to change. But Margaret and Martha are going to be my daughters now, too."

Although the concept of death was still alien to a child of her age, Caitlin did understand on a superficial level that Margaret and Martha were orphans, and realized that they needed a mother. Kathleen, who had always wanted more children, was thrilled to nurture two more.

True to her word, Kathleen cherished the Ratliff girls. Before she arrived on the scene, Margaret and Martha attended public schools even though the Petersons enrolled Todd and Clayton in private schools. Kathleen placed both of the girls in a private Catholic school.

Of course, there were the normal problems of blending a household. Concessions needed to be made for the harmony of the whole. With three girls between 7 and 9 years old, rivalries did arise. One clash was over the Disney placemats. Margaret, Martha and Caitlin all wanted to use the Cinderella mat. Compromise did not come easy. From Caitlin's point of view, she shared her house and her mother with Margaret and Martha; she was darned if she'd share her placemat, too.

Patty, with Clayton and Todd, moved back from Germany after the school year and into the same neighborhood. Although living with Kathleen, Michael had not severed his ties to Patty. When Patty announced at summer's end that she had another job in Germany and was taking the boys with her, Mike had second thoughts about the dissolution of his marriage. He took Margaret and Martha with him and followed her overseas. Now, the two little Ratliff girls suffered loss again—they were torn away from their surrogate sister and another substitute mother.

Not long after Margaret and Martha had settled in with Patty as their substitute mother, Michael decided the marriage was over after all. He brought Margaret and Martha back with him to Durham. And left his two boys in Germany.

Far from his father's watchful eye, Clayton started running amok. He experimented with alcohol and played with explosives. He built a homemade bomb during his senior year in high school, and blew up a phone booth after his application to Massachusetts Institute of Technology was rejected. He also attempted to send chemicals he stole from his school to his father's house in the States. The package did not make it. An acid leak injured several mail handlers and the package was intercepted and destroyed.

Clayton did not pay any price for the destruction caused by his behavior—at least, not yet.

MICHAEL AND KATHLEEN

"With Michael by your side,
you showed us how to rise to every occasion."

–Maureen Berry

23

Kathleen's star continued to rise at Northern Telecom. She visited Russia and the Ukraine to explore the possibilities of her company's expansion into the Commonwealth of Independent States, formerly the Soviet Union.

Kathleen comforted Caitlin through the first loss in her life in 1992. Her great-grandfather on her father's side was a special person to her. Although he was deaf, the two communicated well. He was a patient and gentle man who loved children—especially Caitlin.

Caitlin adored the man she called Super Pop-Pop. He was 104 years old when he died, but his passing still broke the little girl's heart. Kathleen sat by her ex-husband's side during the funeral and held her daughter tight while she shed tears of grief.

Home from Europe for good, Mike Peterson was ready to purchase a home that suited his lofty position as a *New York Times* best-selling author. He had quite a bit of money to invest. He still had a great deal of his $600,000 advance for *A Time of War*, and he'd received additional funds when NBC acquired an option on that book. On top of that, his agent sold his unfinished manuscript, *Peace and Reparations*, to Simon & Schuster for a $450,000 advance.

He found the perfect home in the heart of the Forest Hills neighborhood at the corner of Cedar and Kent Streets. Built in 1940, its 10,000 square feet made it the largest home in Durham. It boasted fourteen rooms, including six bedrooms, a striking spiral staircase in the front of the house, another unique staircase in the back and an elaborate swimming pool.

The house was featured in a movie, *The Handmaid's Tale*, released in 1990 and based on a book by Margaret Atwood. Robert Duvall and Faye Dunaway starred in the movie and three thousand area residents appeared as extras.

The value of the home was listed on the tax records as $1.2 million. Peterson knew he could get it for a lot less. There was just one catch. He did not get a regular paycheck and the bank wanted the signature of his wife, Patty, on the loan.

Patty balked. She wanted nothing to do with that house. Michael took her out to Reno to visit his parents. He prevailed upon them to help him make Patty come to her senses. Michael had not been able to persuade her, but the pleas of his parents did the trick. Patty signed on the dotted line. The deal was closed on July 7, 1992.

Although Patty's name was on the deed, Mike moved into the home with Kathleen Atwater. Living with them were Margaret and Martha Ratliff, Caitlin Atwater and

Clayton Peterson, who had just returned from Germany after graduating from Frankfurt High School. He enrolled as an Engineering student at Duke University.

The move to Cedar Street created a rift in Kathleen's family. Her sister, Candace, thought she was wrong to live with a married man when there were children involved. The two sisters did not speak for more than a year.

Kathleen was a gracious and willing hostess. She often opened her home for after-concert receptions and fund-raising galas for the American Dance Festival, the Durham Art Guild, the Mallarme Chamber Players and the Carolina Ballet. She thought nothing of planning a dinner for one hundred people and preparing all the food herself.

"She was the Martha Stewart of Durham," said Jimmy Gibbs, society columnist for *The Herald-Sun*. "She actually prepared the food for the parties. [. . .] Virtually all her foods were homemade—and they were always wonderful."

Kathleen was also active with the Durham Arts Council, serving a term on the board of directors and with the Historic Preservation Society. She often provided auction items for the Durham Arts Guild. Both she and Michael were involved in the Forest Hills Neighborhood Association.

Filled with thousands of dollars' worth of antiques and collectibles, including 200-year-old furniture from Germany and Japan, and carved vases from ancient Chinese dynasties, the home was a breathtaking sight for first-time visitors. And Kathleen kept it all spotless. She was the queen of clean. She knew the best solution for making short work of any kind of dirt or stain and she used her knowledge like a woman possessed. One of her favorite outside activities was power-washing the exterior of her home until it shined.

Kathleen's other love was shopping. Little thrilled her more than finding a great bargain. When the three girls were going through the stage where their shoe sizes seemed to change every week, Kathleen found a great buy on tennis shoes. She came home with twenty pairs in sizes the girls could grow into.

Todd Peterson returned to North Carolina after his graduation from high school in 1993. Kathleen blended the family of seven together like a magician. She expected all five children to be at the dinner table every night. She sat at one end and Michael sat at the other. The conversation was animated and boisterous. At times, multiple concurrent conversations created an atmosphere of convivial pandemonium.

All these activities, though, did not fill the void Kathleen felt from the disconnect with her family. She wanted to make peace, and planned a family reunion. Her mother and her sisters and brother and their families showed up for the food and fun in Kathleen's beautiful new home.

The reunion also gave Kathleen's family members the opportunity to meet the man who was the root cause of the family uproar. They liked Michael. They found him funny and entertaining.

Former U.S. Representative Nick Galifianakis introduced Michael Peterson to David Perlmutt in 1993 with the idea that the two men should collaborate on a book.

David was a reporter for *The Charlotte Observer*. The year before, he had written an article about Tsui Chi Hsii, a Chinese man nicknamed Charlie Tsui or Charlie Two Shoes by the U.S. Marines who befriended him in 1945.

When the communists took over in 1949, the Marines pulled out and Charlie spent seventeen of the next thirty-five years as a political prisoner because of the suspicions raised by his close relationship to the Marines.

When the soldiers learned of his plight, they moved heaven and earth—and the U.S. Congress—to bring him to the United States. After publishing Charlie's story in his paper, David sold reprint rights to *Reader's Digest* and *Parade* magazine. The hundreds of letters generated by the article in these two periodicals indicated a national audience for a book that would detail the complete story.

At their first meeting, Mike and David sat out by the pool at 1810 Cedar Street and talked for over an hour. Both felt they could work well together and soon they had prepared a chapter-by-chapter proposal, attached news clippings and sent it off to Michael's agent.

They did not find a buyer for the concept until 1996. The Naval Institute Press, a small outfit that had made its mark on the landscape with the publication of Tom Clancy's first book, *The Hunt for Red October*, signed a contract with the two writers. It would be two years of work after the sale before *Charlie Two Shoes and the Marines of Love Company* was finally published.

Michael wrote during the day, then left to work out at the YMCA each afternoon at 4. Sometimes he did not return until 7 or 7:30 at night. Kathleen always kept dinner warm and quieted the impatient children so the whole family could be together for dinner.

Unbeknownst to his wife, Mike's trips to the Y were not always as wholesome as they sounded. The steam room had become a trysting place for homosexual activity. While men engaged in sexual activity inside, a lookout was posted on the bench outside the door to sound a warning if any staff approached. Kathleen had divorced Fred for an extramarital affair with a woman. Surely, if she had been aware of this infidelity, she would have left Michael in a heartbeat.

Some troubles in the Cedar Street household were more visible. During the summer of 1993 when Clayton was between his freshman and sophomore years, Michael found it necessary to send his son to Duke Hospital for counseling because of disciplinary problems at home and at the university. Mike added to the household chaos by being arrested for DWI (Driving While Intoxicated). The charge was later reduced to reckless driving.

Then in 1994, the image of the perfect blended family blew up in their faces. On April 24, in a closet in the Allen Building at Duke University, an administrator discovered a bomb made with a Gatorade bottle filled with gasoline. Someone had lit the fuse, but it burned out inches before ignition. On a nearby table was a note stating that war had been declared on the university. A further search revealed that someone had stolen the equipment the school used to make official identification cards for the students.

Clayton was a suspect. Michael Peterson cooperated

with the police and gave permission for them to search his home. In the attic, they discovered an assortment of model rocket engines, gunpowder, a coffee grinder, lengths of fuse and the stolen I.D. equipment. More telling was the presence of six pipe bombs and the materials to make thirteen more.

Two of the bombs were rigged for aerial assault. They were constructed so that they could be screwed onto an arrow and launched from a crossbow. All of the bombs were designed to send metal projectiles flying in all directions at a very high rate of speed.

Mike Peterson belittled the danger of those devices, telling *The Chronicle*, "Those six little things could fit inside a shoebox."

Upon his return from a trip to Myrtle Beach, South Carolina, Clayton was arrested at his dorm. The state charged him with breaking and entering. The federal government brought one charge against him for possession of an unregistered destructive device.

Mike Peterson rushed to his son's defense, saying that Clayton's only intent was to create a diversion so that he could get away with stealing the I.D. equipment to replace the fake I.D. he lost in mid-April. "There was never an intention to ignite the bomb," Mike Peterson said in a written statement. "There was only an apolitical, hedonistic intent to party." Clayton had even spliced the fuse with electrical tape, his father said, to prevent it from exploding. Some investigators speculated, however, that the electrical tape tactic was a delaying device to allow him time to escape.

At the end of May, a grand jury handed down two indictments for possession of an unregistered destructive device and a third indictment for the manufacture of those devices. Clayton faced up to 30 years in prison and $750,000 in fines.

At the Federal Correctional Institute at Butner, Clayton underwent psychiatric evaluation to determine whether or not he was fit to stand trial. It was easy jail time for the 19-year-old. He had access to the library and a weight room and was not required to wear a uniform.

At the end of June, the psychiatrists at Butner released their report: Clayton was fit to stand trial. Plea bargaining negotiations began at once. In September, Clayton admitted that he broke into the building, planted the bomb and left the note. In exchange for a guilty plea for possession of the bomb, prosecutors dropped the other charges.

Clayton was released to the custody of his parents. He wore an ankle bracelet that confined him to his parents' home with the exception of a medical emergency. He was ordered to receive psychiatric treatment at Duke's community clinic. On the advice of his attorney, he did not go.

At the end of December, Clayton appeared in U.S. District Court in Greensboro, North Carolina. With tears in his eyes, he told Judge William Osteen, "I regret all my actions. I am remorseful. I apologize to everyone, to Duke, to you, to society, to my parents, my friends."

The judge had a broad range of options, from a maximum of 10 years to a minimum of 46 months. Osteen told Clayton, "Goodness knows, I know of nobody in this courtroom who possesses more potential than you."

The judge then handed down a sentence of 4 years and 1 month in the federal prison. He ordered Clayton to pay $1,712.55 for damage caused to the Allen Building by his break-in. After Clayton's release, he would be supervised for 3 years and be required to perform 100 hours of community service each year.

24

While Clayton's troubles were in full swing, Michael Peterson started work on a new book on the Camp Pendleton "porno" scandal. His nine-page description outlined a creative non-fiction work attacking the military's denial of rampant homosexual activity and its fear of the threat it posed. He would detail the forty-three discharges and the imprisonment of one Marine, reveal the cult underground of pornographic films and expose "the records of the men who conducted this witch hunt."

In the conclusion of his proposal, he asserted that "the fear and prejudice of homosexuals is just another in the long line of bigotry, and eventually, it will be overcome also. There is no question of this. The only question is when. What, after all, is there to fear?"

In furtherance of his research, Peterson placed an ad in the personals section of the *Frontiers News Magazine*, a gay-oriented publication in late September 1994. It read: "Well known author, former decorated combat marine officer, doing research for a sympathetic book on the marines involved in the porno videos shoot near Camp Pendleton. If you were involved or know someone who was please contact me. You need not reveal your identity."

Although the address for a response was a post office box, the phone number listed rang at 1810 Cedar Street.

By 1995, Peterson had dipped his toe into the local political waters. He blasted the public school system in a letter to the editor published in *The Herald-Sun* in April. He railed against the principal who saw nothing wrong with all-black schools. He praised re-districting for better racial balance. And he attacked the money spent on perks for school administrators.

He concluded his piece with a battle cry that foreshadowed his formal entrée into politics: "Now that I know where my taxes go, I also know where my vote is going next election: not to those who allow this kind of grotesque waste."

In March of 1996, Peterson's *Peace and Reparations* was 405-page hardback novel re-titled *A Bitter Peace*. The main protagonist was Diplomat Bradley Marshall, who tried to end the conflict in Vietnam in Peterson's previous novel, *A Time of War*.

A Bitter Peace opened in 1972 and involved Marshall in the South Vietnamese peace treaty, the death of the Shah of Iran and the negotiations with the Ayatollah Khomeini. *Publishers Weekly* wrote: "Peterson seems to be trying to do for recent U.S. history what Alexandre Dumas did for the history of France [. . .] It is a mission he performs well, when he sticks to the political; it's only when the personal takes over that his storytelling falls flat."

When interviewed by *The Herald-Sun*, Michael claimed he had finished 300 pages of his next book, which he described as a techno-thriller. He made no mention of his research into the Camp Pendleton homosexual film scandal.

TOP LEFT: Michael Peterson holds his new sister, Ann, as his younger brothers—Jack (*l*) and Bill (*r*)—stand by his side. The siblings paired off: Michael and Bill formed a close relationship because they always shared a bedroom, while Jack and Ann's closeness in age made them tight.

TOP RIGHT: Eugene Peterson's career with the U.S. Army took his family all over America and as far away as Denmark and Japan, where Bill, Ann, Jack, and Michael (*l to r*), are pictured in a park.

LEFT: Michael, Bill, Ann, Eleanor, Eugene, and Jack Peterson are pictured in July 1992, the same month that Michael purchased the 10,000-square-foot home at 1810 Cedar Street in Durham, NC, and moved in with Kathleen Atwater. Michael's estranged wife Patty's name was on the deed, after Eleanor and Eugene convinced her to sign on the loan.

LEFT: Michael Peterson and Patty Bateman were married in 1966 at Fort Belvoir Proving Ground in northern Virginia, just minutes from Mount Vernon, Old Town Alexandria, and Washington, D.C. Michael's brothers, Bill and Jack, are immediately to his left.

LEFT: Patty, Todd, Michael, and Clayton Peterson (*l to r*) in Germany, a few months after Todd's birth in March 1976. The family moved to Germany shortly before Clayton was born in December 1974, and they subsisted only on Patty's salary as a teacher.

Patty, Todd, Michael, and Clayton Peterson in 1990, the same year Michael's first novel, *A Time of War*, was published. The book's dedication read, "To Patty, who suffered all my wounds. To Clayton and Todd, whose suffering, I pray, is only in my nightmares." Though Margaret and Martha Ratliff were living with the Petersons off and on at the time, Michael neglected to mention them in the book.

LEFT: Liz McKee holding Snoopy the Red Baron, a gift from George Ratliff. George and Liz were married in Germany in May 1981.

LEFT: Liz McKee and George Ratliff at their wedding in early May of 1981 in Germany. Patty Peterson was Liz's maid of honor, and Randy Durham, George's close friend from the Air Force, was the best man. George's mother flew out from Texas for the ceremony. *Photo by Randy Durham.*

ABOVE LEFT: Martha (*l*) and Margaret (*r*) Ratliff stand beside the family's Goosy Goosy Gander kitchen lamp in 1984. Since the children's father had died the year before, Liz hired a nanny, Barbara O'Hara, to help her take care of them. *Photo courtesy Randy Durham.*

ABOVE RIGHT: Martha Ratliff at the foot of the stairs in her home in Gräfenhausen in November 1985, the same spot where her mother, Liz, would be found dead later that same month. Martha's father, George, had died only two years earlier while on a secret mission with the Air Force. *Photo courtesy Randy Durham.*

LEFT: The same staircase after Liz's death, which German police declared to be from a cerebral hemorrhage that led to a fall down the stairs. Liz's friend, Cheryl Appel-Schumacher, made the black marks on the photograph to indicate where she had cleaned Liz's blood off the walls. *Photo courtesy Durham Police Department.*

LEFT: Kathleen Atwater and Michael Peterson in 1995. Michael's marriage to Patty Peterson ended in 1996, and she signed over her rights to the house Michael and Kathleen shared.

BOTTOM: The extended Peterson clan celebrated Michael and Kathleen's marriage at their home in Durham. Michael proposed to Kathleen on New Year's Eve in 1996, and they were married on June 21, 1997. Kathleen's sister-in-law Cynthia sat on the terrace by the pool for three days creating bouquets, corsages, boutonnieres and table displays for the event.

Michael Peterson confers with Thomas Maher, a member of his defense team, during his 2003 trial for the murder of his wife, Kathleen. *Photo by Diane Fanning.*

Defense attorney David Rudolf cross-examines Agent Duane Deaver, the SBI's lead instructor on blood-stain evidence. Deaver had testified as an expert witness in over 60 trials, and blood spatter evidence was key in the Peterson trial as prosecutors argued that the patterns were inconsistent with a fall, as the defense claimed. *Photo by Diane Fanning.*

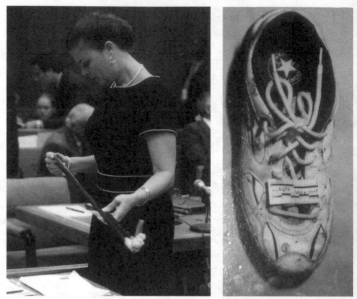

TOP LEFT: Assistant District Attorney Freda Black examines two blowpokes. One was sent from Kathleen Peterson's sister Candace Zamperini who claimed it was an exact replica of the potential murder weapon that had disappeared from the scene of the crime. The second was a surprise exhibit from the defense, who claimed the blowpoke had been found in the Petersons' garage. *Photo by Diane Fanning.*

TOP RIGHT: According to witnesses for the prosecution, the 90-degree angle of the blood spatter patterns on Michael Peterson's shoes were indicative of someone standing over a victim, stains that could not be received just by coming into contact with the body at the bottom of the stairs. Peterson left the shoes by Kathleen's body before emergency personnel arrived at the house. *Photo by Durham Police Department.*

LEFT: Michael Peterson was wearing these bloody shorts when law enforcement arrived at his home following Kathleen's death. *Photo by Durham Police Department.*

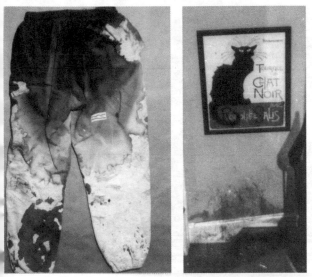

TOP LEFT: Kathleen Peterson was wearing these sweatpants on December 9, 2001, the night of her death. Police and emergency personnel said some of the blood was dry when they arrived on the scene, though when Michael Peterson called 911, he said his wife was still breathing. *Photo by Durham Police Department.*

TOP RIGHT: Michael Peterson said he found Kathleen in this spot after they had been celebrating the movie option of one of his books. He said she fell, but prosecution experts said the blood spatter patterns, including those on the framed *Chat Noir* poster, were inconsistent with a fall. *Photo by Durham Police Department.*

LEFT: Caitlin Atwater came down to Durham, NC, from Cornell University in Ithaca, NY, to attend her stepfather's trial. Liz Ratliff's sister, Margaret Blair, is in the background to the right. She testified for the prosecution. *Photo by Diane Fanning.*

Michael and Kathleen Peterson lived and were married in their home at 1810 Cedar Street. Kathleen also died at the house on December 9, 2001. *Photo by Diane Fanning.*

KATHLEEN HUNT
PETERSON
FEB. 21, 1953
DEC. 9, 2001
JUST WHISPER MY NAME IN YOUR HEART
I'LL BE THERE

Kathleen's daughter designed and erected the gravestone over Michael Peterson's objections about cost. Roses were engraved on Kathleen's headstone because they were her favorite flower. The excerpt from Colleen Hitchcock's poem, "Ascension," was read at Kathleen's funeral. *Photo by Diane Fanning.*

25

Michael's marriage to Patty Peterson was legally dissolved in 1996. Patty may have held the papers in her hand, but she did not accept the reality. Although they were separated and divorced, and her husband was living with another woman, Patty was, in her mind, a married woman. She had no plans to pursue any new relationships. "He's my husband," she said. "I marry once in life." She felt the sanctity of the institution outweighed the actions of an individual.

In protest, she signed papers for Michael once again. This time, it was a quit deed on the Cedar Street home. She signed over any rights she had to that property in exchange for sole ownership of the marital home on University Drive and full ownership of all furniture and other belongings in that home at the time.

On New Year's Day of 1997, Kathleen called her brother Steve and his wife, Cynthia, with her good news. Michael proposed to her the night before at the country club. The wedding would be in June.

Kathleen, with the help of her sister Candace, planned

an elegant wedding in the Cedar Street home. Cynthia, Steve and their three children arrived early to help with the final preparations. For three days, Cynthia sat out on the terrace by the pool, creating bouquets, corsages, boutonnières and table displays for the big event. She got only sporadic assistance from friends of the Petersons who drifted in and out of the home. But Cynthia did not mind—Kathleen was more than a sister-in-law, she was a friend.

The day before the wedding, Steve and Cynthia's twins, 11-year-old Kim and Jack, spent the day with Michael's friend and former professor Richard White Adams, twining magnolia leaves and roses around the banister of the curved front stairway. Richard went out of his way to entertain the children while they created their masterpiece.

1810 Cedar Street was crowded with celebrants: friends, the bride's and groom's families—even George Ratliff's family—were present for the momentous day.

It was an unusual occasion at this home in that Kathleen did not prepare the food for her guests. One of her friends hosted the rehearsal dinner in her own home. Another came to the house the morning after the wedding and prepared breakfast for everyone staying there.

On June 21, 1997, Kathleen floated down the front stairway in a beautiful white dress. Caitlin, Margaret and Martha were the bridesmaids. Kim Hunt and Ashley Zamperini were junior bridesmaids. Richard White Adams and Todd were the best men. After Michael and Kathleen exchanged vows, the party began. Kathleen created a special position for little Hadley Zamperini, dubbing her "candy girl." She handed out bundles of sweet almonds wrapped in tulle and tied with a ribbon to the guests at the reception.

White tablecloths bedecked tables throughout the garden and around the swimming pool. Heavenly aromas arose from the incredible spread of salmon and other edible delights. Sounds of music and dancing filled the neighborhood.

At one point, Caitlin, Margaret and Martha crooned the Dixie Cups' old sixties song, "Chapel of Love." Kathleen joined in, lifting her voice with theirs—her face filled with smiles, her heart bursting with love for the world.

Richard White Adams made a toast to the couple. He dubbed his friend "a man of mystery." Todd followed with a second toast saying that Kathleen was good for Michael—he had never seen his dad so happy.

Kathleen and Michael did not go on a honeymoon right away—they spent that first night in their home full of guests. They followed a path of rose petals to their bed that Caitlin had strewn earlier that evening.

In the morning, they shared an elegant breakfast with family and friends. It appeared to be a marriage made in heaven.

The first indication to Kathleen's family that the relationship had a dark side arose when Lori saw the new yellow pursue that Kathleen brought back from the belated honeymoon trip she and Michael made to London and Paris. Kathleen loved expensive leather goods, but this $2,000 Louis Vuitton piece was a bit extravagant, even for her.

Kathleen told her that it was a gift from Michael. When Lori asked what the occasion was for this atypical generosity on Michael's part, Kathleen told her about an incident that occurred on their trip.

She and Michael fell asleep on a subway in Paris. When they awoke they realized they had been robbed. Michael was furious. He screamed. He raved. He grabbed Kathleen's arms and shook her. In his anger, he left bruises up and down Kathleen's arms. "He was angry at himself. He lashed out at me and hurt my arm," Kathleen told her sister. The purse was his way of saying he was sorry.

Michael Peterson started a new venture in 1997 as a columnist for *The Herald-Sun*. Peterson knew no sacred cows. He attacked everything that moved.

One of his first columns raked the district attorney and the police over the coals for wasting their time busting bingo halls. "The DA and cops can't do anything about those crimes—they can't catch any real criminals in City Hall, so they go after underage voters and bingo players."

He also attacked the city council, whom he referred to as "the thirteen dwarves." "Floyd McKissick proposed entrance signs—gateways—with flowers and shrubs to make Durham look pretty. And Floyd's the smart one on the Council. God help us!"

In another column about the ruling fathers, he condemned proposed tax increases. He wrote, "Your money is not being squandered. It is being stolen."

He came down on the police department and raised a stir. He wrote that cops are woefully underpaid and deserving of our appreciation, but the administration—Chief Teresa Chambers in particular—makes poor decisions.

"As I say repeatedly in this column—stupid is stupid, wrong is wrong, and it doesn't make any difference who commits the dumbness. He or she needs to be outed."

He blamed Chambers for the high rate of unsolved crimes. "The chance of a criminal getting caught is only slightly better than getting hit by lightning."

Police Chief Teresa Chambers flipped when she read her morning paper, and fired off a lengthy email to Michael Peterson. "I have spent a great deal of time stroking bruised egos and hurt feelings of employees who have moved this agency light years ahead in the short span of 18 months. Your assistance in getting out the real story will help our employees put this behind them."

Peterson did follow up with an apology, but heaped on more cynicism at the same time.

Another person to express his annoyance with Michael Peterson's columns was Canine Officer Trent Hall, who would later play an important role at the crime scene. He fired off a few abrasive emails about the dedicated officers who worked hard and were actually catching drug dealers and people breaking into homes in Durham.

Mike's responses were positive—encouraging Trent to want to understand Mike's viewpoint and to have Peterson understand his. After a flurry of emails, Trent asked Mike if he would like to ride with him one night. Mike readily accepted and Trent picked him up at his house at 10 P.M.

Trent spent about fifteen minutes in the Peterson home meeting Kathleen, Todd and Clayton. He left feeling the warmth of Kathleen's smile.

It was not a busy night on patrol. This gave Trent and Mike a lot of time to learn about each other. They had a productive exchange of ideas about Durham, growing up in the town and staff shortages in the department.

Trent pointed out crack houses and prostitutes as they drove the dark streets. Trent felt that Mike was very responsive and open to being educated about the force. When he dropped Mike off at 4:30 the next morning, they parted as friends and their email correspondence continued. Mike even wrote a glowing column about his experience that night.

In October of 1998, the Petersons had three bulldogs: Wilbur, Celeste and her brother, Clancey. That month, Celeste gave birth to Portia and Puck, a pair of twins sired by Wilbur. Celeste did not survive the ordeal. Michael assumed her role. He was up all hours of the night, feeding and caring for the two motherless pups.

On October 23, Mayor Nick Tennyson paid back the jabs of Michael Peterson's verbal assaults in the newspaper by giving him a singular honor. He named that Saturday "Michael Peterson Day" in honor of the columnist's fifty-fifth birthday. Beneath all the officious and high-flown language the mayor inserted his dig: "I hereby urge all of my fellow citizens [. . .] to give thanks that he has been limited to one column per week."

While Mike was irritating the city government with his caustic column, Kathleen was charming its citizens with her competence and grace. At Nortel, a conference room was named in her honor—something that had not been done for any employee before her. She was now in charge of 3,000 employees at offices in Dallas, Ottawa, Toronto and Research Triangle Park. She was amassing stock options like a bandit. And her financial worth on paper skyrocketed as Nortel's stock went up.

At home, her relationship with Caitlin had blossomed. Unlike many girls her age, Caitlin was comfortable seeking her mother's advice about guys, drinking and other personal issues. Kathleen shared with her the life lessons she'd learned from her own faults and errors in judgment.

Caitlin felt that they had developed a mother–daughter respect that allowed Kathleen to trust that her daughter would be honest with her. That gave Caitlin a lot more freedom in her senior year in high school.

When Caitlin succumbed to senioritis, her mother was there to help her get her act together and get back on her feet. Their camaraderie was enhanced by the bottomless sense of humor they shared. The two could be seen giggling together everywhere.

Kathleen was also brightening her neighborhood. On Christmas Eve, she delivered homemade croissants up one street and down the other. She hosted the community Easter egg hunts on her property and first-day-of school parties in her home.

And Kathleen loved roses. She pampered the three dozen rose bushes with their brilliant multi-colored blooms that grew her garden. On the surface, Kathleen Peterson appeared to be a woman who had it all.

26

Calling himself the Jesse Ventura of Durham politics, Michael Peterson paid a filing fee of $156.70 and became a candidate for the office of mayor on August 5, 1999. Peterson was one of five contenders on the ballot vying for the position in an October 5 primary. The two top vote-getters would then go head-to-head in a general election on November 2.

The leader of the pack was 48-year-old Nick Tennyson, the incumbent mayor. He had won the seat in 1997 against four other candidates. In addition to serving as mayor, he was the executive vice president of the Home Builders Association of Durham and Orange Counties.

Brenda Burnette, a city councilwoman representing Ward I was the first person to file on July 2. The 50-year-old single African-American mother had announced her intentions to run in January soon after she had been evicted from her publicly subsidized housing for failure to pay rent. When it came to her fellow candidate, Michael Peterson, she carried a big chip on her shoulder. He often referred to her and her fellow city councilmen as "dwarfs" in his columns. And he singled her out as "brain challenged."

58-year-old Ralph McKinney, Jr., filed the same day as Peterson. He was a familiar face at the meetings of the city council and the county commissioners. Although he had never held public office, this was not his first foray into a political race. He finished third in the Democratic primary for U.S. Senate in 1996 and garnered 520 votes in the mayoral primary race in 1997. He was vocal on issues of racism and sexism—even calling out NBA star Michael Jordan on accusations of discrimination against black customers at his automobile dealerships.

Floyd McKissick, a self-employed attorney, rounded out the list of choices for mayor. The 43-year-old African-American had served on the city council since 1993. His current term was set to expire in 2001. That summer, he had come under fire for a trip he had taken to his alma mater in New England at city expense. With degrees from Duke, Harvard and the University of North Carolina, coupled with his political experience, this Durham native sold himself as the most experienced candidate.

It was a lot of competition for a demanding part-time job that paid only $15,362 per year. At least three of the candidates spent more than twice the annual salary for this two-year job during their campaigns.

To avoid any conflicts of interest *The Herald-Sun* pulled Michael Peterson's columns from their pages after his announcement to run. The candidate responded by purchasing ad space to run his column on Friday each week in the Durham section of the paper. He also posted the weekly column on his Web site.

The site was designed and maintained by a Durham newcomer, Guy Seaberg, a former federal prosecutor and private attorney in Maine. He came to North Carolina in July 1999 after suffering a major setback in court the month before.

Seaberg took on a civil case for Lori D'Amico. He missed key filing dates and, despite numerous warnings from the court, continued to tell his client that all was well. D'Amico's case was thrown out of court because of these late filings and she sued Seaberg.

Maine Superior Court Judge Thomas R. Warren found Seaberg liable for breach of contract, professional negligence and breach of fiduciary responsibility. He awarded Lori D'Amico $1.1 million in actual damages and punitive damages of $25,000. D'Amico said that Seaberg moved to North Carolina where his wages could not be garnished on this judgment.

Peterson ran a tough, no-nonsense campaign, gathering new supporters every day. Fifty-nine percent of his campaign coffer of over $37,000 came from small donors who made contributions of $100 or less. In contrast, the incumbent Tennyson garnered 61 percent of his funding from larger gifts, many of which came from real estate developers and builders.

In the fliers Peterson distributed throughout the city, he proclaimed he'd be a full-time mayor and promised "every citizen will be my special interest." His four-point platform promised that he would stand up against drugs, gangs and illegal weapons, promote racial harmony, merge city and county governments and return the power to the people. He declared that his 120 columns demonstrated that he always told the truth.

To add warmth and local appeal to the advertising bulletin, he had a photograph posed with his wife and five children on the cover, and he wrote "I love Durham. It has been my home for 38 years. My children have grown up here." Conveniently, he neglected to mention that much of that time he was, in fact, away from his home and living overseas.

One of the other issues he put on the table was the need to press Duke University to give back more to the community of Durham. He claimed his criticism of the university's lack of financial commitment to the city did not arise from any animosity caused by his son's incarceration in 1994. To the contrary, he insisted that he attended football games, had given money to the school, donated items to the Rare Book Room and encouraged his three girls to attend Duke.

On another front, he urged the city to realize the necessity of having a full-time mayor and a full-time city council who were all compensated as professionals. He added that if elected, he would not request a pay increase before 2001. Many thought it odd that he would ask for one at all, since he was a strong critic of the city council's recent request for a salary increase.

His issues sparked positive feedback from the voters and he gained some ground drumming up grassroots support. Then, at the end of September, Peterson's public persona collided with reality. He had claimed he had earned two Purple Hearts in combat in Vietnam. He said that he received one because he took shrapnel in his leg when his radio operator stepped on a mine. In truth, the injury in question was the result of an automobile accident when he was stationed in Japan.

When a reporter confronted him with the fact that there was no record of his Purple Hearts, Peterson admitted his story was not true. In parting, he said, "Now I'll have to go home and tell my wife."

Like Patty before her, Kathleen stood by her man. When confronted by a friend about Michael's lies, she walked out of that woman's house and never entered it again.

With the election only days away, Peterson tried to repair the damage with a paid political column published on September 24. Peterson's column was too little, too late. To most of the electorate, it was nothing more than political entertainment. His credibility had been slashed and burned beyond reconstitution in the few days that remained before Election Day.

He still had support in the African-American community, the country club set and the artsy crowd, but the perception of Mike's public persona in other quarters dashed all hopes of salvaging the election. The cynical image Mike presented in his columns splashed on Kathleen, too. Many people in Durham who did not know them personally saw both as somewhat difficult and diffident people with arrogance toward the community.

On September 30, opponent Ralph McKinney was quoted in *The Chronicle*, the Duke University student newspaper, calling for Peterson to withdraw from the race and to "... inform his citizens that they have someone they can vote for that wasn't a coward, a traitor or had a yellow streak down his back and that's myself."

That same day, all five mayoral candidates participated in a political forum at the offices of *The Herald-Sun*. Of the 280 people in attendance, twelve had the opportunity to ask a broad range of questions. One asked each of the hopefuls how they would work with the city council. Four of them talked about developing interpersonal relationships, building consensus, creating a climate of amicability and using bargaining skills. Michael Peterson, though, brushed that query aside. He predicted that his voter mandate would be so large that the city council would have to follow his leadership. The important question, he said, was "How will they work with me?"

After the forum, Peterson and his supporters fled the persistent drone of Purple Heart questions by shoving cameramen and reporters out of the way without comment. The heat of media scrutiny cooled down the ardor of all but Peterson's core constituency. Tennyson got 39 percent of the vote, McKissick 30 percent. Michael Peterson came in third, losing to McKissick by 600 votes or 3 percent of the total. The two top finishers went on to the general election in November. Tennyson predicted that Peterson's supporters would vote for him. He was right—he won that race with 62 percent of the vote.

27

By December of 1999, Kathleen had amassed stock options valued at over $1 million at Nortel where she still used the name Kathleen Atwater. That month, she signed documents to defer 80 percent of her salary and bonuses in 2000. For 1999, the combined household income from salaries, rental properties and military benefits was $276,790. They would not do as well in 2000. Michael would receive $45,000 from military pension and Veterans Administration disability benefits, but he would not earn any money as a writer—or in any other job.

Caitlin Atwater was planning to attend Cornell University in Ithaca, New York, in the fall of 2000. Margaret Ratliff had been accepted at Tulane University in New Orleans.

Liz Ratliff's sisters, Rosemary Kelloway and Margaret Blair, along with Rosemary's daughter, Keri, traveled down from Rhode Island for Margaret's graduation ceremony. During the visit, they stayed at Maureen Berry's house across the street. Members of George Ratliff's family had rooms in the Peterson home.

One morning, Rosemary, Margaret Blair and Martha were sitting out by the Peterson pool relaxing and talking. Frolicking in and around the pool were the four English bulldogs: Puck and Portia, Celeste's offspring, now nearly 2 years old; their father, Wilbur; and their uncle, 4-year-old, 70-pound Clancey, nicknamed Fat Boy.

Clancey was up to his usual routine—jumping into the pool and swimming across it. He'd then step on the cooler fastened to the bottom of the pool as a step stool and make his way up the rungs of the ladder. After a quick shake, he'd pad back around to the other side and do it all over again. The other three bulldogs entertained themselves by running up and down the side of the pool barking at Clancey. Margaret, Martha and Rosemary were not paying much attention to the dogs' antics.

They did not notice when Clancey jumped in and grabbed the hose attached to the hard plastic fountain and dragged it to the deep end of the pool. But they could not ignore the horrible scream that erupted from the house as Michael barreled through the outside door to his office at a full gallop. His face was flushed as red as the roses blooming in the garden. The veins popped out on his forehead and in his neck. He looked like he was about to stroke out.

"You stupid dog!" he screamed. "I've replaced that thing three times already because of you!"

He raced past the three women to the other end of the pool. He reached into the water and grabbed the hard plastic fountain with one hand and jerked Clancey out of the pool with the other. He beat Clancey over the head with the fountain, again and again and again.

Poor Clancey whimpered and whined as he cowered at Michael's feet. Margaret jumped up and screamed,

"Stop it! Stop it! Stop it! Hit me! Leave that poor dog alone!"

His anger vented, Michael stopped, panting and out of breath. He stomped back into the house, telling the three by the pool, "Don't go near the dog. I'm teaching him a lesson. Don't go near him."

Margaret ignored his command and rushed to the poor dog's side. She and Clancey were both trembling all over. The blood vessels in Clancey's face had ruptured, making him a bloody mess. Margaret was outraged. After comforting the injured animal for a moment, she headed to the house to get a towel to clean his face. She stomped through the kitchen and up the stairs to the linen closet. She pulled out the nicest towel she could find.

Michael screamed, "Who's in the house?"

She did not answer. She stomped back outside, slamming the door as she left. While Margaret cleaned the blood off of Clancey's head, Martha sat with no expression on her face at all. She said, "The dog bleeds like that a lot."

Margaret was horrified by Martha's flat acceptance of the brutality she had just witnessed. With deliberate intent, Margaret left the bloodstained towel in a heap by the pool as a testament to Michael's cruelty.

The experience distressed Margaret Blair. She was not only concerned about the dog, she worried that Margaret and Martha could have been victimized by Peterson's violent temper, too. That fear intensified when Caitlin confided that Margaret had asked Michael why he had never adopted them and he said it was because it saved him a lot of money the way things were.

As long as the girls were classified as orphans, higher benefit payments came into the household, and college was cheaper.

On September 1, 2000, Kathleen's stock peaked at a value of $2,439,630. The Petersons' financial future could not have looked brighter.

Then, without warning, the bottom fell out. The stock prices plummeted. Nortel began its optimization program—a fancy phrase that meant they were downsizing and laying people off left and right. Even employees on Kathleen's executive level were being let go as departments merged and positions became redundant. By the end of the year, Kathleen's huge nest egg had shrunk to a value of less than $900,000. Still she maintained her 80 percent deferral on salary and bonuses.

In April, Michael and Kathleen applied for and received a second mortgage on the home at 1810 Cedar Street. In the previous year, their expenditures had exceeded their income once again—this year by nearly $100,000. Their credit card debt had skyrocketed. They now carried a balance of more than $114,000.

Kathleen was stressing out over her job and crumbling under the financial burden she carried with little help from her spouse. But when her mother needed her, she was there.

Veronica Hunt, a widow after forty years of marriage, had lived with Carl Schnitzer, her companion for the last fourteen years. In April, he died at the age of 90. Kathleen planned the memorial service and made the arrangements for his cremation.

All of Veronica's children—Steven, Kathleen, Candace and Lori—traveled to Florida without spouses or children to be with their mother for the service. Because Veronica lived in a two-bedroom home, Kathleen and Candace were farmed out to a nearby friend's house, where they shared a bedroom. It was the most one-on-one time they had together in years.

Kathleen unburdened her troubles to her sister during that visit. She bemoaned the millions of dollars she lost on paper. She was counting on that money, she said, to fulfill her dream of having a second home in Paris.

She spoke of her distress about the people being laid off. She worried they would not find jobs. She missed them. She was afraid that she would be next.

An ugly pattern was developing at Nortel, she told her sister. You would be promoted and your first task was to lay off your division. Then you would have no job. She was also worried that it was just part of a larger plan to move all the executive positions to the home office in Canada.

Candace asked her why she continued to put up with all the stress. Why didn't she get another job and leave Nortel?

"I will stick it out to the bitter end," Kathleen said. She knew she could not find another job in Durham that offered the same status and salary.

Kathleen talked about the stresses caused by the demands of the children. Three of them would be in college in the fall—they needed money for tuition, room, board, clothing and books. On top of that, Michael's grown sons were still demanding financial support.

The only bright spot in their finances was the reinstatement of Margaret's scholarship. In her freshman year, like many new college students, Margaret had neglected schoolwork for her social life. Tulane cancelled her scholarship because of the resulting bad grades. Margaret appealed and the grant was renewed.

Kathleen told Candace that she loved her home at 1810 Cedar Street, but she did not know how long she could stand the stress of living there. Because of its age and size, the expense and physical work required for its upkeep was staggering. She had very little help from the children or Michael. They had had a housekeeper off and on, but could not afford one now.

On top of the day-to-day upkeep, Kathleen continued, the house needed major repairs. There was a colony of bats in the attic. They had caused a leak in the house and now the roof had to be replaced. Termites had invaded the home and caused $10,000 worth of damage to the living room. The plumbing was a mess—Kathleen had not been able to take a shower for months.

Kathleen was desperate to simplify her life and relieve some of the financial pressure. She wanted to move from Cedar Street to a newly constructed, low-maintenance home in nearby New Hope Valley. But Michael refused.

"I am always tired," Kathleen complained, "and I don't have time to go see a doctor." She added, "I am not enjoying what I am doing. I am not enjoying life."

Candace was very concerned about her sister and

frustrated with Michael for not helping more with the financial situation.

In the spring, Mike sent an email to Martha's uncle, Thomas Ratliff, an oncologist at the University of Tennessee Cancer Institute in Memphis, to find funds to send her to the University of San Francisco.

"Apparently everyone is coming for Martha's graduation including Aunt Margaret Blair, who has personally spoken in Tongue with the Virgin Mary." He went on with additional scurrilous remarks about the family. "What a circus. So why aren't you coming? Or is the answer self-explanatory? Coward! Come save me. Bring Demoral!"

Then, Michael got down to the business at hand: He asked for $5,000 per semester toward tuition. "I know this is awful but I need to ask for it—either from you personally, or an advance on her share of the future estate." He said he could cover the expense of a local state school, but felt it was important for Martha to experience more of the world.

Thomas Ratliff responded without commenting upon the disparaging remarks Michael had made about his family. He agreed to pay the requested amount and promised he would try to come to the graduation.

When Margaret Blair and her niece Keri Kelloway came down to Durham again for Martha's high school graduation, Michael was very solicitous and put them up in his home. They had no idea that Michael held them in such deep disdain. Margaret saw Wilbur, Portia and Puck, but there was no sign of Clancey. She asked Michael where he was.

"Oh, oh, oh. It was a terrible thing. A horrible thing," he replied.

"What happened?" Margaret asked.

Michael would not look her in the eye. He talked fast. And he rambled. He told her that it was just terrible. Clancey had a heart attack and drowned in the pool. The kids found him floating there. Dead.

A chill went through Margaret as Michael prattled on. Her stomach churned as possibilities tumbled through her mind. She witnessed one episode of violence with Clancey. Was there another?

Candace Zamperini was uncomfortable with the story, too. When she asked Kathleen how Clancey died, her sister said that it was too painful to talk about and changed the subject. That was not like Kathleen and it made Candace very suspicious about the circumstances surrounding Clancey's death.

Soon after this visit, Puck disappeared. It was suspected that he had run away, since he had gone off once before. None of the family ever saw him again.

Looking back, Candace and Margaret both wish they had done something—anything—to prevent the death of a dog from becoming the foreshadowing of Kathleen's future.

28

Candace saw Kathleen and Mike again when Candace hosted a family get-together at her house on July 3. During this celebration, her concern for her sister escalated to alarm. Kathleen was agitated and nervous. She was far too stressed out by the ride up from Durham. She was even more stressed about the situation at Nortel than she was in the spring. The lay-offs had continued and the stock's dramatic drop kept worsening. The value of her nest egg, once $2.4 million, was heading below $50,000. As the two sisters talked in the kitchen, Kathleen popped a Valium and washed it down with a glass of wine.

Steve noticed that Michael's behavior was off and that Kathleen was stressed. He put it all down to their current financial situation and let it go.

Lori was concerned about her older sister, too. She visited Kathleen's home on Cedar Street with her two sons, William and Eddie, and her mother, Veronica Hunt. Eddie had just turned 5 and the blowpoke by the Petersons' fireplace was irresistible. He loved swinging it around like a sword. Lori retrieved it from him several times, concerned that he might break the glass-top table or chip the slate on the fireplace.

William noticed that Wilbur would not stop licking Portia's neck. Lori investigated and discovered a raw and oozing line under her collar that had to have been there for quite some time. She pointed it out to Michael, who removed the leather strap from her neck. She had thought Michael was attached to those dogs. She had seen him playing and swimming with them. The neglect made no sense to her.

Michael Peterson spent a lot of time at his computer. That was not unusual for a writer. It was unusual that a married man spent a great portion of that time browsing homosexual pornography.

One day in August, someone gave him a phone number for Brad, a male-to-male sexual escort, who was serving in the Army and stationed at Fort Bragg in Fayetteville. When he called Brad, the escort directed him to his Web site to check out his references.

Mike visited the site and discovered photographs and the following description: "I am jock-masculine and carry the same attitude. I'm a 25-year-old regular athletic guy. I'm 6'1" and 185 lbs, with a 32" waist and 42" chest. I am NOT a bodybuilder . . . yet. If you want some muscle worship, I am not your guy. I have short brown hair (lighter in the summer) and blue eyes. I have bright white teeth and I am clean shaven. My body is smooth and shaved in most places. I am tan, clean-cut, and have great skin." He continued in this vein with praise of his genital endowments.

His standard rates were posted: $150 per hour and $700 for an entire day. He even had a special vacation rate of $2,000. There was also a page containing testimonials from satisfied customers.

Mike was pleased with what he'd found and sent an email to Brad. "You have great reviews and I would like to get together with you." He suggested a daytime rendezvous and encouraged Brad to audition for Dirk Yates, a major player in the porn business, when Brad traveled to Palm Springs. A graphic description of the sexual activities of interest to Peterson completed the message.

But Brad was not familiar with Dirk Yates. Michael responded with a description of the autoerotic and homosexual films the man made with Marines in San Diego. "Some of my friends did films for him but I never did (though, I was better looking and better hung) because this was way before 'Don't ask, don't tell.'"

Mike told Brad that he thought Brad had the potential to be a star in the porn industry—a potential Mike felt they shared. Mike encouraged him to visit next week and concluded with a few vulgar statements about their future sexual escapades.

The next email concerned the logistics of their encounter and a comment about Kathleen. "Evenings are not great for me anyway; I'm married. Very happily married with a dynamite wife. Yes, I know, I know; I'm very bi and that's all there is to it."

Brad's radar detected too much friendliness in that email and made sure Michael understood that this was a financial arrangement. In his response, Mike made it clear he was aware that their relationship was all business.

On September 3, Mike urged him to come up to

Durham for the 6 A.M. flight he had the next morning. He suggested they could meet close to the airport and Brad could sleep on the plane. Two more emails followed with increasing urgency about the arrangements for their rendezvous.

In the end, Brad stood him up. He was tired and wanted to get some rest before his flight. On September 30, Brad emailed an apology to his would-be client. Michael never responded.

In October, during fall break, Caitlin drove down to Durham from Cornell with two of her college friends. She timed her departure to arrive on Cedar Street at 8:30 in the evening. Kathleen promised Caitlin that her favorite—chicken Parmesan with prosciutto—would be waiting for her when she arrived.

Caitlin encountered horrendous stop-and-go traffic on the way down. The worst of all was in the Washington, D.C., area. She called her mother and let her know she would not make it for dinner.

The girls arrived after 11. They had not stopped for dinner and were famished. They hoped to scrounge through the kitchen and find something to eat. To their surprise and delight, Kathleen greeted them with a set table and more delicious chicken Parmesan than they could possibly consume.

Kathleen enjoyed the visit. It gave her the opportunity to set aside her worries and pretend she was a college girl once again. On a shopping trip to Costco—Kathleen was nuts about that place—they all slipped one arm into children's Halloween costumes and held masks to their faces, laughing at their silliness and having a great time. Kathleen squeezed the paws of every giggling stuffed animal she could find to embarrass Caitlin. Caitlin turned red, but delighted in every second.

The morning the girls were leaving to drive back to Ithaca, Kathleen rose early and prepared a sumptuous breakfast of bacon, eggs and pancakes to send them on their way. It was the last time Caitlin would ever taste her mother's cooking.

29

On July 31, 2001, Michael Peterson, now president of the Forest Hills Neighborhood Association, had thrown his hat into the political ring again. This time, he ran for a city council seat against incumbent Howard Clement. Unlike the fat campaign chest he had for his run for mayor in 1999, Peterson raised only $800 in contributions this time. The negative residue from his last race covered his candidacy like an oil slick.

Despite the incessant attacks and accusations that Michael's muddy hands lobbed at the eighteen-year incumbent, November 6 was not Peterson's day. He only received 11,442 votes. His opponent brought in 18,324 votes—a clear victory. Peterson did not take this loss very well. He spouted venom in his column in the Duke University newspaper, *The Chronicle*, and on his Web site.

Kathleen had thought about having all the family in for Thanksgiving, but when Candace demurred, she changed her plans. Instead, she and Michael went down to Florida to visit Kathleen's mother for the holiday.

Ever the happy hostess, Kathleen planned and prepared a dinner for two dozen of her mother's friends on Thanksgiving eve. She called Candace and crowed about the success of the event. Candace noticed that her sister sounded upbeat and her stress level seemed down. When she asked about it, Kathleen said that although she was still unhappy with her life, what with the lay-offs and the stock prices, the Valium she had started taking in the summer was helping her a lot.

During the visit, Veronica sat down with Michael and Kathleen to discuss her will and funeral arrangements. She wanted Kathleen to serve as executor for her estate. She informed them that she wanted to be cremated when she died and that she had a living will stipulating no life support.

Kathleen was willing to follow her mother's wishes, but told Veronica and Michael that was not what she wanted for herself. "Do not cremate me," she said. "Bury me in the ground. And do not ever disconnect my life support. I'm going to go out of this world kicking and screaming."

Upon his return to Durham, Michael emailed his ex-wife about the financial woes of their grown sons. He wanted Patty to take out a $30,000 home equity loan to help support them. Clayton's rent and the interest payments on his credit card consumed more than he made from NC State with his teaching fellowship, and left him nothing for other expenses. Todd was paying about $300 a month in credit card interest and not reducing the principal.

Mike offered to pick up the payments on the home equity loan in two years after he paid off Todd's car.

"Please let me know what you think. It would be a huge relief off my mind because I am worried sick about them. It is simply not possible for me to discuss this with Kathleen."

A few days later, Michael sent an email to Margaret and Martha's uncle, Thomas Ratliff. He bragged about Clayton graduating at the top of his class at NC State in Computer Engineering and expressed concerns about Clayton's future prospects.

"Poor Kathleen is undergoing the tortures of the damned at Nortel," he wrote. "They've laid off 45,000 people. She's a survivor and in no trouble, but the stress is monumental there."

Despite the confidence he expressed about Kathleen's survival, her immediate supervisor at Nortel was laid off in early December and Kathleen was on an optimization list for a short time.

On Wednesday, December 5, Mike sent an email to Kathleen at work. "Here's the scoop on the Independent [a Durham news weekly]. There were no invitations, but we can still go. Let me know if you want me to call in. Or we could just show up at the door Friday night. You looked great last night. If ONLY we hadn't gone to Pao Lim. Let's work on our marriage tonight."

When this email was retrieved by forensic computer experts, it raised a lot of questions. To the investigators, Michael sounded like a man in the doghouse. They wanted to know what had happened at Pao Lim and what was wrong in the marriage.

• • •

Money was quite tight in the Peterson household, prompting Kathleen to make a change to her deferred income plan on December 6. Instead of socking away 80 percent of her salary and bonuses every year, Kathleen reduced that amount to a 10 percent deferral for the calendar year of 2002.

Kathleen used a vacation day on Friday, December 7, and went shopping with Michael that morning. They went to Costco and a few other places buying Christmas gifts for the kids, a TV for the house and a Christmas tree. That afternoon, they put the tree up in the living room, strung it with lights and hung a few of their ornaments.

Early that evening, Kathleen answered a telephone call from David Perlmutt. He had good news to share and spoke with both Kathleen and Michael. Stratton Leopold, a major Hollywood producer, wanted to option *Charlie Two Shoes*. Stratton's most recent film success was a movie based on a book by Nelson DeMille, *The General's Daughter*, starring John Travolta and Timothy Hutton. After a long dry spell, Michael would earn some money for his writing.

Friday night, the Petersons went to the party Mike mentioned in his email. It was thrown by the *Independent*. They danced and socialized till 1 A.M. when the party broke up.

The next morning, Kathleen went to work to prepare for a business trip. She was scheduled to meet with a colleague at the home office just outside of Toronto, at 9 A.M. that Monday morning. At 4 P.M., she left the office.

Michael spent the day writing and prowling the

Internet. A few minutes before Kathleen was expected home, he left to go to the YMCA.

In the car on her way home, Kathleen called her sister-in-law, Cynthia. They talked about Cynthia's new job, the holidays and the kids coming home. Kathleen told her about a new wave of lay-offs at Nortel that would include some people who were close to retirement. She worried that she would be next.

At 6, Mike called Kathleen from the Y and she expressed her annoyance about all the time he spent at the gym. Her husband was conciliatory. He suggested that they stay home that night and celebrate the good news about *Charlie Two Shoes*. He offered to pick up a romantic movie.

Just before 7, Michael rented *America's Sweethearts* starring Catherine Zeta-Jones, John Cusack, Julia Roberts and Billy Crystal at a Blockbuster near his home. According to Christina Tomasetti, she and Todd Peterson stopped by the Peterson home around 9:45. Kathleen and Michael were drinking white wine and champagne while watching the movie. Both of them appeared very happy. Forty-five minutes later, Todd and Christina left for a Christmas party in the neighborhood.

Just after 11 P.M., Kathleen returned a call from her Canadian colleague about the conference call scheduled on Sunday morning. They exchanged home email addresses—Kathleen gave her Michael's address so they could share documents on line before the call. Kathleen's voice did not slur on this call—her demeanor was professional. There was no indication that she was impaired in any way.

The next three and a half hours are shrouded in

secrecy. Michael Peterson claimed that the two of them were sitting by the pool talking. Kathleen went inside between 1:45 and 2 A.M. Michael stayed outside in his shorts in 55-degree weather. He claimed that when he came in forty-five minutes later, he found Kathleen dead at the bottom of the stairs.

Was his story true? The investigators looked at the evidence and concluded that it was not. They saw indications of a brutal attack on Kathleen that they believed happened at midnight or a little earlier.

Prosecutors and investigators wondered: How could the peaceful scene of a couple watching a romantic movie erupt in violence in the span of a couple of hours? Had Kathleen found evidence of Michael's infidelity and bisexual lifestyle while waiting at the computer for Helen's email? She left her first husband because of his adulterous acts; they did not think she would tolerate that same behavior in Michael.

Did she confront him? they speculated. Did he lose his temper and erupt in a violent rage? Only one person survived that night at 1810 Cedar Street. Michael Peterson had told his story, and he was sticking to it.

MICHAEL PETERSON

"It's awful for the people who know them. I guess everybody feels the way I do. You just feel very helpless because you don't know what to do. I guess there's nothing anyone can do to help them get through this."

—Lou Galifianakis

30

Kathleen would not make it to the holiday function for 100 under-privileged children that she'd planned to attend on Sunday, December 9. She would not be present at her business meeting in Toronto the next morning. She would not see the special viewing of *The Nutcracker* at the Executive Mansion on Wednesday evening. She would never go back to Bali to celebrate her wedding anniversary on June 21. All her plans and her dreams, all her hopes and fears vaporized on that stairway at 1810 Cedar Street.

Michael Peterson was shut out of his home as the investigators, the district attorney and the medical examiner sought the truth of what happened that night. He did not, however, spend the time alone. His family, Kathleen's family and his neighbors and friends rallied round him in support. No one gave any indication that they thought Michael was responsible for Kathleen's death. Two of her siblings kept their negative thoughts private.

The average person has a difficult time believing that

an innocent man would hire an attorney before any charges were filed. Naturally, Peterson raised eyebrows outside of his immediate circle when he lawyered-up within hours of Kathleen's demise. His first attorney was his long-time friend, Kerry Sutton. She brought Barry Winston into the case. In days, Mike exchanged both of them for the high-powered legal team of David Rudolf and Thomas Maher.

Rudolf had a stellar reputation as a defense attorney in North Carolina even though he was a transplanted Yankee. He earned his law degree from New York University in 1974. After graduation, he worked as a federal public defender in New York City.

Rudolf moved South to teach at the University of North Carolina at Chapel Hill and opened a private practice there in 1982. He represented the mail order company, Adam & Eve, against obscenity charges and Robert J. Kelly, Jr., in the Little Rascals Day Care child molestation case—both high-profile cases in North Carolina.

The spotlight of the nation turned on Rudolf when he defended the Carolina Panthers' wide receiver, Rae Carruth, against charges that he killed his pregnant girlfriend. Although Carruth was found guilty and sentenced to 18 years in prison, it was on the lesser charges of conspiracy to murder and shooting into an unoccupied vehicle. Rudolf saved Carruth from a possible death sentence.

His co-counsel in the Peterson case, Thomas Maher, was one of the brightest people to ever practice law in North Carolina. He graduated cum laude with his B.A.

in American Culture from Northwestern University near Chicago, Illinois, in 1979. He then went on to law school at the University of North Carolina at Chapel Hill, where he performed even better—graduating magna cum laude—in 1982. He clerked for two years at the Seventh Circuit Court of Appeals in Chicago. He had been an Adjunct Professor of Law at Duke University since 1990 and at the University of North Carolina since 1992.

In Rhode Island, voices of the present and echoes of the past tormented Margaret Blair. She found the name of the lead investigator in the Peterson case, Art Holland, on the Internet. Should she call and tell him about her sister? Or should she let it go and not dredge up a past that would surely darken her days?

She turned, as she had so often in her life, to her trusted friend and priest. He told her that making that phone call was the right thing to do. These were the words Margaret needed to hear. On December 13, she spoke to Investigator Holland. She told him that her sister had died the same way and that Michael Peterson had told her that he was the last person to see Elizabeth Ratliff alive.

Pat Finn left her last job in Germany a few months earlier. She was settled in Chicago when she heard the news that Michael Peterson was accused of killing his second wife. She was not surprised.

• • •

On the day of Peterson's arrest, Rudolf and Maher submitted a twenty-page motion for his release on $1 million property bond. Former U.S. Congressman Nick Galifianakis, Michael's friend and neighbor, agreed to assume responsibility for him and insure that Peterson did not flee. The defense asserted in the motion that Kathleen either died in a drunken fall or was murdered by someone other than her husband.

He had the best legal team money could buy, but Michael Peterson could not buy his release from jail. Superior Court Judge Ron Stephens did not entertain any testimony or arguments on the afternoon of December 21. He ruled that Peterson would remain in jail without bond until a January 22 hearing, where it would be determined whether the state would seek the death penalty.

Caitlin Atwater, who had returned to Cornell after the funeral, was now back in Durham. She and Todd Peterson expressed their shock and dismay about Mike's continued incarceration to the media gathered outside of the courthouse.

Behind bars, Michael Peterson wrote the "Jailhouse Journals." His first piece was about Christmas Eve in custody and it dripped with self-pity.

On Christmas Day, Peterson's location in the jail dictated that he had no visitation. The five children gathered at 1810 Cedar Street, still in shock. Caitlin spent some time with friends that day. The next morning, she drove to Northern Virginia to visit her two aunts. Veronica Hunt, her 81-year-old grandmother, was there, too. After the funeral, she had gone home with Lori. Now, she was staying at Candace's house for a while. The death of her daughter hit harder during the holiday season. It was not a time to be at home alone in Florida.

Caitlin then returned to Durham, where her father picked her up and took her to his home in Washington, North Carolina. She couldn't bear to stay in any one place for long. She felt an irresistible urge to keep moving.

On the morning of December 28, Investigators Art Holland and Mike Harris met with Patty Peterson. The language she used in her statement to the officers was odd. She talked about the evening before Liz died. Liz had been at her house for dinner. Instead of telling them that Michael walked Liz and the girls home, she said, "Elizabeth went home and Michael left also."

She mentioned that George Ratliff had a life insurance policy when he died. However, when Liz's assets were listed two years later when Mike filed her will in Texas, there was no reference to these funds at all. Liz had told her family that she had not touched that money, but put it aside for the girls' education.

The Zamperinis received a phone call from Bill Peterson after Caitlin left their home. He wanted to inform them that Michael was a practicing bisexual. With the computers in the hands of law enforcement, he knew it was only a matter of time before the police knew. He didn't want the family to learn about it from a reporter calling to get their reaction.

On New Year's Eve, Michael called Candace collect. She motioned for Mark to get on the line. Then she asked Michael, "Are you homosexual?"

He responded with a denial.

"Are you bisexual?"

Again, he answered no. "Why are you asking me this?" he said.

"Because Bill told us you were bisexual. Is it true?"

Peterson blustered about his telephone time being up—and then, he was gone. It was the last time Candace ever spoke to Michael.

Candace's head pounded with this new revelation. She'd thought Michael was heterosexual. She'd thought he was monogamous. She'd believed that he loved her sister—that he was madly in love with her.

Her siblings, Steven and Lori, had suspected Michael was responsible since the moment they heard Kathleen was gone. Candace had defended him to them again and again. Now she faced the possibility that Steven and Lori were right. The Michael Peterson she thought she knew did not exist.

She wondered if Michael and Bill had wanted her to make the funeral arrangements just to keep her out of their hair. She cast a jaundiced eye on the actions and words of all the Peterson men. She suspected they were not being open with her.

In Rhode Island, Liz Ratliff's 92-year-old mother Elizabeth McKee received a belated Christmas greeting from Patty Peterson. It was postmarked January 2 and mailed from Durham.

> *I pray you will rest in peace concerning your daughter, Liz, my beloved dearest best friend. She, Elizabeth, died a natural death; her life was not taken from her.*
>
> *I held vigil over her body and was with her longer than any other person, official or civilian, German or American. The last days of my dear friend Liz were happy and shared with friends.*

It was an odd missive with an unusual definition of "vigil". By all other accounts, Patty spent the day of Liz's death sitting in the kitchen and staring out into space.

The police called Caitlin at Fred's house in eastern North Carolina wanting to talk to her. She hesitated to make a commitment to stop by for an interview when she returned to Durham because she was so confused about her feelings toward Mike. No other family member had talked to the police yet. She still subscribed to the principle that Michael was innocent until proven guilty. But the barricaded stairway gnawed at her, stirring up a sense of uneasiness with his story.

She turned to her father for advice. He said that it could not hurt to talk. And it might help her better understand the situation. He impressed on her the importance of not hiding from problems—because when you avoid them, they only get worse. She agreed to meet with police when she returned.

On the drive back to Durham with Caitlin, Fred's cell phone rang. On the line was David Rudolf looking for Caitlin. He told her to be careful what she said to the police. In his assessment, they wanted to drive a wedge between family members and push the family apart. He advised her not to talk to police at all.

Fred interrupted, "Are you representing Caitlin?"

"No," Rudolf replied, "I was just advising her of what was going on."

"You're representing Michael?"

"Yes."

"You are looking out for his interests and his interests only?"

"Yes," Rudolf admitted.

That one word said it all. Caitlin and Fred went directly to the police station and talked to investigators. The police did not supply much information to the two, but they did tell them that they knew it was not a fall. And that they knew they had the right person, but could not yet tell them why.

The possibilities of what had happened to her mother screeched through Caitlin's head. She was full of doubt and was no longer comfortable staying with the family on Cedar Street. She picked up her car and headed back up to Northern Virginia.

Todd Peterson arranged a television interview and wanted all five of the children to talk to the cameras about their dad and how distraught they were that he was in jail. According to Fred Atwater, Todd was belligerent and demanding when he talked with Caitlin.

Caitlin did not want to participate because she no longer felt certain about her feelings. She had reflected a lot on her relationship with her stepfather. In high school, she thought they had a strong bond—they talked and joked with each other and Michael often gave her good advice. At times, she had balked at sharing him with her mother, but she thought his love for her was genuine, even though he never verbally expressed it. Looking back now, it seemed more like care than love. Michael, she believed, was not a very loving person and she blamed that character flaw on Vietnam.

The situation between them had taken a dramatic turn when Caitlin went away to college. It was bad enough that he never wanted to come to Ithaca to visit. What really bothered Caitlin was that he tried to talk Kathleen into not visiting her either. Caitlin now reflected on his hair-trigger temper and his frequent bouts of yelling. She thought about this man's controlling nature, which she had overlooked in the past.

She did not know what to believe. She only knew that her mother was dead. And no matter how Kathleen had died, Caitlin's pain would last forever.

Todd phoned her repeatedly telling her she had to participate in the interview. His pleas sounded more and more like demands with each call.

When the interview was videotaped, Todd, Clayton, Margaret and Martha were there, along with Clayton's girlfriend Becky. She was not identified. She did not speak. Some viewers who did not know Caitlin were left with the impression that the silent young woman in the living room was Kathleen's biological daughter.

31

On December 31, the defense submitted a request to move up the bail hearing date. The district attorney agreed a week later. A new date was set for January 14. Three days before the hearing, Durham Superior Court Judge Ronald L. Stephens recused himself from the case on the grounds of conflict of interest. His youngest daughter, now a freshman in college, was in the same high school graduating class as Martha Ratliff. She knew all three of the girls in the Peterson household and had spent considerable time in their home. Visiting Superior Court Judge Henry Hight, Jr., of the Ninth Judicial District was selected to preside.

Fifty people with candles gathered outside of the Durham County Jail on the evening of Friday, January 11, to demonstrate their support for Michael Peterson. Martha Ratliff carried a sign that read: "FREE OUR FATHER." Other signs in the crowd included: "A MAN WITH A FAMILY CAN ONLY RUN HOME" and "PETERSON WON'T FLEE."

The icy wind filled with whispered words, carried them through the crowd and out to the media, who encircled them: *The district attorney will not seek the death penalty*. Hardin would not respond to this rumor, reserving his comments for the courtroom the following Monday.

Michael Peterson could not see the crowd of well-wishers from his cell, but he passed a message out with his son Todd. "I want to thank everyone here and so many others who have shown their support," Todd read. "I can't express what it means to me."

Another rumor flashed through Durham that weekend. Michael Peterson's trial had caught the attention of Court TV. The cable network confirmed this story, but said the degree of their interest had not yet been determined.

Waving and smiling at his friends and neighbors, Mike Peterson entered the courtroom on Monday, January 14, escorted by deputies. He shuffled to his seat in shackles and a blue blazer. He sat between his two lawyers and never uttered a word on his own behalf.

The judge had letters from Peterson's supporters. They endorsed Todd's contention that Kathleen was a heavy drinker, insisted that Michael was no threat to the community and swore that the relationship between Kathleen and Michael was "idyllic." And, of course, urged Mike's release from jail.

Several people testified in person, including former U.S. Representative Nick Galifanakis. Tears coursed down Peterson's face as they spoke on his behalf.

District Attorney Hardin responded by presenting autopsy photographs proving, he said, that Kathleen's death was not an accident. He gave the court a power of attorney document drawn up the day after she died which he suspected was written to allow Michael's sons to aid in gathering the cash that would enable Peterson to flee the country. He also announced his decision not to seek the death penalty.

He surprised the courtroom by calling Todd Peterson to the stand. He questioned the witness about the power of attorney. Todd refused to answer, calling the questions baseless and irrelevant.

Judge Hight told him to respond. After a bit of squabbling and a flash of Todd's temper, Hight snapped, "Son, quit being smart and answer the doggone question."

In the end, the judge released Michael Peterson on $850,000 bond. Mike signed papers on his home to cover the bail, relinquished his passport and agreed not to leave North Carolina.

A little after 6 P.M., he emerged from the jail carrying his possessions in a plastic bag. He told the gathered members of the press, "I really want to go home to see my kids. This is the first opportunity I have to grieve my wife and I'd really like to have that time."

Friends came by the Cedar Street home with groceries and stayed to cry together and reassure one another. Live broadcast media trucks rumbled on the street while reporters looked in on the Christmas tree and its colored lights gleaming from the living room window.

Within a week, Margaret was back at Tulane and Martha returned to the University of San Francisco. Caitlin Atwater was not present for the hearing or the post-jailhouse reunion. In weeks, the one thin remaining thread that supported her belief in Michael Peterson's innocence would snap.

32

On January 26, Mike Peterson filed a claim on Kathleen's assets with her employer. In ten days, Nortel Networks issued the first check for $29,360—the balance after taxes were deducted from Kathleen's long-term investment funds. In the past two years, the value of this account had suffered a dramatic drop.

David Rudolf moved to have Kathleen's autopsy photos sealed and not released to the public. He claimed that the release violated the privacy of the victim's family. He lost that battle with this response from the attorney general's senior deputy on February 8: "The status of autopsy reports as public records was established more than 25 years ago by this office. Since then, it has been the attorney general's consistent opinion that autopsy reports constitute public records. Our office opined in 1995 that legislation would be the appropriate avenue to clearly exempt autopsy reports from the public records law." The existing law dictated that only District Attorney Jim Hardin could have the records sealed.

Three days later, Candace sent a fax to Investigator Holland with a description and a drawing of a possible murder weapon—a blowpoke, a gift Candace gave to her sister years earlier. She described it as a forty-inch-long hollow tube of solid brass. She explained that when you blow through the top, air comes out at the bottom through a small hole. It got airflow into a fire and was strong enough to move logs around in a fireplace.

She ended her fax with a solemn encouragement: "Be Careful!" Fear of Michael Peterson was now a constant and stressful presence in Candace's life.

Peterson's attorneys intensified the defense's efforts in February by hiring Dr. Henry Lee as an expert witness—a man many considered the world's foremost forensic scientist and whom others insisted was nothing more than a "hired gun" in the worst definition of the phrase. He was well known to the public at large from the work he did for O. J. Simpson's defense and the assistance he rendered to the prosecutors in the JonBenét Ramsey murder in Colorado. In the pasty thirty-five years, he had testified in more than a thousand cases.

Lee arrived in Durham on February 13, his face hidden by reflective sunglasses as he emerged from behind the tinted windows of a chauffeured limousine and entered the Cedar Street home. He spent the afternoon at the mansion examining the stairwell and other points of interest.

On Monday, February 17, the state medical examiner's office released Kathleen Peterson's autopsy report. In Ithaca, New York, Caitlin Atwater sat down at a computer in the Kappa Alpha Theta sorority house at Cornell University. She steeled herself and went on line to view the document.

Bile rose in her throat as she glanced through the 11 pages of the report. She went back to the beginning and read each page slowly enough to absorb every word. A numbness settled in her mind as she detached the words from her emotions.

The diagram did not make sense to her. Although she understood some of the report, the technical language in other places obscured her understanding. One thing she knew with certainty when she finished reading was that her mother had not died from an accidental fall.

She placed a call to Tulane to talk with her stepsister, Margaret. She gave Margaret the Web site address for the autopsy and pleaded with her to look at it. "You need to read this. You need to understand this. Mom did not fall down the stairs. She was beaten to death."

Margaret refused. First Caitlin's mother had died. Now, her childhood bond with Margaret was shattered, and like an old mirror, it left only distorted reflections of what used to be.

Soon, she received a telephone call from Michael Peterson. She refused to take it. She would not speak to him or see him until the trial. In an interview with Raleigh's *News & Observer* she said, "I don't want to see into the eyes of someone who could have done that to my mother."

The defense responded with passion to the document from the medical examiner's office. Peterson denied the allegations in the report that he called other people before he dialed 9-1-1. He insisted that his phone records would prove that he did not place those calls. The local telephone service provider said that local, toll-free calls cannot be traced at a later date and would not appear on the records.

Peterson also denied the medical examiner's contention that Kathleen lay bleeding for hours. "I had nothing to do with Kathleen's death," he insisted. The lawyers urged the press and the public not to jump to hasty conclusions.

Candace Zamperini dropped a bombshell on the defense the week following the publication of the autopsy report and photographs. She said she felt that the release would lead to the discovery of the truth. She added, "Mr. Rudolf does not represent Kathleen's family, nor has he ever spoken to any family member. Although Michael Peterson was Kathleen's husband, he also stands accused of her murder. Therefore, the assumption that he is Kathleen's 'family' no longer applies."

On February 19, Nortel Networks released another check to Michael Peterson for Kathleen's pension fund. After taxes, he netted over $94,000. He went on a manic shopping spree. He bought items for every room of the house—rugs, artwork and furniture. He enhanced the family room with the addition of a $10,000 large-screen plasma TV. He bought a room full of exercise equipment and a small refrigerator for his bedroom to keep white wine chilled and his wine glasses frosted—all right by his side.

. . .

On March 1, 2002, at 10 A.M., Christina Tomasetti, Todd Peterson's date on the night of Kathleen's death, was scheduled for her third interview at police headquarters. Instead of Christina, a letter arrived for Investigator Holland. Thomas Loflin II, Christina's new lawyer, was the author of the correspondence.

He advised Holland that the meeting was cancelled and that all communication would now be with him. Loflin requested all notes of the prior interviews and a list of questions that the police would like to ask his client.

The defense submitted paperwork on the afternoon of Monday, March 4, claiming that there was not enough evidence to obtain a search warrant and that police withheld evidence from the magistrate who issued it. The document also asserted the sole motivation of the police was retaliation against Michael Peterson for the critical columns he penned about the department. It called the whole search process invalid and demanded that all evidence seized be thrown out of court.

On March 31, Judge Hudson ruled that Peterson's rights were not violated in the searches of his home. The evidence the defense wanted suppressed would be part of the trial.

Nortel Networks issued a final check for $212,790 to Michael Peterson for the amount of Kathleen's deferred income. Michael Peterson received about

$340,000 from Nortel as a direct result of Kathleen's death.

He still had hopes of getting his hands on his wife's $725,000 life insurance policy, which paid double for accidental death. Yet the defense team maintained from the time of Michael's arrest and all throughout the trial that no financial motive existed.

Wacky rumors about the Michael Peterson case raced up and down the streets of Durham and rippled through Internet chat rooms. Not one person, not one shred of evidence ever surfaced to give the least bit of credibility to the lethal stories that circulated. It did, however, point to one truth—Durham was obsessed with the most sensational case in recent memory and the residents had no clue yet of how much more was in store.

33

ABC's *20/20* aired a profile of Dr. Henry Lee on April 5, 2002. In it, there was footage of the forensic specialist walking through the Peterson house. The stairway where Kathleen died was the focus of that portion of the program.

Kathleen's family was outraged. Although the show did not identify the crime scene, the sisters recognized it. Veronica Hunt did not see the show, but she heard all about it, and she felt betrayed. She spoke out to Sonya Pfeiffer of WTVD news about the letter she received from Michael Peterson protesting his innocence.

"Things in the letter were totally new to me. My family has kept me sheltered from many details of my daughter's gruesome death." She said that now that the crime scene and all the blood in it was shown on television, she was more aware and wanted to know the whole truth.

Patty Peterson granted an interview to the same reporter. Her selection of words was peculiar. She did not say that she knew her ex-husband did not kill Kathleen. Instead she said, "My assumption and my hope is they are going to find the truth and that he is innocent."

When asked if she had ever known her ex-husband to

lie, she said, "No, not directly. I have no knowledge of that."

"Did he ever hit you?" Sonya asked.

"I would say no," Patty answered.

The reporter wanted to know if she would still support Michael if he admitted his guilt. Patty said, "It would be totally contrary to my experience with him as a human being for forty years. I've known him in his youth, his middle age, as a soldier serving his country, as a loving father, as a man who has loved me and other individuals."

Her answer left questions in the air. Was the crime or a confession contrary to her experience? And would it be contrary to her experience with him as a husband?

In direct opposition to the families of victims of other crimes, Candace Zamperini appeared before the North Carolina legislature to urge them not to pass a bill that would limit public access to autopsy photos. It was these photos, she told the assembly, that convinced her that her sister was murdered. She knew if the law they were considering had been passed already, she would have never seen them, because Michael Peterson would refuse to allow their release. After her appearance at the hearing, Mike blasted her for sensationalizing the issue and for putting herself above medical experts.

The value of Kathleen's estate—over a quarter of a million dollars—was announced in early May 2002. She died without a will, making Michael Peterson and

Caitlin Atwater her heirs. Michael renounced his right to administer his wife's estate and the responsibility fell to Caitlin.

Then the other shoe dropped. The media learned of the death of Elizabeth Ratliff in 1985. They knew that the Durham police were looking into her demise and its possible connection to the murder of Kathleen.

All of Durham was atwitter. They could talk of nothing else but the similarities between the two women's deaths. Both suffered injuries and severe head trauma. Both were found at the bottoms of stairways. Michael Peterson, by his own admission, was the last person to see both of them alive. But strangest of all was the eerie physical resemblance of the two women whose deaths were separated by sixteen years and two continents.

Eleanor Peterson was shocked by the new information she learned about her son. Ann peered through a shroud of denial that now hung about her like a tattered veil. But to the media, the family presented a united front protesting Michael's innocence.

In early May 2002, Judge Orlando Hudson announced that he would be the jurist for the trial of *State of North Carolina* vs. *Michael Iver Peterson*. He warned attorneys to be more temperate in their comments to the press, but stopped short of issuing a gag order.

He granted Michael Peterson permission to leave the state to attend the sixtieth wedding anniversary celebration of his parents in Reno, Nevada, in July. Michael Peterson would take a trip to Reno that summer. But it would not be in July. And no one would be celebrating.

34

In early June, Judge Hudson set Michael Peterson's trial date for May 12, 2003, with the week before scheduled for jury selection. Once again, he warned the lawyers to limit their comments to the media. He also ordered them to comply with the law in sharing information.

Ann Christensen received a call from her mother, Eleanor Peterson, in the last week of June. She called to tell Ann she had broken her hip and was in the hospital. Ann suspected all was well, but doubt propelled her to book a flight and head to Reno.

Wednesday night, June 26, Eleanor was quite ill. As Ann kissed her goodnight, Eleanor grabbed her arm and said, "I don't think I'm going to make it out of this one."

At 6 A.M. the next morning, Bill called Ann from the hospital. "Get here right away."

Eleanor had slipped into a coma. By that afternoon, it was clear that Eleanor was not going to survive. Ann told the nurses that they had to keep her alive until Michael arrived. "You won't believe this, but he just lost his wife. He has to be able to say goodbye to his mother."

Eleanor's youngest child, Jack Peterson, arrived from Las Vegas. Both he and Bill wanted to let their mother go. By now, her body functioned only by the grace of the machines. Ann refused to allow the equipment to be disconnected. She wanted to wait for her oldest brother.

At 10:30 that night, Michael arrived at the hospital. He held his mother's hand. He kissed it with tenderness. Then he said, "Enough of this nonsense. Let's turn it off."

The plugs were pulled at 10:45 and Eleanor Peterson slipped quietly into the eternal night. Michael stayed in Reno for the funeral. None of Eleanor's children discussed the courtroom awaiting Mike back in North Carolina. They did not mention Kathleen. They talked only about their mother. And they cried in each other's arms.

While Michael mourned the death of his mother, the Durham police—armed with a search warrant—were back in his home. Under the watchful eye of David Rudolf, they took measurements of the stairwell and other pertinent locations throughout the house. They retrieved fibers from a kitchen rug and from a blanket on a sofa.

In August, Caitlin talked to her stepsister Margaret one last time. Margaret had no interest in talking about Kathleen's death or Michael's impending trial. When Caitlin pushed, Margaret responded, "I don't need that in my life."

She might as well have told Caitlin that her mother was irrelevant. Conversation over. Relationship done. Destruction accomplished—courtesy of Michael Peterson.

It was now eight months since the death of Kathleen Peterson and her gravesite still had no headstone. The plot was in Michael's name and, legally, that small piece of land was his property. No one but the owner could erect anything on it.

Kathleen's family begged him to put up a marker. He did not. Candace tried every trick she had to lay a guilt trip on him and make him take action. She failed.

According to the contract with the cemetery, a headstone had to be put up within six months of the internment. That time was up. Candace asked what would happen now.

Their first response was: "We don't know. It's never happened before." They checked their policies and told her that they would have to put up a small marker and bill the estate for it. Candace pleaded with them to give her a little more time. Recognizing the unusual circumstances, they agreed.

Candace was nervous about the outcome of the upcoming primary elections in Durham. She requested an interview with Sonya Pfeiffer of WTVD on September 6, 2002.

She had nothing against opponent Mark Simeon. It was just that she wanted an experienced D.A. to present the case before the jury. She also told the reporter that a murder weapon had been identified by the state.

Peterson's attorneys threw a hissy fit. They presented motions in court accusing Hardin of hiding evidence, using the case to his political advantage and attempting to influence the pool of potential jurors. Hardin denied that the interview was his idea in timing or substance. Candace insisted that she acted on her own. She admitted that the murder weapon theory was hers and that no one in the district attorney's office had told her that they had identified the weapon.

The drama of the *State of North Carolina* vs. *Michael Iver Peterson* hit an even higher pitch in October. In court early that month, it was revealed that police and prosecutors wanted to know whether Todd Peterson was involved in an attempted cover-up in the death of his stepmother. They did not, however, uncover grounds to take any legal action against Todd. That same day, the attorneys bickered once again about the sharing of information and were admonished—again—by Judge Hudson.

In the middle of October, the public learned that the media frenzy had exceeded their expectations. Denis Poncet and Jean-Xavier de Lestrade of the French company, Maha Productions, were on the scene. Maha— a Sioux Indian word meaning "he who swims against the tide"—received national recognition in the States earlier that year. Their HBO movie, *Murder on a Sunday Morning*, won an Oscar for Best Documentary Feature Film. The cable show involved racial profiling, police oversights and a wrongfully accused 15-year-old boy.

Maha did not have a movie deal for Kathleen Peterson's Sunday morning death yet, but they were already taping, certain that a deal would evolve soon. Many, however, were not confident that the product would be unbiased. Word spread through town that Denis Poncet was in Vietnam at the same time as Michael Peterson and that he was at UNC–CH when Michael was in law school. Poncet denied knowing Michael Peterson, but the extraordinary access he got to the defense made Durham wonder.

While everyone else was focused on Kathleen's death, D.A. Hardin had filed a request in the Texas courts for permission to exhume Elizabeth Ratliff's body at the end of the month. Caitlin Atwater trumped that with her dramatic move on October 29.

Her attorney, Jay Trehy, knocked on the door of 1810 Cedar Street just after 9 A.M. He served a court order and directed movers to retrieve Caitlin's belongings—bedroom furniture, clothing and personal effects. He said his client was too fearful to enter the home herself.

Just before 3:30 that afternoon, Trehy filed a wrongful death lawsuit in Durham against Michael Peterson. The suit asked for compensatory and punitive damages for the daughter of Kathleen Peterson.

A claim had also been filed on Caitlin's behalf in a courtroom in Greenville, North Carolina. In it, she requested that she receive the proceeds of her mother's life insurance policy. Kathleen had submitted a change of beneficiary form on her policy, removing her ex-husband Fred Atwater, and adding her new husband, Michael Peterson. She forgot, however, to sign the form.

Documents filed by Caitlin's attorneys concluded that if Fred Atwater was not the beneficiary, then Kathleen's daughter should be. North Carolina's slayer statutes prohibited Michael from receiving the money, since it did not allow a person convicted of killing another to profit from the death.

Michael Peterson carried a double burden—the death of his wife and his indictment for murder. That stress would be enough to induce writer's block in the most

seasoned and productive scribe. Not for Peterson—he
sent the first one hundred pages and an outline of a new
book to his agent. In March, HarperCollins made a six-
figure offer for the book Mike would co-author with
Colonel Arthur Boyd. Then the publisher discovered
that one of the writers was indicted for murder. They
withdrew their offer quicker than a Marine could shout
"*Semper Fi*."

When the first anniversary of Kathleen's death rolled
around in December, Kathleen's sisters, brother, mother
and daughter were in agony about Kathleen's still-
unmarked grave. Candace's patience had expired. She
took her case to the press. She said that although
Michael sold the plot to the estate, he would not sign the
papers to make the transfer legal.

Through his lawyer, Mike proclaimed his devotion
to Kathleen and attacked Candace for ordering and
attempting to install a marker that was totally out of
character for Kathleen. He said he and his children were
appalled.

Candace slapped back. She told *The Herald-Sun*, "I
have never drawn on paper any design for a monument
for any grave. My sister is still in an anonymous plot,
which is heartbreaking to me. She's in a potter's field
because he did not mark it."

Michael signed the papers at long last.

On February 6, 2003, Margaret and Martha Ratliff wrote
a bitter letter granting the district attorney permission to

exhume their mother's body. They attacked Hardin's character and decried his persecution of Michael Peterson. "We only hope that you treat our mother's remains with more respect than you have treated her memory."

Caitlin, too, faced a sad task with her mother. She consulted with family members and purchased a black granite headstone. Because her mother loved roses, she had that flower entwined with ivy and engraved on the stone. She then added one line from "Ascension," the poem by Colleen Hitchcock that was read at Kathleen's funeral: "Just whisper my name in your heart, I'll be there."

Stuart Johnson, Steven Hunt's roommate at Virginia Military Institute, created a special wind chime for Kathleen. It was engraved with her name and hung in the stately branches of the tree that shaded her grave.

The minister who had presided over Kathleen's funeral service came to Maplewood Cemetery to lead a prayer service to bless her grave and her headstone. Nortel employees surrounded the last resting place of Kathleen Peterson for the somber ceremony. And at last, the hearts of Kathleen's family rested in peace.

But they would not rest for long. In two months, they would take the next step in their grief-filled odyssey in a courtroom in Durham where they hoped to find justice for Kathleen and closure for themselves.

35

In mid-April, Investigator Art Holland took the first airplane flight of his life. He flew to Texas with another investigator and a forensic technician to supervise the exhumation of Elizabeth Ratliff.

The gravesite, undisturbed since 1985, was sprouting wild flowers. Taylor Brothers Funeral Home began the morbid task at 8 A.M. on Monday, April 14, at the Cedarvale Cemetery in Matagorda County. In the wispy remnants of a lifting heavy fog, the workers and Bay City police officers erected yellow police tape around the area and across the service road. The forensic technician videotaped the official record. Outside, television cameras and reporters recorded the event for the evening news.

At 8:15, workers pried up the granite and bronze marker and set it to the side. An iron dowel was forced into the earth until it made contact with the concrete vault two feet below. With a small backhoe, the equipment operator dug down to the top of the sarcophagus surrounding the casket. Workers then dug the rest by hand, wrapped a chain around the two-ton container and pulled it and its contents out of the ground just before lunch.

The tightly sealed lid was forced off the top, leaving a trail of stringy glue in its wake. The coffin was removed, wrapped in plastic and placed in the back of a blue Chevrolet Suburban. Elizabeth Ratliff and the three men from Durham traveled to Meridian, Mississippi, where they stopped for the night.

Early the next morning, they were on the road again, determined to get their precious cargo back to North Carolina that day. The autopsy was scheduled for Wednesday at the state medical examiner's office in Chapel Hill.

The white plastic-enshrouded silver-gray coffin of Elizabeth Ratliff rolled into the autopsy suite on a gurney at 9 A.M. on Wednesday, April 16. Yellow police tape secured both ends. When the lid of the casket was lifted, the musty smell of old news flew into the faces of the observers. Dr. Werner Spitz, a well-known and respected forensic pathologist, was present on behalf of the defense, along with Investigator Ron Guerette, who always seemed to be everywhere—many on the prosecution side of the case joked about getting him a "Where's Waldo?" tee shirt.

The autopsy team of Dr. Aaron Gleckman, forensic neuropathologist, and Dr. Deborah Radisch, forensic pathologist, examined the exterior of the body in its coffin. The disintegrating lace of Liz's wedding gown added a delicate poignancy to the macabre moment. She was surrounded by an array of items sufficient to melt a seasoned and inured heart. There was a book—one well loved by Dr. Radisch's children—*The Little Rabbit*, a white stuffed lamb, a stained and broken seashell, a ballet slipper charm and soft brown plant material that once shone brilliant with the color of life.

Opening the book, the doctors discovered a metal unicorn window hanging, a card with a picture of a church in Frankfurt and inside the card, a photograph of two small girls. On Liz's fingernails, a tired gloss of nail polish blushed in an unnatural burst of color.

Using a mechanical winch and straps, they transferred the body to a stainless-steel table and more photographs were taken. Dr. Radisch was eager to find the answers to the questions that rose in her mind when she reviewed the original autopsy. In twenty years of experience, she had never seen a cause of death listed as a sudden unexpected death due to a spontaneous intra-cranial hemorrhage caused by von Willebrand's disease. Her curiosity was also inflamed by the absence of any diagrams to indicate the number and location of the lacerations.

The body itself was in an excellent state of preservation. The skin on her face had a layer of make-up and looked quite normal. When the cosmetics were removed, the pathologists uncovered bruising under Liz's left eye and a laceration on her eyebrow. Even this late, the bruising was distinct. The embalming process preserved the bruising because, although it removed the blood from the circulatory system, it could not retrieve blood from surrounding tissue.

In Liz's mouth, there was an area of small bruising and a tear on her upper gums. The skin on her body was dark and leathery with a small amount of mold on its surface. Dr. Radisch found evidence of bruising on the back of Liz's left hand and on her left wrist.

The doctors shifted their focus to the head—Dr. Gleckman's area of specialty. The multiple lacerations were all glued and sutured in the autopsy and embalming in 1985. He found and described seven distinct lacerations to Liz Ratliff's head—the same number found during Kathleen Peterson's autopsy. The number could be mere coincidence, but the biggest surprise was their location. One was on the very top of her head—its position made it more condemnatory of Michael Peterson than any found on Kathleen.

Dr. Radisch removed the thick cotton sutures from six of the lacerations on the head with great care. She then tackled the more difficult task of the fine blue suture material on the remaining laceration.

They observed a distinct fracture along the base of the skull that corresponded to the angled laceration on the top of her head. The fracture traveled from there down to where the spinal cord connects. Inside the skull were flecks of dried blood indicative of a pre-mortem injury.

When Dr. Gleckman and Dr. Radisch completed the procedure, they informed the observers that, pending a neurological consult, they believed that Liz Ratliff's death was caused by blunt force trauma to the head—the manner of death: homicide.

Investigator Art Holland paced the halls and peered through the windows throughout the procedure. Now, he had a phone call to make. When Margaret Blair picked up, he asked her, "Are you sitting down?"

She answered, "Yes," but dread surrounded the word and muffled her response.

"Your sister didn't die from a fall down the stairs."

Eighteen years of sorrow, eighteen years of uncertainty, eighteen years of loss crashed down on Margaret Blair with the intensity of a Nor'easter. An intense anger at Michael Peterson and a savage lust for justice burned a hole in her heart. She would not rest until the world knew the whole truth of her sister's death.

36

Elizabeth Ratliff's body was back in Bay City, re-interred at her husband's side in the Cedarvale Cemetery by the time the doctors microscopically examined sections of the brain.

The conclusion in the autopsy report was unequivocal. Dr. Gleckman wrote that the injuries were inconsistent with a fall and not consistent with a natural disease process. The cause of death was blunt force trauma to the head. The manner of death was homicide.

Margaret Blair needed to talk to Liz's friends in Germany. She located Amybeth Berner, who provided names and numbers of others. Margaret urged Amybeth to contact Investigator Holland. Soon after that call, Amybeth heard from Barbara Malagnino. "What kind of bloody mess have we gotten ourselves into?" Barbara asked.

"We knew this was going to come back at some point," Amybeth said. "We knew it wasn't finished."

• • •

Defense Attorney David Rudolf demanded that the results of the autopsy be sealed. The media screamed in outrage. The decision, though, was in the hands of Judge Orlando Hudson. He sealed the records until and unless the evidence was introduced into court.

A hearing was held to determine if the Elizabeth Ratliff evidence and the evidence of Michael Peterson's bisexuality were to be allowed in the trial. Initially, the judge ordered it to be a closed hearing. The media screamed again, this time using a legal expert on constitutional law to argue their right to be present.

The judge relented. And in that hearing, he also reversed his earlier decision and allowed the results of the autopsy to be released to the public. Motions arguing against the admissibility of evidence submitted by the defense that month bore a whiff of desperation. Not content to make a simple argument about his client's innocence in the death of Liz Ratliff, they pointed the finger of responsibility at someone else.

The document accused Barbara O'Hara Malagnino of being a prime suspect if Mrs. Ratliff was murdered. This reckless statement overlooked the fact that there was no evidence, suspicion or motive connecting Barbara to Liz's death.

Barbara was outraged at the allegation, but felt she knew the reason for it. The summer before, Rudolf paid a visit to her in Germany, believing that Barbara would make a good defense witness. After returning to the States, he sent her a letter asking her for an affidavit. He

enclosed columns from *The Herald-Sun* written by
Tom Gasparoli and told her how awful Gasparoli was.
Barbara did not respond because she thought Rudolf
would send her an affidavit to sign. Now, Barbara
thought, he wanted to scare her out of coming to
Durham to testify for the other side.

But Barbara had no desire to speak for *either* side. All
she wanted to do was tell the truth—she owed that much
to Liz.

The district attorney would not make a commitment
one way or another on the possibility that he would
introduce the Elizabeth Ratliff autopsy or the testimony
about Michael's sexual lifestyle into trial. Because of his
equivocation, the judge delayed any ruling on the
admissibility of it.

In response to the media clamor over the autopsy
report, Margaret Ratliff spoke to Sonya Pfeiffer at
WTVD. "I know Dad is innocent. He didn't kill either
one of my mothers. It's just ridiculous." She added, "I
can't believe any jury will convict my dad after all the
evidence is laid out. There's just no way."

District Attorney Jim Hardin was ready for battle. His
character and determination were forged and hardened
in the crucible of childhood tragedy. Jimmy—as he was
known to family and friends—was the oldest son of Jim
and Carolyn Hardin. The couple met at Duke, which the
older Jim Hardin attended on a football scholarship.
They married after graduation—Jim with a degree
in Engineering, Carolyn with an Education degree.
Carolyn taught third grade for one year and then quit to
start a family. They had four children in the span of four
years—Jimmy, David, Mary Elizabeth and Carol.

In 1971, when Jimmy was 12 years old, the family lived out in the country on a farm filled with ponies for the children and Thoroughbred horses for breeding. In the middle of the night, a fire broke out in the Hardin home. Carolyn and Jim tried to open their bedroom door to get to their children, but fire and smoke drove them back. They jumped out the window and tried to get to the children from outside. Again their efforts met with failure.

Jimmy tied his bedsheets together and lowered himself out of his room and joined his frantic parents. In the barn, the horses, panicked by the smell of smoke, screamed and kicked the sides of their stalls. David, Mary Elizabeth and Carol did not find their way out of the home. And no one could get in to them in time. They died in the fire that night—their deaths scarring and strengthening the sorrow-filled survivors.

As if he felt compelled to fulfill the hopes and dreams his parents had for all four children, Jimmy was driven to achieve. The bonds of shared tragedy knitted the three remaining members of this family together in a way nothing else could.

He graduated from Duke in 1979 and after a year's hiatus, he continued his education at Mercer University School of Law in Macon, Georgia. In his first year, he met Lori Thomas, a senior at Macon's Wesleyan College from Annapolis, Maryland. They were married in Jim's last year of law school.

He went into private practice as a defense attorney when he graduated. He was not well suited for this work. If he believed his client to be guilty, he lost sleep at night worrying about the ramifications of what he had done.

After a year, District Attorney Ron Stephens offered him a job as an assistant district attorney and he accepted the position with great relief. The focus of Hardin's work was as a drug prosecutor. He took to this endeavor with intense fervor—riding out with the police on raids to round up dealers. When his boss took a judgeship, Governor James B. Hunt appointed Hardin to finish Stephens' term.

In his first election in 1994, Hardin faced stiff opposition. Support of defense attorneys and the African-American community put him on top. In 1998, he faced no opposition in his re-election. He won his third race in September 2002, besting opponent Mark Simeon. Hardin had a clear understanding of his responsibility. "Using the law to find the truth is our mandate. I believe that to my core," he told *Herald-Sun* columnist Tom Gasparoli.

Jim Hardin was not content with success in one arena; he also was a member of the Army Reserve. One weekend a month was dedicated to serving his country. He had risen to the rank of Lieutenant Colonel a year before jury selection began. The specter of a possible call to active duty haunted the pre-trial preparations. After all, he was overdue—he had not been called up since the Persian Gulf War.

Now Hardin faced another trial by fire. Although this one was merely figurative, it would prove just as intense.

37

Hardin's partner before the bench was Assistant D.A. Freda Black, a graduate of Campbell University School of Law in the village of Buies Creek, less than an hour from Durham. After law school, she went into private practice as the only female defense attorney in Lumberton, North Carolina. In her court-appointed cases, she defended everything from worthless checks to first-degree murder—even two capital murder cases in her three years there.

Black moved to Durham to work in the public defender's office as chief assistant, then switched to the Durham County District Attorney's Office in 1991. Her experience in domestic violence homicides and successful record in prosecuting first-degree murder cases made her addition to the prosecution team a foregone conclusion.

Some said Freda Black had a natural persuasive ability. Others said that she was a drama queen. One thing was certain, she threw herself into her cases with a passion that resonated in the Southern soul, but often was mocked by Yankee-based media outlets. Black and Hardin were backed in the Peterson case by the ever-present David Saacks, a veteran litigator from Texas.

On May 5, 124 citizens of Durham County—nearly double the usual number—filed into the courthouse as potential jurors. Jury selection was expected to last two weeks, with the trial beginning on May 19. However, it was May 20 before the first juror was empanelled. The selection of twelve jurors and four alternates was finally complete on June 23.

Assistant District Attorneys Freda Black and David Saacks traveled to Germany with Investigator Art Holland to meet with German authorities, visit Liz's home in Gräfenhausen and interview potential witnesses. They asked to review police records and collided with a serious obstacle. Such a request required the approval of the Minister of Justice. In addition, German prosecutors wanted assurances that Peterson would not be charged with Elizabeth Ratliff's murder in the United States and that he would not be subject to the death penalty on the other charge.

Opening arguments were scheduled to begin on July 1, 2003. Satellite TV trucks circled the courthouse like a high-tech wagon train. Court TV erected cameras in the courtroom, where they would broadcast the trial live for its duration.

The Big Top was erected. The circus was about to begin. Two disparate definitions of justice would reside on opposite sides of the courtroom. Only one would prevail.

THE TRIAL

"This is an adversary system.
There can't be but so much love here."

—Judge Orlando Hudson, September 2003

38

Durham, North Carolina, was a blue-collar city with a population of 227,000. Despite the presence of Duke University and its world-acclaimed medical research facilities, tobacco was the king in this town.

Durham got the nickname "Bull City" when the Blackwell Tobacco Company introduced their bull's head logo on their "Bull" Durham products. That logo was the most famous one in the world at the end of the nineteenth century. Its pervasiveness spawned additions to the American vernacular like "bullpen" and "shooting the bull."

The discovery of brightleaf tobacco, and the subsequent industriousness of Washington Duke and his family to capitalize on it, led to the birth of one of the world's largest corporations, consisting of companies like American Tobacco, Liggett & Myers and R. J. Reynolds. This industrial development drew more manufacturers to the central North Carolina town. The first factory to produce denim was here at one time, as well as the largest hosiery maker in the world.

The courthouse nestled in the heart of the Downtown Durham Historical District. Beyond the flashy cluster of the media, the backdrop of downtown Durham looked abandoned. Across the street, a monument to the Confederate dead stood proud and defiant in front of the old courthouse. In the basement, a cafeteria fed bland but decent food to many of the participants in the trial.

A couple of blocks away, a shabby storefront on Parrish Street housed Ron's Foods, where the tangy taste of genuine North Carolina barbecue sandwiches was the highlight of the menu. For caffeine addicts, it was a long walk to the Blue Coffee Company—but fueled by a lust for lattes, it was a trip many in the courtroom made multiple times each day. It was also a spot where they could order lunches of sandwiches and salads—an alternative a bit more upscale than the nearby hot dogs and barbecue.

Back in the courthouse, lunch was served in District Attorney Jim Hardin's office. His mother, Carolyn Hardin, brought in a meal for the prosecution team and witnesses every day. In no time, her menu was a daily feature of the coverage on Court TV.

In the courtroom itself, a long pew-like bench stretched behind the defense and prosecution desks. The prosecution table was stacked with papers and exhibits. The defense table was piled high with computer equipment and gadgets manned by disbarred attorney Guy Seaberg.

Behind that bench were rows of red theater seats—a comfort appreciated by those who filled the courtroom. The middle seat of the first two rows was designated as a press seat to form a line of embarkation between the two sides. Two rows of pure press followed, and the remaining seats were open to spectators.

A frenzy of activity erupted early in the courtroom, as cameramen taped down electrical cords, attorneys organized their materials and court personnel made last-minute preparations. A pall of silence descended when Judge Orlando Hudson entered and the deputy called the court to order. The trial of *State of North Carolina* vs. *Michael Iver Peterson* had begun.

Jim Hardin approached the podium and faced the jury. His soft Carolina drawl demanded edge-of-the-seat attention. "I anticipate you must be asking yourself, 'Regardless of how much I know about this case, what is it really about?' From a legal perspective, it is very well defined. We talked about that in our selection process with you. The sides are diametrically opposed. The defendant says that Kathleen Peterson's death was caused by a tragic, accidental fall down stairs in their home. And we say, on the other hand, that she died a horrible, painful death at the hands of her husband, Michael Peterson."

Hardin walked up to the juror rail and held up a photograph of a living, vibrant, smiling Kathleen Peterson. "You can see from this photograph—you can feel from this photograph—that she is a very genteel, warm person. It does not take much time to see that, from just viewing one photograph, but there it is."

The next photo the prosecutor presented to the jury was one of Kathleen Peterson bloodied and sprawled on the back stairway of her home. "Now, on December ninth, 2001, at 2:48, when EMS personnel first arrive, [. . .] they see Kathleen Peterson in a completely different way. They see her lying at the bottom of her steps, just as you see in this photograph."

Hardin then showed the jurors a photo taken at the medical examiner's office. He walked the length of the jury box with this gruesome image of Kathleen lying on a steel gurney. "This is where the rubber meets the road, ladies and gentlemen.

"They," he said, pointing to the defense table, "say it was an accident that was caused by a couple of falls in that stairwell, and we say it's not. We say it's murder, and you will have to decide that. They say this is three or four lacerations. We say it's at least seven, and you're going to have to be the judge of it."

Hardin picked up an oblong package covered in brown butcher block paper and unraveled the covering as he spoke. The jury was captivated—all eyes entranced by the mysterious item in his hands. The crinkling of the paper crackled through his words.

Inside was Candace Zamperini's blowpoke. Harden told the jurors it was just like the one Kathleen's sister gave to several family members. The one she gave to Kathleen was missing.

"This is not the actual weapon. [. . .] But the primary mechanism is something like this. It is hollow. It is light. It's easily used, and we will contend to you that this, or something like this, is the article that was used to inflict these wounds."

Hardin paused as the jurors contemplated the vicious-looking hook on the end of the blowpoke.

"[T]his case is about pretense and appearances. It's about things not being as they seem. As this case begins to unfold, you see the grandeur of the Petersons' ten-thousand-square-foot mansion that is located in a very affluent area of Durham. You will see the appearance of a storybook marriage between a couple who had a blended family that appears to have it all.

"In particular, you will hear about what some have described as the success of Michael Peterson as a writer and columnist. You will also hear about Kathleen's success as a Nortel manager, as a patron of the arts, and as the quintessential hostess for all occasions. And doesn't she look like it?" Once again, Hardin drew the jurors' attention to the victim's smiling face. "She looks like a very loving, warm person—the quintessential lady, genteel, exactly what you want your daughter to be.

"From all the appearances, this was a perfect family. But as the old saying goes, appearances can be very deceiving. [. . .] Like a storm cloud, many pressurized conditions in the Peterson house began to converge, and on December ninth, 2001, they erupted."

Across the courtroom, Michael Peterson slouched in his chair with the disinterested attention of someone viewing the proceedings for their educational value only.

Hardin highlighted the dependence of the family on Kathleen's salary and benefits because Michael had made no income as a writer since 1999. Even with her salary, the family was living on credit and now her employment was in jeopardy because of Nortel's deteriorating financial condition.

"Kathleen and Michael both knew that the loss of Kathleen's job and the loss of her salary and benefits would have a devastating effect on an already difficult financial situation."

The level of Hardin's voice rose and indignation etched around its edges. "But Mike Peterson, the creative thinker, the writer of fiction, was able to figure out a perfect solution. That solution was to make it appear as though Kathleen accidentally fell down her steps and died. And, like magic, no more money problems. Like magic, Mike Peterson goes from a point where they are going to have to sell assets and live on credit to survive to, all of a sudden, with her death, has one point eight million dollars in his hand. That's a lot of money. That solves a lot of problems. What a wonderful solution. There's only one catch: He's got to kill Kathleen Peterson to get that one point eight million. But Mike Peterson, with that money, was going to be able to pull himself out of the financial fire he had built for himself. Kathleen's death, accidental death, would then have allowed him to continue to live the affluent privileged life to which he had become accustomed even though he had no job."

Hardin told the jurors that when Peterson placed that 9-1-1 call, he gambled that the police were as dumb as he always claimed. He urged them to listen carefully to that tape and hear how evasive and deceptive Peterson was.

The prosecutor's tone softened as he talked about the thoughts of one of the first responders to the scene. "There's blood on Kathleen, under Kathleen, beside Kathleen. It's all dry. So he says when he gets there, he sees all this dry blood, and based on that assessment of Kathleen, and based on the observations that he makes of the area, he concludes that she's been dead for some time. He can't say exactly how long, but she's been dead for some time."

Hardin summarized for the jury the list of witnesses that he would call and the evidence they would present. "This is not a case of the battle of the experts. This is a case about your exercise of your good reason and your common sense. And it's going to be a battle against what this defendant contends happened, what he wanted it to appear as having happened."

He picked up Kathleen's photograph and walked toward the jury box. "Up to this point, we have talked a lot about Mike Peterson, but when you really get down to it, it's about Kathleen. About Kathleen."

He reminded the jurors that it was their responsibility to determine the truth and asked them to return a verdict of guilty to the charge of first-degree murder.

After a ten-minute break in the courtroom proceedings, David Rudolf began his opening statements without a word. He pressed a button and the voices of dispatcher Mary Allen and Michael Peterson filled the courtroom. The recording of the 9-1-1 call etched pain across the faces of Margaret and Martha Ratliff. Todd Peterson sat with a steel jaw and inscrutable eyes. Michael Peterson cried as he listened. But at the front of the courtroom, Rudolf listened with dramatic intent—his stance and expression filled with the anticipatory glee of a producer the night his play opens on Broadway.

"That, ladies and gentlemen, was the voice of Michael Peterson right after he found Kathleen Peterson at the foot of the stairs. I want to take you back with me before that terrible night, before that terrible phone call."

Rudolf sketched out the beginning of Michael and

Kathleen's relationship. Then with unfathomed insensitivity, he read a 1999 letter from Caitlin—a letter
praising the man whom she now believed killed her
mother.

He told the jury that the Saturday before Thanksgiving,
Kathleen's co-worker Donna Clement said that Michael
and Kathleen were "very affectionate and in tune with
each other."

Behind the defense table, Michael Peterson's lips
moved when Rudolf read that line as if he had mem-
orized it.

"If the prosecution is correct, how do you go from
soulmate and lover to cold-blooded killer? The answer is
very simple: You don't. Nothing was different that
weekend."

Rudolf painted a portrait of a normal weekend in the
Peterson home, enlivened by Christmas shopping, a
holiday party, a romantic movie and big news about
Michael's movie deal.

He spoke of Kathleen's intoxication that night she
died, though in far more delicate terms than her own
stepson, who referred to her as a weekend drunk in a
media interview. He told the jury about her headaches
and dizziness. He promised them that they would hear
testimony from friends and from her doctor about her
medical condition.

He described Michael's discovery of his wife at the
foot of the stairs and his calls to 9-1-1. "Now, they went
there, and initially it was treated as an accident because
that's what they initially thought it was. [. . .] And so
Todd Peterson was allowed to go up to Kathleen's body
and hold her in his arms and get blood on his clothing.

And Michael Peterson was allowed to go up to Kathleen. In fact, he had to be physically pulled off of her."

Rudolf then alleged that if this accident had occurred in any other household, it would have been treated like an accident to this day. It was not, in this case, because of the bias of the Durham Police Department toward Michael Peterson. As a columnist for *The Herald-Sun*, Peterson's criticism of the police department was unflinching.

"And so, for the Durham police investigators who arrived at that scene, it wasn't very hard for them to look at the blood and assume the worst about Michael Peterson. And it was based on that altered and contaminated scene and blood evidence that they decided the death was suspicious."

He accused the police department of tunnel vision— of looking for evidence that supported their view and ignoring anything that did not.

"What our experts will testify, in short, is, the lacerations on her scalp are much more consistent with a fall than with a beating. And that's confirmed by the lack of certain injuries. I mean, can you imagine," he said, shaking his head as he approached the prosecution table, picked up the blowpoke and checked its heft in his hand, "someone beating somebody over the head?" He hauled back his arm to its full reach and slammed it forward. "Whacking them as hard as they can? I mean, you don't whack someone like this when you are trying to kill them." He scratched the air with puny swings.

"Imagine that there's no skull fracture," he said with incredulity as he cropped the blowpoke with noisy disdain back on the table.

"There's no brain contusions. There's no swelling of the brain. There's no internal hemorrhage, no subdurals, things that you would see from that kind of injury. No. None of it.

"And it's confirmed that it was a fall by other physical evidence that, as we said, Kathleen Peterson sustained those injuries to her head at least thirty minutes before Michael Peterson walked in and found her and called 9-1-1."

Rudolf then used video clips of the experimentation done by Agent Duane Deaver to duplicate the blood spatter in the stairwell. He selected the cuts with care, showing the jury those he could mock the best.

"What our experts are going to say is that the amount of blood spatter in that stairway—as horrific as it is—is not consistent with what you would get from a beating. It's consistent with what you'd get from hitting your head in various places.

"You've all seen dogs shake water off and it goes all over. Well, that happens with blood as well if it's wet, or hands or your clothes coming in contact with the wall. Or coughing up blood. Or sneezing blood. That's what causes all the blood spatter, you see. As bad at it is, that's what our experts will testify."

Rudolf then disparaged the financial motive presented by the prosecution. Wrapping up that argument, he journeyed into hostile territory, the death of Elizabeth Ratliff. The judge had not yet ruled whether or not this evidence would be admitted in trial. The defense took a calculated gamble based on the old adage that the best defense is a good offense and dragged the elephant in the room up to the jury box.

"Now I'm going to talk about Elizabeth Ratliff," Rudolf began. "Interestingly enough," he said, placing his left hand on the side of his face, "Mr. Hardin chose not to. I'm not sure why he chose not to. He said before that it was a critical part of his case, but he chose not to. So let me address it."

He stretched his arm toward the two frightened young women sitting on the front row on the far side of the courtroom. "We're talking about the mother of Martha and Margaret Ratliff. She died eighteen years ago in Germany. And you all have heard a lot—not everybody, but most of you—have heard a lot about that in the news."

Rudolf continued. "The police learned of her death in December 2001. How do we know that? Well, they asked Patty Peterson, who was Elizabeth Ratliff's best friend in Germany. They asked her about it in December 2001."

He pointed out that the prosecution did not seek to exhume the body until fifteen months later, in March of 2003, and then held back the autopsy for another six weeks.

"And we will submit to you," he said, pounding his finger into the podium again and again to drive his point home, "that the reason it was delayed for that long was to create a barrage of negative publicity to prejudice Mr. Peterson's right to a fair trial in this case just before the trial was to begin. And they succeeded. He was tried and convicted in the media."

"Objection," roared Hardin.

"Sustained," answered Judge Hudson.

Rudolf continued, launching attacks on the series of

coincidences, claiming they were false. Hardin objected to numerous statements. Some Hudson overruled, others he sustained on the grounds that the defense's comments were argumentative. As his attorney spoke, Michael Peterson pulled his glasses on and off his face again and again. And he popped Tic Tacs as if his very survival depended on devouring as many as possible in the time allotted.

Up on the large screen behind Rudolf's back, Michael and Kathleen smiled across the room at the jury. "The truth is that Kathleen Peterson, after drinking some wine and some champagne, and taking some Valium, tried to walk up a narrow, poorly lit stairway in flip-flops and she fell and she bled to death.

"What Michael Peterson brought to Kathleen Peterson was true happiness over thirteen years. That's the picture—that's not posed—that's Kathleen sitting on Michael's lap."

Across the courtroom, Michael Peterson bowed his head. When he raised it, he spotted a camera, turned toward the photographer and grimaced.

Rudolf reiterated his claim of their loving marital relationship and insisted that everyone knew Mike had nothing to do with Kathleen's death. He then asked for a verdict of not guilty.

After lunch, the case in chief began. The first witness called to the stand by the prosecution was Jay Rose, a paramedic with Durham County Emergency Medical Services. Jay sank hard into the witness chair, outfitted in the protective coloring of his uniform. From the look on his face, there were a lot of other places he would much rather be that afternoon.

He sported a buzz cut in his pale hair and even though he was only 30 years old, the thinning process was taking its toll: his hairline receded on both sides of his forehead and on the top of his head. As if in compensation, his full moustache stretched down on both sides of his mouth. The arms of his wire-frame glasses pinched into the sides of his head, punctuating his obvious discomfort on the stand.

He walked the jury through his arrival at the scene, his assessment of Kathleen Peterson and his amazement at the large quantity of dried and drying blood. On cross-examination the next morning, Thomas Maher questioned Rose's honesty about the state of the blood.

Then, on re-direct, Hardin asked, "Now with respect to your observations of the scene and based on your experience and training as a paramedic, do you have an opinion on how long Ms. Peterson would have been dead when you arrived?"

Maher was on his feet in a flash. "Objection."

The bench responded, "Overruled."

Jay answered, "As I say, due to my experience, we were, I would say anywhere between thirty and forty-five minutes."

"Okay. Based on your training and your education and the experience that you've had, do you have an opinion as to how long there will be activity in the heart after a patient dies?"

An indignant Maher stopped the proceedings,

"Objection. Now, can we be heard on this? Approach the bench?" And with those two questions, contentiousness introduced itself into the courtroom and did not leave the premises until the verdict was delivered.

After a lengthy argument outside of the presence of the jury, Judge Hudson responded. "All right, your motion to strike the testimony is allowed. I will instruct the jury that the witness has testified that Ms. Peterson had been dead for thirty to forty-five minutes. The jury is ordered to disregard that testimony, as the court has determined that the witness is not qualified to give such an opinion."

David Rudolf told the judge that he wanted to confer with co-counsel about cross-examining the witness before the jury on that testimony.

"Well, you discuss that with Mr. Maher," Hudson responded in his quiet drawl. "But when you ask the court to request the jury to disregard something, the presumption is that the jury disregards it."

"Yes, sir."

"It wouldn't make much sense to the court . . ."

"I understand."

". . . if you allowed them to cross-examine about something that they are to disregard."

After lunch, the other paramedic and two first responders from the fire department related their viewpoint of the night's events to the jury. David Rudolf's cross-examination of one of the firefighters appeared to be designed more to make the witness appear stupid than to poke holes in the prosecution's case. It was not a pretty picture.

. . .

Assistant District Attorney Freda Black took control of the court to establish a financial motive for the murder of Kathleen Peterson. She questioned four Nortel Networks employees as well as an expert from the Durham County Probate Department.

Then she extracted the lengthiest and most complex testimony from a financial specialist for the North Carolina State Bureau of Investigation. Between them, the witnesses disclosed that Michael Peterson was the beneficiary for Kathleen's pension plan, her deferred income and her life insurance policy—together worth more than $1.8 million; that the couple had spent far more than they'd earned in the last three years; and that by the end of 2001, the couple had managed to accumulate more than $140,000 in credit card debt.

Black dressed for court in a manner some more conventional woman prosecutors might find frivolous. One dress trumpeted an uninhibited garden of orchids. Others were in more subdued colors. But all had a distinct feminine style. Her jewelry assortment was more restrained, favoring gold and pearls.

One bad hair day, Freda stumbled across a godsend right in her building and right off her witness list, Glenda Lilly from the probate department. Although Glenda worked in the courthouse, she came from a family of hairdressers. She could whip up a French twist or French braids quicker than most people could yawn. On days Freda could not get her hair to sprawl with calculated wildness past her shoulders, Glenda came to the rescue.

Beneath this decorative exterior beat the heart of a competent, ruthless member of the prosecution team. Freda extracted testimony about the financial status of Kathleen Peterson at Nortel Networks with great finesse. She guided each witness through a maze of numbers and benefit packages with focused, step-by-step explanations. And she was prepared. She provided the jurors with a copy of every financial document she discussed to facilitate their ability to follow along.

Pity the defense attorney who judged this woman to be an ornament for the prosecution.

Fiscal details that often make a juror's head swim had been laid in front of the panel in stunning clarity by the time Freda took her seat. The defense team, in contrast, seemed disorganized and confused. Their cross-examination was disjointed and abstract. And thus, it was easy to ignore.

Liz Ratliff's sisters, Margaret Blair and Rosemary Kelloway, agreed to participate in a television interview with Camille Whitworth at their homes in Rhode Island. Margaret received a call from her niece, Margaret Ratliff. Crying and sobbing, she begged them not to do any interviews. Moved by her tears, the sisters cancelled it.

For the next few days, Margaret Blair ran the conversation through her head and a realization dawned on her. Margaret did not believe her niece made that call on her own initiative. She felt certain someone was pulling her strings.

She called her niece back and told her that she and Rosemary would be granting interviews and asked her to give a message to Michael Peterson: "Tell him the next time he wants something from me, tell him to call me himself instead of using you." Margaret ached for her niece. The young woman had expended an incredible amount of energy defending her guardian. She insisted she had her act together, but Margaret Blair could tell she was falling apart.

39

After the financial testimony, 9-1-1 telecommunications operator Mary Allen took the stand. Now it was the prosecution's turn to hit the PLAY button and fill the courtroom with the voice of Michael Peterson. Once again, Peterson displayed tears and a tormented face for the jury.

The faces of Margaret and Martha Ratliff radiated acute distress. Margaret shook and sobbed as she listened. Todd Peterson tried to comfort her by putting an arm around her, stroking her hair and rubbing her shoulder.

Corporals Juanita McDowell and Scott Kershaw, two of the first Durham police officers to arrive at 1810 Cedar Street followed Allen. They related the people and events they encountered on the scene that night.

On direct examination, Freda Black walked Sergeant Terry Wilkins through the early morning hours of December 9, 2001. On cross-examination, David Rudolf was intent on proving that the Durham police had botched the scene to such a great extent that no information they had to offer was reliable and that none of their conclusions were valid.

"You know that telephone that was on the counter there?"

"Yes."

With a heavy tone of accusation in his voice, Rudolf asked, "Did she [Corporal McDowell] ever tell you that she asked Todd Peterson to get her that phone?"

"I believe I do remember hearing her mentioning that she needed to use a phone from the residence because as a corporal, she did not have a city phone to use."

"And you're aware, are you not that generally speaking—by the way are you familiar with this book, *Practical Homicide Investigation*?"

"Somewhat familiar with it."

"That's sort of standard—I won't say *standard*—but a lot of police departments use this as a reference?"

"I would say they do," Wilkins admitted.

"Are you familiar with the fact that one of the things that this book talks about is never using the telephone at the scene?"

"Yes I am."

"Because that's a problem in terms of possible contamination, right?"

"That's correct."

Rudolf pushed him harder. "So that wasn't an appropriate thing for Corporal McDowell to do?"

"It was not the perfect thing to do," Wilkins conceded.

"Okay. Um. She should have observed where Todd Peterson got that phone, right?"

"Yes. I would have preferred that."

"If you had been there you would have required it, right?"

"If I had thought of it, I would have required it."

"And, particularly if that phone was sitting in the stairway? In blood?" the defense attorney emphasized. "That would have been something you would have wanted documented as Todd Peterson was permitted to go and get that, right?"

"That's correct."

"Indeed, you would not have let him go and get that phone, would you?"

"No, sir."

Using the report that Wilkins filed, Rudolf pointed out all the places where he had mentioned blood in his report and got him to admit that never once had he described it as dried blood.

He then handed him Corporal McDowell's report and asked the same about her report.

"I don't see any mention of it being dried, no," Wilkins replied.

Rudolf slapped two more scene reports in front of Wilkins and his identical line of questioning produced similar answers in response. Satisfied that he had laid enough foundation for doubt with this witness, Rudolf ended his cross-examination. After a lunch break, Black rehabilitated Wilkins with a few brief questions. Then the defense attorney wrapped up the witness's testimony with a masterful re-cross.

"If you had been present at 2:50 A.M. on December ninth, would you have allowed Heather Whitsun to walk in that door saying she was a medical doctor and not even asking for her name or her I.D.? Would you have done that?"

Trying to prevent the path of probing she saw ahead, Freda Black was on her feet. "Objection. Speculation."

The judge squashed her attempts with just one word: "Overruled."

If Wilkins could have fled the courtroom at that moment, he would have done so with great joy. He knew where this line of questioning was going and his reluctance to follow that road was etched across his face and punctuated by his stiffened body language. Nonetheless, he answered, "I probably would not have. Again, I don't know what Corporal McDowell or Corporal Kershaw had been told, so I couldn't base my assessment unless I knew exactly what they had been told."

"I wasn't asking you to criticize them. I was simply asking what you would have done."

"I probably would not have."

"You wouldn't have allowed Todd Peterson to go up to Kathleen Peterson's bloody body, correct?"

"I wouldn't if I could have stopped him in time."

"Right. You certainly wouldn't have given him permission to do that?"

"No."

"You certainly wouldn't have given Michael Peterson permission or allowed him to go up to Kathleen Peterson's body?"

"No I would not."

"You certainly wouldn't have allowed Michael Peterson and Todd Peterson to embrace after Michael Peterson was covered in blood?"

"No."

Rudolf continued to pound on Wilkins, forcing him to condemn one judgment call of a colleague after another. He wrapped up with one final question: "And the reason why you wouldn't have done any of that [was] because each one of those had the potential for contaminating the scene, didn't it?"

"Correct."

"That's all I have."

Relieved that the ordeal was finally over, Sergeant Wilkins rose from the witness stand and took his place on the bench behind the prosecution table. He gave a sympathetic look to the former police officer who took his place to corroborate the official version of the night's events.

Next to testify was Sergeant Fran Borden, the criminal investigation division officer on call on December 9, 2001. His head of thinning white hair, a bushy white moustache, wire-rimmed glasses and round face gave him the aura of a young, kindly grandfather. The now-retired fourteen-year veteran of the homicide division had been to more than 500 death scenes. He stood before the jury and used a diagram of the house to describe his actions and observations.

He spoke of Kathleen being coated in blood. As he proceeded to describe in further subjective detail, Rudolf interrupted with "Objection to commentary. There are pictures that will show what was there." It was an odd comment for that attorney to make. It directly contradicted his argument during the defense opening where he explained that a picture has a point of view, but the narrative tells the whole story.

Borden continued telling the jurors that he had never seen a serious fall where the neck aligned with the spinal cord. It did not make sense to him. That was one of the reasons that he'd made the decision to officially label the area as a crime scene. He took the jury through the steps he'd followed after that declaration until he'd left the home after 9 that morning.

On cross-examination, Rudolf established that Borden was the spokesperson for the police department in 1998 and 1999. He got Borden to admit that at one point, the chief of police had cut off all official communication with *The Herald-Sun* because of her displeasure with Michael Peterson's columns.

Rudolf asked Borden questions about other articles critical of the department, but unfortunately for the defense, the jury, once riveted to every word of Borden's direct testimony, now slouched or rested their heads in their hands and appeared to lose interest in this line of questioning.

Then, Borden loaded his gun and took aim at the defense allegation of bias by the Durham police. "Actually, Mr. Peterson's columns, a lot of officers agreed with them—especially his columns referring to what he called the Thirteen Dwarves of City Council. And he recommended that police officers and teachers and other public servants obtain higher raises at a time when the city council was giving themselves a pretty substantial raise."

"Of course," Rudolf interjected, "what you didn't agree with were his columns that were critical of the police department. [. . .] When he would say things like the Durham Police Department intentionally didn't reveal rapes because they were hiding the crime rate, you didn't agree with that, did you?"

Borden looked the defense attorney dead in the eye. "You stand corrected, sir. Part of the reason I was let go as the media officer is because I wanted better communication—open communication—with all our news sources. Why? Because through the news media we were solving much more crime back when we were [. . .] more in tune with each other—when we liked each other. Chief Chambers came in and had a problem. And because I advocated more cooperation, I lost that job."

Finally, Rudolf switched the examination to questions about the fatal night at 1810 Cedar Street. "Before you went inside there, when you spoke with McDowell and Wilkins, were you told, for example, that Todd Peterson had been allowed to go up to Kathleen and hug her?"

"No, I was not."

[. . .] "Were you told that Michael Peterson was allowed to go up to the body and hug her?"

"No, I was not."

Were you told that Michael Peterson and Todd Peterson, both having blood on them, were allowed to embrace each other?"

"No, I was not."

Rudolf continued hammering away, his voice stretched thin with exaggerated impatience. "Did you say to either of the officers there: 'Listen, did anyone other than the people giving first aid go up to the body?' Did you ask that question?"

"No, I did not *ask* that question."

"That would be an important thing to know," Rudolf badgered. "Wouldn't it?"

"[. . .] I would certainly hope I would receive that information."

"But you didn't ask for it?"

"Sometimes we don't have to ask, Mr. Peterson, we just get . . . Excuse me, Mr. *Rudolf*."

Rudolf kept up a relentless attack on the credibility of his conclusions and the appropriateness of actions taken at the scene. "By the way, when you were considering the scenarios of how Kathleen Peterson could have fallen, [. . .] did you consider or ask yourself how she got blood on the bottom of both her feet?"

"I wondered about that. I wondered— I wondered about a lot of things, Mr. Rudolf. [. . .] We did not have the luxury of information because no one was talking to us."

Freda Black began her re-direct by establishing from Sergeant Borden that all officers on the scene wore protective gear and that he had experience at scenes where individuals had fallen down stairs. Then she asked if anyone took a statement from Christina Tomasetti so that she could go home to her husband.

"I believe so. I don't know," Borden answered.

"You do know she was having an affair with Todd Peterson that night, don't you?"

An outraged Rudolf shouted, "Objection to that."

"Sustained," Hudson replied.

Black continued, "Now you were also asked . . ."

"Move to strike," Rudolf interrupted.

A smug grin crossed Todd Peterson's face as the judge sent the jury out of the room. Bill Peterson gave his nephew an exasperated glance of disbelief.

Once the jury was out of hearing, Rudolf argued,

"Judge, as far as I know, what Ms. Tomasetti did that night was to go to Mr. [Todd] Peterson's parents' home, meet him, go to a party with a very large group of people, come back to the house to pick up her car, found the police officers there. And then, unless some police officer got her together with Todd Peterson that night, I believe she spent the night quite by herself."

"So, I don't think she would have had an affair with anyone that night, assuming that she even were so inclined. Moreover, Ms. Tomasetti is married. [. . .] It was an improper question. It demeaned and slandered Ms. Tomasetti, who is in fact married. That goes over the airwaves. For all I know, her husband is watching."

Judge Hudson tried to hide his amusement at this turn of events by holding finger-laced hands before his face, but the twinkle in his eye gave him away. "Apparently, you know something more than Mr. Rudolf, Ms. Black."

"I know Todd Peterson told members of Kathleen Peterson's family that his intention was to come home and have sex with her at the Peterson home."

Hudson interrupted and told the prosecution to save that line of questioning for Todd Peterson if he took the witness stand. The judge struck that bit of courtroom theatrics from the record. Todd Peterson's face glowed from this notorious moment in the sun.

Caitlin's eyes drifted over to Margaret and Martha, the two young women she once regarded as sisters. They seemed like deer caught in the headlights. She tried to be empathetic, but it was hard. Mike was the only parent they had left. But what about her mother?

Her mother had meant so much to them. In fact, since Kathleen's death, Martha had referred to her as "the best mother I ever had." Caitlin was surrounded by support from her family, her sorority sisters and other friends. But it was not the same. There was a large place in her heart reserved for her mother. And there was a second spot that was also lonely and bereft—that empty hole belonged to Margaret and Martha Ratliff.

40

A parade of police officers filed through the witness stand. They testified about searches of the house and the grounds, the time Peterson spent checking and sending email in the hours after his wife's death, and the discovery of Mike Peterson's power of attorney document granting authority to his sons, Todd and Clayton.

Forensic meterologist William H. Haggard made his way to the witness stand with the help of a cane. The top of his head was bald and fringed round the sides with longish white hair. He wore a hearing aid, glasses, and a blue suit, and moved with slow deliberation.

The judge allowed the defense to question Haggard outside the presence of the jury. They launched an attack on his credentials and credibility. The judge then granted the defense additional time to review Haggard's documents and studies before he testified before the jury. Slowly, the elderly man made his way across the courtroom—his appearance this day a total waste of time.

In a blue suit and red tie, Lieutenant Connie Bullock took the stand radiating an aura of comfort and security. He listened to every question with intensity—often sucking his bottom lip into his mouth to aid in his concentration.

He explained his arrival and his responsibility to coordinate the activity at the scene. Hardin then directed his questioning to Bullock's role in the search of the home on December 12. Bullock testified that the warrant was obtained that afternoon and served at 6 P.M. He told the jury that they executed the search at that time because it would be less disruptive, since most people would be at Kathleen's viewing.

The defense flew at Bullock about the timing of the December 12 warrant. Rudolf ridiculed the contention that a search during the wake would be less intrusive. "You were going in the hopes of finding the house empty?"

"Of not having to displace people."

"You are talking about finding no one there, right?" Rudolf asked.

"When we execute a search warrant, any resident that would be present would be secured by the police, meaning either they would have to be held up in a particular location or escorted out of the residence."

"Well, the truth is, what happens is, you can ask them to step outside while you conduct the search, right?"

"Yes, sir."

"That's what usually happens, right? Right?" Hostility had crept into Rudolf's tone, but no reaction to it was visible in Bullock's placid demeanor.

"[. . .] Now were you expecting Michael Peterson to be there when you got there?"

"I had no earthly idea who would be there," Bullock replied.

"All right. And how were you going to get into this house if no one was there?"

"If no one was there, the Constitution and the search warrant would allow for a forced entry," the witness stated.

"Forced entry?" When he uttered these two words, Rudolf etched the edges of each syllable with outrage. "You think it would be less intrusive and upsetting to Mr. Peterson to come home from a wake and to find out that the police had rummaged through his house?"

"[. . .] I don't know if it would be more or less upsetting to Mr. Peterson. I don't know."

"[. . .] Two or three days after his wife dies in the house, what he finds is that someone—he doesn't know who—has been in the house and maybe rummaged through it, right?"

"That's correct."

"And your view was that that was less intrusive than simply coming to his house, say at one o'clock in that afternoon, and knocking on the door?"

Nodding his head, Bullock said, "It was an option."

"And what you all chose to do instead was to come to his house at the very time that the wake for his wife was scheduled, correct?"

"Yes, sir."

"And, as a result of that, because he chose to— He was put in the position, basically, of choosing between going to the wake right then and there or sticking around and seeing what you guys—or at least trying to figure out—what you guys were doing in the house, right?"

Bullock denied knowing what Peterson was thinking. Rudolf launched an attack on the officer about the rape kit obtained from Kathleen's body on December 11. "And the people at the funeral home said, 'We're not going to let you do that unless you go get a warrant.' Isn't that what happened?"

"Yes, sir."

"And they called Mr. Peterson to tell them that you all were now wanting to take a rape kit from his wife? Didn't they?"

"I was told that he was called," Bullock answered.

With a look of disdain, repugnance dripping from his voice, Rudolf said, "And then you all actually went and got a warrant and that was done to his wife's body, wasn't it?"

"It's my understanding that it was," the witness admitted.

On re-direct, Hardin established with the battered witness that the discovery of a used condom and a towel that appeared to have semen stains on it was what motivated investigators to obtain that search warrant on Kathleen Peterson's body.

41

After the lieutenant was excused from the witness stand, the courtroom fell back into tedious testimony from an attorney who taught finance and law in the department of Business Management at the University of North Carolina at Chapel Hill. He presented the deadly dull details of how Kathleen's property would be divided since she died without a will.

The direct, cross-examination and re-direct of this witness were so mind-numbing that it prompted a quip from the judge at the end of the day. After the jury had been dismissed, he turned to the attorneys and asked, "Did you all enjoy your law school property review?"

The next morning began with evidence technician Dan George on the stand. Part of his testimony included Resusci Anne, the life-size dummy used as a CPR training tool. She was dressed for court in a red turtleneck, navy shirt and pants. She wore a blonde wig and was about the same size as Kathleen. As the demonstration began, Todd Peterson sat in the audience popping Tic Tacs like a maniac, with an amused expression across his face.

George propped the dummy on the step beside the witness box in an approximation of the position of Kathleen's body, and pantomimed Michael Peterson's impulsive race to his wife's body. He demonstrated how the defendant put an arm around her, but did not hold or caress her. He then described how the combined efforts of an officer and Todd Peterson forced Michael Peterson from the stairwell and to the sofa in the breakfast nook.

Black questioned George about his interaction with other members of the police, the removal of Kathleen's body, the gathering of evidence and the videotaping he had done throughout.

A short break in the proceedings gave the prosecution time to set up their next exhibit. When the jury door opened, laughing and giggling wafted into the courtroom. Unaware of the drama about to unfold, many of the jurors took their seats with smiles on their faces.

At the push of a button, all of that changed. The prosecution played the videotape of the crime scene. They elected to run it without any commentary. The courtroom filled with a hush so deep it echoed in the spectators' ears.

The video opened with a shot from the circular driveway and up the brick walk toward the Kent Street door. The camera paused to zoom in on a droplet of blood on the walkway. Then, it traveled onto the slate porch and focused on the smear of blood on the doorway.

The jury was rapt. Brows furrowed, hands stroked beards, cheeks flushed. As the camera entered the house and moved ever closer to the body of Kathleen Peterson, the darkness of the jurors' thoughts was written in their expressions and their body language.

Hands flew to mouths. A number of jurors squirmed in their seats. At times, some flinched away and then forced their gaze back to the monitor. The pale face of an older woman developed a progressive look of distaste. The lines beside her mouth deepened from shallow furrows to infinite crevices.

A young blonde juror looked on the verge of bursting into tears. Another woman sank deeper and deeper into her seat until she almost disappeared behind the rail. A young male juror held his chin against his throat, forcing him to view the video with an upward gaze as though he could not bear to face it full on. A middle-aged woman sucked her lips into her mouth and blew them out over and over again.

A gray-haired man blinked his eyes in rapid rhythm. His hand rose to his mouth, formed a fist, and his teeth latched onto his ring finger. An older man removed his glasses, wiped his eyes, rubbed his forehead and clenched his jaw with enough force to distort the line of his face.

When the tape ended, the panel looked as if their collective heart was full of an intense desire to fly away—the devout wish to be anyplace, anywhere but the jury box. When they had filed out for lunch break on previous days, they would go in pairs, chatting together, exchanging grins—the anticipation of an hour of freedom splashed across their faces.

It was a different jury that headed out of the courtroom that day. They were as somber as a hanging judge. Their eyes cast down, their movements sluggish—their mood and the ambiance of the courtroom underwent a dramatic transformation that weighed down on everyone for days.

. . .

Large cardboard boxes were lugged into the courtroom and piled on the bench behind the prosecution table. Hardin and George began to empty them of the presentation of evidence seized or collected by the evidence technician from the home of Michael Peterson. The process of revealing these items was a tedious but necessary step in courtroom procedure. It demonstrated that the chain of custody was clear and constant.

They started with State's Exhibit 1, a brown paper bag covered with writing. George donned a pair of latex gloves and, with a small pink utility knife, sliced open the bag. From it, he removed a roll of brown paper. Spreading that open, he revealed a pair of shorts belonging to Michael Peterson. Holding the shorts, he walked before the jury displaying the blood-soaked front and the lightly spattered back.

That Friday afternoon, he also presented Michael Peterson's blood-smeared shirt and his blood-spotted shoes. On Monday morning, he continued his introduction of evidence. When he finished, the defense battered him about evidence that was not seized—the telephone, the towels beneath Kathleen's head, the keys in the door.

Tuesday morning, the cross-examination of Dan George was preceded by a hearing with one of the jury members. She had ridden on an elevator with Michael Peterson and his family. After determining that she had not heard anything that would affect her ability to be fair, the judge called the jury back into the courtroom. He instructed them to use the back elevator to avoid people involved with the case. At times, the unreliability of the old courthouse elevators made it impossible for the jurors to comply.

The cross-examination of Dan George continued throughout that day and into the next. Rudolf attacked his experience, the decisions he made and the contamination of the crime scene by first responders, police personnel, the defendant and others.

On re-direct, Hardin focused on the reality that crime-scene contamination is a fact of life in every investigation. "Have you ever been to a scene," he asked George, "where everything was absolutely frozen in place? The defendant was still standing there?"

"No."

"The weapon still in his hand?"

"No, sir, I haven't."

"Do you have an opinion whether that the second he moves around in the scene, that scene's altered?"

"In every case," George agreed, "it probably would be. Yes, sir."

The prosecutor established that George was aware of the time line of events prior to his arrival at the scene. George admitted that he had no knowledge about the positioning of the body before he got to the scene. Hardin then walked him through a list of injuries to Kathleen's body and George acknowledged that he only observed an injury to her eye.

"But you still processed the scene?" Hardin asked.

"Yes, sir, I did."

"And no one whatsoever," Hardin emphasized, "gave you any information about what Mr. Peterson was doing before EMS got there, did they?"

"No, sir, they did not."

On re-cross, Rudolf disputed George's previous testimony that no one had sprayed luminol in the lower stairwell. He produced a photograph that depicted a white residue in the area of the stairway that George admitted looked like dried luminol.

On re-re-direct, Hardin held up the same photo Rudolf had shown and elicited the opinion of George that it was not a photo taken by the Durham police. He told the jury that if luminol had been sprayed there during the investigation, it would have been tracked off the stairs by someone. When Hardin asked if it were possible that one of the defense experts sprayed the area, the defense went ballistic.

"Object to that as an outrageous allegation," Rudolf shouted.

The judge upheld Rudolf's objection, but admonished him about editorializing.

On re-re-cross, a squabble erupted between counsel over the appropriateness of questioning the evidence technician on the contents of the autopsy report. The prosecution prevailed and, to his great relief, Dan George was released from the stand.

It had been a difficult day for Candace Zamperini, too. She sought healing and strength at the Maplewood Cemetery. The day was still, the air hot and moist. No earthly conditions were present to make the chimes by Kathleen's grave sing. However, when Candace stood by the side of her sister's resting place, the light, bright tinkling of the chimes filled the air. It did not stop until Candace walked away.

Candace experienced this inexplicable phenomenon many times throughout the trial. Kathleen was speaking to her. And Candace was listening.

42

The rest of the morning of July 24 and all of that afternoon was filled with the testimony of ID Tech Eric Campen. He exuded self-confidence on the stand. His pleasant demeanor and frequent eye contact with the jurors built a high level of rapport.

The district attorney, using his own witness, laid the foundation for evidence and established the chain of custody of numerous pieces of evidence just as he had done with Dan George. The monotonous process crawled along until they reached State's Exhibit 12, the substance Campen removed from an indentation on a lower step.

In front of the jury box, Campen opened the envelope, unsealed and uncapped a small plastic container to reveal the contents—but there was nothing there. The witness stammered, insisting that there was a silver-colored object in there when it was sent to the state lab for analysis. But now nothing was there. Hardin was stunned. Both men knew that the missing sample had been transformed into a weapon for the defense. And they knew Rudolf and Maher would use it.

On cross-examination, Rudolf first questioned

Campen about the photos of the laundry room that were
stills taken from the videotape. He attempted to force
Campen to admit that it was a mistake or an oversight
not to take those shots with a regular camera. Campen
dodged that inference every time it was made.

Rudolf moved on to questions about luminol spraying
and attacked Campen's knowledge base, experience and
credibility. Throughout, the sharp edges of sarcasm
and exasperation scratched across Rudolf's voice. His
raised eyebrows and pursed lips telegraphed disdain. On
Court TV, experts were amazed. They told their viewers
that, in many courtrooms, an attorney could be sanctioned
or fined for emotive facial displays, but Hudson allowed
it all to slide.

As he was questioned, Campen's eyes focused on
Rudolf, his brow furrowed in serious concentration. But
when answering, the corners of his mouth made a subtle
upturn and the light of amusement sparkled in his eyes
as he sent knowing looks in the direction of the jury.

Then Rudolf went in for the kill over the missing
piece of evidence. "Remember before, when you took
out that little container that had that little particle?"

"Yes, sir."

Holding the round, squat cylinder in his hand, Rudolf
pantomimed the actions as he asked about them. "And
you cut it open, right?"

"Yes."

"And you explained how you had sealed it up in there,
right?"

"Yes."

"[. . .] And then when you opened it, there was
nothing there."

"There were a couple of small, tiny specks in there, but not the same item I placed in there," Campen answered.

"And do you know where it is?"

"No, sir, I do not."

"Do you know why it wasn't in there?"

"No, sir. When I sealed up that item," Campen explained, "that item was submitted to the state lab for analysis and they analyzed the item that was in there. There have been many people who handled that item. Your staff . . ."

"Excuse me," Rudolf interrupted.

"I guess— I'm assuring your staff has looked at all the evidence."

"My staff?"

"Yes."

With a face screwed up in a tight grimace that looked as if he were in physical pain, Rudolf asked, "You're assuming *my staff* looked at that evidence?"

"You looked at that evidence at police headquarters on occasions."

"You know who was there when we looked at it? Do you know if we opened that particular container?"

In contrast to Rudolf, Campen's expression was as peaceful as a cat stretched out in the sun. "I just said, I know you have looked at the items of evidence. Whether or not you opened the packages, I have no idea."

Campen fielded the questions well, but the impression left was clear—the state had misplaced a piece of evidence. It may have been the most powerful point for Rudolf to conclude his cross with, but he pressed on. He asked questions about bloody towels, contamination and Campen's responsibilities at the scene.

Next, the jurors heard the testimony of three officers about procedures at the scene and at the jail when Peterson was arrested. Then a special agent with the SBI took the stand. Most of her testimony was a mundane recital of her analysis of the fingerprints from evidence taken at the scene. But then she dropped a bombshell. She showed the jury the clear mark of a footprint on Kathleen's sweatpants. And she added that the foot impression was consistent with the design, elements, size, and wear pattern of Michael Peterson's shoe.

Serologist Suzi Barker was the last person to testify on July 29. She went through the items she tested and the results on the testing for blood and semen. Her long brown hair with sweeping bangs framed a pair of lively brown eyes and a winning smile. It was apparent that she had captivated the jury. When David Rudolf cross-examined her, it seemed as if she had him under her spell, too. The questioning seemed more like a flirtation than an inquisition.

After her testimony, an agent testified about DNA evidence and a hair analyst presented evidence that the hairs clutched in Kathleen's hands and from the steps were forcibly removed from her head.

Over renewed objections from the defense, forensic meteorologist William Haggard got to say his piece at last on August 6. He testified that on December 9, 2001, it was simply too cool outside for Michael Peterson to relax by the pool in shorts and a tee shirt—the temperature was between 51 and 55 degrees.

Then, Dr. Kenneth Snell of the North Carolina

Medical Examiner's Office described his observations at the scene and at the autopsy. His facial expression was relaxed and his manner was focused, reflecting an innate honesty and intelligence. But the dark look in his eyes spoke of a man who spent too much time in the company of death.

The next day, Judge Hudson delivered that long-awaited decision about the admissibility of the pornography and homosexual email as evidence in the trial. He first addressed the defense. "Mr. Maher, I agree with the state's presentation. The court is going to find this evidence proffered by the state is relevant. It goes to the issue of motive. It also goes to attack the idyllic marriage that the defendant has set forth through his counsel in his opening statement."

The jury would now be exposed to photographs more sexually explicit than some of them had ever seen.

Computer experts educated the jury about the specifics of Michael Peterson's computer. They introduced the exchange of emails between Peterson and pornographic film producer Dirk Yates about his homosexual Web site. They pointed to the lack of any literary work or book proposal in progress, even though the defense contended that all the pornographic material on the computer was there for the purpose of research for a book.

They detailed the hundreds of files deleted from the computer between December 8 and December 12, and a long list of pornographic Web sites accessed on that computer. Most of the sites had homoerotic names, but a few indicated that the focus was on sexual activity with teenagers below the age of consent.

The jury had a lot to contemplate over the weekend. And a big question loomed for Monday—would Brad, the male escort, testify or would he take the Fifth?

The courtroom audience was eager for some titillation on Monday, August 11. The judge had denied the request from Brad's attorney Thomas Loflin to conceal his client's real identity. But Loflin was successful in obtaining immunity from state prosecution for his client.

Brent Wolgammott, aka Brad, was born in a small town in Indiana to a Southern Baptist minister and his wife, who worked as a secretary in an automobile plant. He disclosed his homosexuality to his parents when he was 17, but he never told them about his escort work.

Before court was in session, Brent was in the district attorney's office with Freda Black looking at the evidence photos of himself. When they flipped to a back view of his naked body, Brent said, "I wish my ass still looked like that."

Freda did not know where to begin to respond to that remark. He then expressed concern about the photographs becoming public documents. Freda couldn't figure that one out—he had these photos splashed over the Internet for the world to see and now he worried that people will see them?

Looking at his naked front view, Brent said, "It's a good thing I'm well hung."

"I wouldn't go so far as to say that," Freda quipped.

"You don't think so?" a distressed Brent asked.

Freda just stared at him. She couldn't believe she was having this conversation.

Brent took the stand with self-assurance. His blonde brush cut and lantern jaw labeled him military as well as a uniform could have. A half-formed smirk was constant on his full, sensuous lips. With little provocation, that smart-aleck look would transform into a warm, wide grin.

Freda Black smiled and laughed a lot during the cross-examination of this witness—sometimes from amusement and at other times from embarrassment. "What types of services did you perform?" she asked.

"Oh, wow, that's pretty broad," Brent replied. "Basically it's companionship for other males of legal age."

"All right. Did that involve sexual activity?"

"Sometimes it does."

Black used the witness to introduce photographs and reviews from the Web site as well as emails and phone call records from Michael Peterson. "During your conversations with Mr. Peterson," she asked, "did you all actually even discuss a price for your services?"

"I believe we did."

"And what was the price that you quoted him?"

"I believe that it was one hundred-fifty dollars per hour."

She asked him about Michael Peterson's positive comments about Kathleen and about the setting of the date for their rendezvous. Then she asked, "Tell us, please, did you all actually discuss what you were going to do when you were to get together on September fifth, 2001?"

"Yes, ma'am."

"And what were you all planning on doing?"

"Having sex."

On cross-examination, Rudolf asked, "Was that an unusual occurrence for you to have or plan to have sexual relations with married men?"

"To the contrary, I mean, married men are in the majority of most the clients I saw when I was an escort," Brent said.

"With regard to the kinds of men that you tended to have escort relationships with, can you give us some indication of their professions, for example?"

"Sure. Usually they are professionals because my fees were so high. I saw doctors, attorneys. One judge."

The courtroom erupted into boisterous laughter.

With exquisite comic timing, Judge Hudson allowed a perfect pause before he said, "It was not this judge."

The audience roared in appreciation.

Rudolf followed up with: "I think we can stipulate to that."

The defense attorney established that Brent did not have a personal relationship with Michael Peterson and that he did not have sex with him. Then he asked, "Do you know anything about the death of Kathleen Peterson?"

"I know diddly. Diddly," he said with a laugh and a smug expression.

Judge Hudson put him in his place. "I take it that means nothing?"

Brent straightened up at his command and said, "I know nothing. Zip."

Brent Wolgamott was dismissed. Courtroom observers shook their heads in disbelief. They had anticipated a serious person involved in a provocative profession. Instead, they got a refugee from a comedy skit who seemed to have no sense of the gravity of the situation.

When the next witness took the stand, he wiped away all lingering amusement from the spectators' faces. The SBI forensic chemist was all business as he told the jury about his analysis of Michael Peterson's khaki shorts. He found eight defined spots of blood deposited on the inside of the right leg. This spatter was consistent with that on the test shorts created when a blood source was straddled and impacted with a blunt object. His testimony invoked an image of a bloodied Peterson looming over the body of his wife.

A downtown Durham power outage prevented court from beginning until noon on the next day of the trial. When it did, it moved at the speed of cold molasses. The courtroom sat in a whispered, shuffling impersonation of silence for more than an hour while the jury reviewed the photographs and documents submitted into evidence. The judge's eyes hung heavy as he fought off the desire to lapse into catnap. At moments, it appeared as if he might lose the battle.

When Agent Duane Deaver of the State Bureau of Investigation hopped into the hot seat, the jury got its exercise. Deaver was to testify as an expert on the meaning of the blood spatter in the stairwell. The judge sent the jurors in and out of the deliberation room as the defense turned cartwheels to have Deaver disqualified.

As a bloodstain analyst, Deaver's testimony centered on his findings and interpretations at the scene and in the evidence room. His direct testimony consumed the rest of that Wednesday. On Thursday, the prosecution wheeled a wood and Plexiglas model of the complete stairwell into the courtroom. It was made to scale, with 12 inches equaling 62 inches—Kathleen's height.

Using this model and photographs from the scene, Deaver detailed every blood drop, transfer stain and cast-off to the jury. He then testified about the clothing of Michael, Kathleen and Todd Peterson.

Outside the courtroom, the Court TV staff hustled. They lost all contact with the mother ship. Soon they learned about the massive northeast blackout that spread over New York City, into Southern Canada and as far west as Ohio and Michigan. They would not regain contact with New York until late on Friday.

On Friday morning, Rudolf questioned Deaver outside the presence of the jury. Rudolf's repetitious questioning was designed to ridicule. Deaver's drawn-out answers were as dense as a textbook, as if the agent believed that if he just kept talking, the questions would fade away.

43

The action in the courtroom during the week of August 18 divided into two distinct sections. During the regular court day, the prosecution witnesses' testimony continued. Once the jury was dismissed, the hearing on the admissibility of the Ratliff evidence began.

Agent Deaver presented the conclusions of his blood spatter analysis to the jury on Monday. On Tuesday, David Rudolf cross-examined him. He played the videotape of Deaver's experiments to the jury, ridiculing what the SBI expert had done.

Looking at the videotape out of context, it might look more like a child playing in a mud puddle than serious experimentation. But when seen through the eyes of an experienced blood analyst, questions about the location of blood spatter were answered. Theories about how it occurred were supported or destroyed by the re-enactments. Alternate possibilities that could be forwarded by the defense were considered and eliminated. Rudolf hoped the jurors would not have enough sophistication to see beyond the superficial appearance.

After an exhausting day of cross-examination, Agent

Deaver reflected on his ordeal. He videotaped every step of his experiments to be fair—so that the defense team could review and perhaps replicate the complete sequence of events. He knew they would use it to question his conclusions. He did not expect it would be used to attack his character, competence and credibility. He mourned the loss of a court system where seeking the truth was the main objective on both sides of any case.

Rudolf battered Deaver again on Wednesday. Deaver maintained a cool, professional demeanor throughout. His opinions in old cases were thrown at him like an endless barrage of spitballs—but none of his opinions were presented in proper context. To Deaver, it was as ugly and deceptive as an old-fashioned political mud-slinging contest.

On Thursday, the cross-examination of Duane Deaver continued. The judge expressed impatience with the length and repetitiveness of Rudolf's questioning.

While Deaver presented the conclusions of his blood spatter analysis to the jury by day, the late afternoon was devoted to a hearing on the admissibility of the Ratliff evidence outside the presence of the jury. On the first day, Cheryl Appel–Schumacher took the stand. Her quivering chin, halting voice, and moist eyes showed a trauma that was deep, a memory that still had the ability to shatter after eighteen years—even her smiles were caressed with pain.

She testified about the lengthy process of cleaning up Liz's blood in the stairwell. Thomas Maher tried hard to get her to discredit the testimony of upcoming witness Barbara Malagnino. At the time of Liz's death, her name had been Barbara O'Hara. In the intervening years, she had married and divorced cab driver Salvatore Malagnino and still retained his name. Cheryl insisted throughout that she had no opinion on Barbara's credibility.

The next afternoon Cheryl was on the stand again. She told of theories of murder that drifted through her circle of friends, but she did not share their suspicions. "The overriding feeling for me was sadness and confusion and doubt," she said. Her face collapsed inward and reddened as tears spilled down her face. She choked as she finished her sentence. "Doubts about the reasons why these two beautiful girls do not have parents."

Thomas Maher was not diverted by her display of emotion. "I don't mean to keep pushing the same question, but you said there were discussions of a lot of feelings or possibilities. Did any of those possibilities involve Michael Peterson being involved in the death of Liz Ratliff?"

"I think you have to ask somebody else."

Judge Hudson intervened. "He's not really asking you about how you felt. I think you made it clear about how you felt."

"That's all I want to say about it," Cheryl told the judge.

With a smile, Hudson said, "Well, it's not always about what you *want* to say."

"Yeah, but he's trying to make me remember things from 1985."

I don't think he's trying to make you remember anything. He's asking you. Do you know?"

After a moment's pause, Cheryl said, "No." And that was the last word of her testimony in the hearing.

After the jury went home the following day, Freda Black read into the record the proffered statement of Margaret Blair, Liz Ratliff's sister, about the similarities in Liz's and Kathleen's deaths that compelled her to contact the Durham police. Margaret then took the stand for a cross-examination by the defense.

The judge announced his ruling on the Ratliff matter first thing Friday morning. Thomas Maher's ruthless mocking of the thirty coincidences presented by the prosecution did not impact his decision—he sided with the state. Judge Hudson found enough similarities in the two deaths to deem the Ratliff evidence appropriate for this trial.

The prosecution began the presentation of this evidence immediately, as if they feared the judge might change his mind if they dawdled. Cheryl Appeal–Schumacher dragged her sorrow back onto the stand and recounted her previous testimony before the panel of Peterson's peers. Freda Black talked to her about the blood. "And over what period of time did you clean?"

"It seemed like we cleaned blood most of the day." Cheryl's face shriveled into a tight ball as she fought off tears. She put her index finger to her lips and looked down as she tried to regain control. "It was a slow process."

Her face cracked a nervous smile as she wiped her eyes with a tissue. "It was overwhelming to my senses many times during the day. When I actually thought of what I was doing, then I couldn't manage. It took a while because I was slow at it." Cheryl's face contorted in pain. "But there was a lot of blood."

"Did you clean it all up?"

"The purpose of cleaning the blood was so that the baby girls would not see this, this place. And it would not be a part of their memory. I wanted the place to be clean so they couldn't see it."

Under cross-examination, Cheryl told the jurors about the two-hour telephone call she and her husband had with Michael's detective in December of 2002. She discussed the face-to-face interview she had with that detective and a German detective at Patty Peterson's home in Gräfenhausen in May of 2003.

Judge Hudson interrupted her testimony to clarify to the jury that the men were not detectives—they were private investigators.

"If they hadn't contacted me, I wouldn't have contacted the prosecution and we wouldn't be here today," she said.

Tom Appel-Schumacher, Cheryl's husband, was the next on the stand. He confirmed his wife's statements. After he stepped down, the current owner of the home where Liz died slipped into the box. She introduced the statement from Liz's neighbor about seeing Michael Peterson flee from Liz's house. She also brought an excuse from the neighbor's doctor that stated her recent surgery made her unable to travel.

The original statement was written in German. The defense demanded an interpretation by a court-certified interpreter. This was an expensive and time-consuming demand for the prosecution—the nearest person with

certification in German was in Virginia. The defense
rejected the state's compromise offer of a Duke University German professor as translator. The judge ruled
that the statement would be admissible if a translation
agreeable to both sides was provided. Next week, the
prosecution announced their decision not to pursue the
matter.

The state called Dr. Larry Barnes, the clinical
pathologist who performed Liz Ratliff 's original autopsy,
on Monday morning. They used him to establish that he
was not trained in forensics and that the review done by
the Armed Forces Institute of Pathology (AFIP) was only
cursory.

The goal of the cross-examination by the defense was
to reinforce the credibility of this doctor's original
autopsy conclusions and to elevate the perception of
competence of AFIP. Barnes did not give the defense
much help.

On re-direct, Hardin asked him, "The new autopsy
indicates death caused by blunt trauma. Do you dispute
the conclusion of the medical examiner?"

"It is at significant odds with what I thought at the
time. But, no, I don't dispute it."

"Can you say that the external bleeding was
spontaneous vessel rupture or blunt trauma of a fall
down the steps?"

After an objection by the defense and a sidebar, Dr.
Barnes answered, "No. I cannot say 'spontaneous.' I
can't definitely say it was caused by a blow to the head.
No, I can't say it was caused by a fall down the steps."

[. . .] "If you had been told that there was suspicion
about the cause of death other than as an accidental or

natural cause, would you have handled it in the manner that you did?"

"Definitely not."

"What would you have done?"

"I would have appealed to higher command that this be taken from our section and given to someone more qualified to do it."

"More qualified? In what way?"

"With forensic training."

Margaret Blair was the next witness to face the jury. When Freda Black presented Elizabeth Ratliff's will to her, she said, "I recognize the will—the only thing I don't recognize here is my sister's handwriting. But the will, yeah."

"Do you know your sister's handwriting?"

"Well, my sister was left-handed like I am, and she always wrote with a backwards slant, and that's a cursive with a total right-handed slant, so I've never seen—I've never seen her write like that."

After the trial, Margaret compared the signature on Liz's will to a letter written to her by Michael Peterson. The similarities she found sickened her. The letters were squished together in an unattractive way so unlike the artistic nature of Liz, and it appeared to be missing an "e" and an "a" in "Elizabeth." To her eyes, the loop on the "R" in "Ratliff" looked the same as Michael Peterson's loop on the "k" in "talk." The little curls in the "a's" and the shaping of the "f's," "l's" and "t's" were identical in the signature and in Michael's letter. Margaret was convinced and expressed her suspicions to the Durham District Attorney's office. In her eyes, the document filed in Matagorda County, Texas, in 1985 was a forgery.

44

Arguing that contact between the lay witnesses for the prosecution may have altered their testimony, Rudolf requested the opportunity to question Barbara Malagnino and Amybeth Berner out of the presence of the jury. He based his objection on the heavy email correspondence between those two witnesses and the viewing of the Peterson home video at the district attorney's office, but reserved the bulk of his outrage for the dinner party over the weekend attended by out-of-town witnesses and arranged by Assistant District Attorney Freda Black.

David Rudolf implied nefarious intent on the part of Ms. Black. The Northern media outlets and the defense attorney guests sitting in a studio in New York echoed Rudolf's sentiments. They just didn't get it. For folks south of the Mason–Dixon Line, the intent was clear. It was nothing more than old-fashioned Southern hospitality at its finest. It was darn near required to welcome strangers to North Carolina with a good meal. Freda Black had even brought along her two children to ensure that conversation did not drift to the discussion of murder.

The judge had Southern sensibilities, too. At the end of the testimony by Barbara and Amybeth, and the arguments by counsel, he ruled that no violation of ethics or law occurred.

The prosecution called to the stand Steven Lyons, a special agent for U.S. Army Command at the time of Liz's death. He reported that he saw no significant blood, but admitted that he interviewed no one, took no photographs and did not examine the body.

After Lyons was excused, Barbara Malagnino took the jurors on a journey to that distant, dreadful morning she arrived at Liz Ratliff's home. She entered the house with trepidation—uncomfortable because of the atypical lighting. She saw a body and her mind fled into the shadows of denial. She was forced to accept reality when she looked into Liz's face. She also testified about all the blood on the stairway.

Amybeth Berner followed, relating her memories of her friend's demise. She told the jury that she was suspicious from the start that the official cause of death was not correct. At first, she told them, she did not suspect Michael Peterson. As time went by, however, her doubts about that night frequently turned to him. There was his talk about his CIA connections and all the death and rape that oozed from the pages of his book, *The Immortal Dragon*.

Then she spoke of blood—massive quantities of blood—spattered high and low, far and wide. Tears filled her eyes as she ran the memory of that vision through her head, but she soldiered on.

The next witness to face the jury was Dr. Aaron Gleckman, a neuro-pathologist involved in the second autopsy of Elizabeth Ratliff. He pointed out that the cuts to the brain tissue in the original autopsy were not at all conventional. Although some of the brain tissue was missing, he was amazed that after seventeen and a half years, the remaining tissue was remarkably well preserved.

He read his conclusion from his report that Liz Ratliff had died from blunt force trauma to her head. That trauma, he testified, was the result of a beating.

On cross-examination, Rudolf tried to make Dr. Barnes appear as a superior authority on the death of Liz Ratliff, but Gleckman was non-plussed.

"Based on what you were able to see in 2003, you cannot rule out the possibility that Elizabeth Ratliff had a vascular malformation that burst in 1985, correct?"

"I can't rule it out," Gleckman agreed, "but it wasn't the cause of her death."

Next, Dr. Thomas Bouldin, neuropathologist, testified about his role in the neurological examination of Kathleen Peterson. He was the doctor who made multiple sections of the brain to search for abnormalities and discovered the presence of red neurons. In brief, he told the jury that injuries to Kathleen's brain were consistent with head trauma. The red neurons proved that she lay on the stairs for hours before she died.

Two days earlier, Candace Zamperini was in the witness box for *voir dire* examination before the judge. On September 3, she repeated her ordeal in front of the jury. During cross-examination, it was clear that there was no love lost between her and David Rudolf.

Rudolf attempted to destroy her credibility by pointing out inconsistencies in some of her previous statements. Many on the jury, however, were not buying it. With every jab he threw, their empathy for Candace grew.

Rudolf handed Candace photographs of the stairwell stained with Kathleen's blood. Under direct testimony, she had marked the places where she had cleaned.

"Just so we're clear, can you initial next to the areas you said you cleaned up, what you say you did in terms of the area you cleaned up?" Rudolf asked.

Candace's face contorted in anguish as she looked at the pictures. Her head bobbed from side to side as if her mind were rebelling against her vision.

When Rudolf pushed her for specifics, Candace interrupted. "Do you want me to go before the jury and show this?" The pitch of Candace's voice was rising as her level of stress increased. She now sounded more like a distressed child than a grown woman. Hearts broke for her all over the courtroom.

"Well," Rudolf said, "what I would like you to do is write on here, if you could, the areas that you feel like, as best as you can recall right now, that you cleaned up and then we'll try to identify it for the record."

As he spoke, Candace's ragged breath echoed like a background bass beat through the crowd of riveted spectators.

"I realize this is hard on you," Rudolf said, "and I apologize, but you've indicated that you were spraying on the step area there were you put 'X's' now."

Candace, her forehead resting on her hand, answered, "Yes." She struggled to answer questions on the locations of her cleaning, but her emotional stamina was disintegrating with every response.

"Are you okay?" Rudolf asked as Candace blotted away tears.

A deep sigh blew through the silent, transfixed audience. "It's her blood! It's just unnerved me."

"Maybe we should take a brief recess, Your Honor," Rudolf said.

As the judge dismissed the jury for a five-minute break, Candace collapsed forward on the stand.

To many present, it seemed as if Rudolf had crossed that delicate line. Any doubt he raised in his earlier questioning was now washed downstream on a river of empathy for Candace Zamperini.

Candace's testimony reverberated far outside of the courtroom. In California, Michael's sister, Ann, discarded her denial and tossed aside the Peterson public persona of a family united. She had told *Herald-Sun* columnist Tom Gasparoli a few months earlier, "I don't think anyone could easily believe one's brother could be a murderer. It's just something you don't fathom." After the last few days of testimony, her perspective had changed. "I'm not keeping it a secret that I think he killed both Kathleen and Liz."

Ann also called Patty Peterson. "Don't you get it, Patty? He killed your friend."

"I know his character," Patty said, "and I know he didn't."

"What about all the blood on Kathleen? What about all the blood on Liz? Can't you see she was beaten to death?"

"No. It's not true."

. . .

The prosecution followed Candace's emotional and moving testimony with cold, hard facts. Dr. Deborah Radisch of the medical examiner's office was now in the hot seat. Certified in anatomic, chemical and forensic pathology, she had performed more than 3,200 autopsies—most of them forensic.

On direct examination, Hardin walked her through in-depth descriptions of every abrasion, contusion and laceration on Kathleen's head.

When he handed her the blowpoke and asked if the injuries to the scalp were consistent with injuries caused by a similar fireplace tool, Radisch agreed. "It's not solid—it has weight to it, but it is not solid. Since there are no skull fractures, a hollow metal object like this could cause severe laceration without fracture."

"Are they collectively consistent with a fall down stairs?" Hardin asked.

"No."

"With respect to these injuries cumulatively?"

"In my opinion, the injuries were the result of being struck by an object or against an object." She added that some of the injuries may have been caused by striking the stairs or being struck against the stairs by force.

She then testified about the fracture and bleeding of a small piece of cartilage in Kathleen's neck—an injury that is present with attempted strangulation. She also pointed out the many defensive wounds on Kathleen's hands and arms.

Hardin shifted the questioning to the autopsy of Elizabeth Ratliff. Dr. Radisch's conclusions were succinct: "In my opinion, the cause of death of Ms. Ratliff is blunt trauma to the head. In my opinion, the manner of death in Ms. Ratliff's case was homicide."

On cross-examination, David Rudolf started off on the wrong foot. "Ms. Radisch," he said.

"*Doctor* Radisch," she responded.

That afternoon, Rudolf badgered Radisch without making much headway. She admitted that she made mistakes in her life, but conceded nothing else.

In the next day's questioning, though, Rudolf sought payback. He brought two enormous white three-ring binders containing records from 1991 through 2003, and set them on the rail of the witness stand. "Obviously you're not going to be able to read these all, but I want you to just tell me if they appear to you to be, just by looking at them, a collection of all the autopsies involving blunt trauma to the head for this time period?"

She lifted up the cover of one book and flipped pages. She shook her head. She pulled one book toward her with a rueful grin at the jury.

"Objection, Judge, grounds of relevancy," Hardin interrupted.

Radisch gave the judge a pleading look.

Rudolf said, "I think she can look . . ."

Judge Hudson responded, "He asked her to look at them. I think she can respond however she wishes."

Radisch flipped a notebook open. She sighed. She looked at the jurors and grinned again. "I don't really think I can give you an accurate answer to your question," she said with a laugh.

"All right," said Rudolf.

"Not today."

"Well . . ." before Rudolf could complete that sentence, the courtroom's decorum dissolved in a tidal wave of laughter. David Rudolf had met his match.

Radisch expected a tough cross-examination. After all, she had consulted with David Rudolf when she wanted pointers on testifying years ago in her early days as a witness. What she did not expect was what went on outside of the courtroom. It seemed Peterson's friends spread unfounded rumors and insinuations that attacked her professional credibility.

On Friday, September 5, after fifty-one witnesses, the prosecution rested. The defense made the perfunctory motion to dismiss. As usual, that motion was denied. Rudolf responded, "We don't know if we'll put on evidence. We'll know on Monday."

No one doubted that he would. The only question was who?

45

The defense opened its case on Monday, September 8. Their first witness was Dr. Jan Leestma, a forensic neuropathologist. At the request of the prosecution, he was first questioned outside the presence of the jury.

"With regard to Kathleen Peterson, do you have an opinion whether or not injuries she sustained both externally and internally are consistent with a beating?" Rudolf asked.

"Yes, I do have an opinion."

"What is that opinion?"

"That they are not consistent with that scenario," Dr. Leestma said.

Rudolf waved the blowpoke around in the air. Dr. Leestma examined it and declared he disagreed with Dr. Radisch's testimony that it could inflict the wounds of Kathleen Peterson.

"Dr. Radisch also testified that, in her opinion, the injuries, both internal and external, on Mrs. Peterson were not consistent with an accident in that stairwell. Do you agree or disagree with that?"

"I disagree with that interpretation."

While the district attorney cross-examined, boisterous

laughter and loud voices emerged from the jury room. The noise had begun as a distant murmur, now it was the dominant sound in the courtroom. Judge Hudson stopped the proceedings to have the jurors moved to the jury pool room upstairs.

Broadcast pundits seized on this incident. Some thought it indicative that the jury did not take the case seriously. Others expressed the opinion that if the jury was in a good mood at this point of the trial, they would never convict Michael Peterson.

After lunch, the jurors were seated again in the courtroom. Dr. Leestma reiterated his disagreement with the opinions of Dr. Radisch in both autopsies. He expressed the view that there were four lacerations on Kathleen's head—the result of two falls causing two impacts each.

When Rudolf asked, "Could Radisch and Gleckman, with just half a brain, overrule the decision of AFIP and Dr. Barnes?" the doctor said, "No, I think she had a stroke."

He claimed that there were abnormalities in Kathleen's heart tissue that could account for dizziness. He concluded by repeating his assertion that Kathleen Peterson's injuries were inconsistent with a beating—that they were not typical wounds from a round object and that they were not consistent with blows of any sort. He insisted that there was, "robust and reliable evidence that her injuries were the result of a fall."

After the defense portion of Leestma's testimony, Rudolf and Michael Peterson looked at each other and grinned hard. Michael Peterson slapped Rudolf on the back. They were certain of victory.

Jim Hardin took the offensive when he began the cross-examination. "How much do you charge per hour for sworn testimony in the courtroom?"

Leestma testified that his in-court testimony rate was $500 per hour. He charged $350 per hour to review records and $75 per hour for travel during a normal workday. He had billed for services two or three times since inception of the case—for a total of about $10,000.

Next, Hardin attacked his conclusions in Kathleen Peterson's death. Leestma equivocated about the number of falls and in his certainty that all of her injuries had been caused by those falls.

When asked about the injuries to Kathleen's face, he said, "One possibility I considered, and I have no way to go with it any more than saying, 'Well, maybe something like this happened,' is that she ended up somehow on her hands and knees trying to get herself up after one of these falls and somehow either she fainted or she slipped and her face went down on the stairs. I really can't do much better than that, and that borders on speculation on my part."

"Well, how many times would she have to do that to cause these?"

"Uh, it could be one or two times. I don't know."

"Could it be more?" Hardin pressed.

"That's possible."

"Can you say with certainty that she wasn't struck with some instrument to cause them?"

"Those don't look like, uh, blows with some instrument. There's virtually no pattern to them— they're just bruise-like things. Could there be some instrument of some sort that could do that? Sure, there could. I just don't know what the impacting surface is."

Asked about what surfaces would cause the injuries to her left shoulder and down to her left hand, he replied, "These look like blunt impacts to something. The floors, the stairs, the wall, who knows?"

"[. . .] At least it's possible that each of them is individually caused?"

"I suppose it is possible. I think that's unlikely," Leestma said.

Dr. Leestma stated his belief that original 1985 Elizabeth Ratliff autopsy results were correct. "So, are you eliminating completely the possibility that Elizabeth Ratliff was struck by some instrument?" Hardin asked.

"I think it's unlikely," Leestma said. Then he blathered about the wounds, trying to avoid giving a direct and definitive answer.

"Okay. So— But at least it's possible that Elizabeth Ratliff was struck by some instrument?" Hardin pressed.

"I'll never say never and never say always. So, it's there. It's a possibility."

The defense next called Major Timothy Palmbach to the stand. He was an employee of the State of Connecticut Department of Public Safety. He also worked part-time for Dr. Henry Lee's Forensic Research Training Center.

The whole purpose of his arrogant testimony was to slash and burn the Durham Police Department and the North Carolina State Bureau of Investigation. He criticized the collection of evidence and the length of time it took to tape off the scene and restrict movement near Kathleen's body. But he saved his most vicious attacks for

Agent Deaver. He disputed Deaver's conclusions and ridiculed his technique.

When questioned about Palmbach's testimony, some state police officers across the country expressed dismay. They insisted that there is a procedure to follow if another officer suspects wrongful conclusions by a crime scene analyst. There is an official protocol for cleaning up concerns between jurisdictions. Regardless of the merit of his opinions, they professed, revealing this information as a witness for the defense in a murder trial is not one of the methods members of the police force would ordinarily use. However, in the State of Connecticut, there is no official policy and no existing law that prohibited or discouraged Palmbach from presenting this testimony. Due to scheduling difficulties, Palmbach's cross-examination was reserved for a future date.

Following his testimony, the judge ruled that a statement from Christina Tomasetti could be read into the record. Christina was Todd's companion on the night of Kathleen's death. Now she lived on the West Coast, was pregnant and, according to the defense, her doctor did not want her to travel. Many suspicions were raised about the real reason for her absence in the courtroom.

Nonetheless, a member of David Rudolf's staff read her description of the early morning hours of December 9, 2001. Her statement concluded: "Mr. and Mrs. Peterson were in good spirits and very happy when Todd and I left the house at 10:20 P.M., Saturday night. I gave this statement of my own free will."

In response, the prosecution read the following statement into the record: "On January 8 at 1600, I, Art Holland, interviewed Ms. Christina Tomasetti.

Ms. Tomasetti said she did not see Ms. Peterson while she was in the house."

Then Ron Guerette, the investigator for the defense team, took the stand. He explained how he had ordered the boarding-up of the stairwell and the additional actions he had taken there. He said that he was present every time the plywood was removed for a defense expert to view the stairwell.

With the judge's permission granted, it was now time for the jury to inspect 1810 Cedar Street for themselves. A journalist from the Raleigh *News & Observer* was selected as the press representative at the scene. In his report, he said that the jury members went into the house in two groups of eight. Jury members went one by one to the staircase. Some of them walked all the way up the stairs and down—others walked halfway up. Some walked three steps up and looked back to see what it would look like to fall from that position—some made swinging movements as if the blowpoke were in their hand. Many of them crouched down to look more closely at the blood spatter in the lower level.

The defense hoped that the jurors would perceive that the space was too tight to swing a blowpoke. And they did. But some of them came to another conclusion as well—that the space was too small for someone to sustain such massive injuries from such a short fall.

46

When the celebrated Dr. Henry Lee walked to the front of the courtroom, he nodded his head, smiled at the jury and wished them a good morning. He tried at first to project the image of a typical witness, but his Hollywood-enhanced persona overshadowed his pleasantries. The only testimony capable of creating more anticipation than his was the possibility of Michael Peterson facing cross-examination.

Lee testified that medium velocity spatter comes from many things other than impact—shaking hair, a swinging hand. He stood in front of the jury box to demonstrate, telling them he would not use real blood, just red ink.

With a full dropper, he dripped red onto a horizontal white board and then a vertical one, showing examples of low velocity spatter. Using a piece of hair dipped in the red ink, he flipped his wrist and slung medium velocity spatter on a white board held by Rudolf on the edge of the table where Lee performed his demonstration. When he swung a second time, his arm flew upward and flying red ink spattered the defense attorney. Dr. Lee laughed, but Rudolf was not amused.

He then explained that that type of spatter could also be the result of someone coughing, sneezing or wheezing. He held up a bottle and said, "I'm not going to drink ink. I'll use some ketchup. He swigged it into his mouth and coughed onto the white board. The ketchup was diluted and a fine mist flew far and wide around the board and landed on the prosecution table, staining some of the papers there.

Freda Black fumed. When the experimentation continued and she had to duck to avoid the onslaught, she was ready to throttle him.

Lee told the jury that the pattern would be radically different if the person were lying down. Laughing, he said, "I'm not going to lie down." He turned to the defense table. "Anybody want to lie down? Nobody want to lie down? So we won't do demonstration of lie-down."

Photographs of Kathleen in death were important evidence. When the prosecution team showed the horrific pictures from the stairwell or the autopsy suite, they held photos up to the jury, but did not display them to the whole courtroom. The defense, however, demonstrated total insensitivity to Kathleen's family members by displaying these photos on a large screen.

Guy Seaberg pressed a key on the computer and there was a close-up of Kathleen's agonized face, larger than life. Dr. Lee pointed out the evidence of blood or a darkish stain around her mouth and on her lip. That, he said, proved that much of the blood on the walls was coughed up by Kathleen.

Rudolf wound up the direct examination of Dr. Lee with a long-winded question that had one succinct point: Was the evidence more consistent with a beating or was it more consistent with an accident?

Lee answered, "It's more consistent with an accident."

The defense released its witness, but one of Dr. Lee's statements hung like a cloak of deception around the witness box. "There's too much blood for a beating," he said. This counter-intuitive statement stunned jurors and spectators alike. For some, it was a fatal blow to Dr. Lee's credibility.

On cross-examination by Jim Hardin, Lee confirmed that he did not believe Kathleen died from a beating, but did agree with Agent Deaver's finding of three points of origin in space—seemingly contradictory conclusions. He then tap-danced around questions posed about the cause of the lacerations on Kathleen's head.

He testified that a void spot on the wall was not the result of cleaning, but was caused by Kathleen coughing while holding a closed fist to her mouth. He could tell this, he said, because of the ghosting—the round circles of blood with empty centers.

Hardin asked Dr. Lee if he tested those spots for the presence of saliva.

"Not my responsibility. That's something your local laboratory crime-scene people should do. If they do their job properly," Lee banged his fingertips on the wood railing, "I don't need to come here. You cannot blame me. Say I did not do test."

Hardin pushed the issue, causing Lee to get even touchier.

"How many time I have to repeat it?" Lee turned to the jury and smiled. "That's not my job. In Connecticut, I guarantee I would do it."

Hardin asked him about different photos and blood spatter patterns and what they meant, getting him to admit that the prosecution scenario was possible. Hardin used a photograph to point out stains in the crime scene and to ask Lee if he tested any of them.

Lee laughed and asked, "You want me to work for you? Sure, you can offer me a job in North Carolina." During direct examination, Lee often made eye contact with the jury, but during cross, the façade of charm slipped.

On his next day of testimony, he discredited Agent Deaver's experiment model in the stairway because Deaver used a head-shaped piece of Styrofoam with a wig in lieu of a human head. He also said that he did not use stringing via a computer model or any other method to determine point of origin. He just used his visual observation.

At first, Lee claimed that he had not used the stringing method since he was a rookie. On further prodding from Hardin, he admitted to using the method in a 1992 case as verified by the photographs in his book. Then, Hardin forced him to acknowledge that he had used the process as recently as a year ago.

After Lee agreed with Agent Deaver's analysis of bloodstains on shoes, Hardin moved on to Peterson's shorts and Lee disparaged the use of experiments at all. He said that it was impossible to reproduce real life and any effort to do so was useless.

Using Lee's book, Hardin went through the cycle process of crime reconstruction iterated there and read a quote from the book about the need for testing to corroborate the reconstructive hypothesis. "You wrote that, didn't you?"

"Yes," Lee admitted.

When Hardin asked him about any testing he performed on clothing or on any other evidence seized, he argued again that it was not his job.

Hardin continued, "Well, Dr. Lee, you did produce an eight-page report called a 'reconstruction report,' didn't you?"

"Yes, I did."

"And you did that without going through all the phases of the fact-gathering process that you indicated in your book are very important to go through in order to produce a reconstruction?"

"No. I did gather the facts."

Pressured by Hardin, Lee admitted that Deaver did a good job, but had not considered all the possibilities.

After a break, Hardin asked, "Based on all you saw and all you did, all you didn't do, is it your testimony before this jury that you can absolutely, conclusively exclude that Kathleen Peterson was beaten on her head?"

"My conclusion more consistent with an accidental fall."

"But you can't exclude that she was beaten?"

"Nobody can."

Hardin continued to pummel the witness after lunch. He questioned him about a conversation Lee had with Agent Deaver in which he said that what Deaver did was some of the best work Lee had seen.

In response, Lee dithered without giving a real answer to the question.

Hardin pushed harder. "Okay. Do you recall telling him that his work and his conclusions were very close to yours, but that you differed on how some of the blood spatter occurred? Do you recall that?"

Lee insisted he did not recall.

"Well, let me show you a copy of your book. You recall giving him a copy of your book, don't you?" Hardin asked.

"Yes, I generally give everybody a copy of my book. I want them to learn."

[. . .] "Do you recall signing an inscription with a note to Agent Deaver in this book?"

"Yes."

[. . .] "If you would please read what the note says."

"It says, 'To Duane Deaver, one of the best,'" Lee read. "'Keep up with your good work. With warm regards, Henry Lee.'"

"Okay."

Lee objected that his courtesy was just the result of his Chinese culture and upbringing. "I cannot say he did not try to do good work."

A Cheshire grin crept across Hardin's face. "So you are agreeing then that he did good work?"

"I just . . . What, you want me to say he do lousy work on the book? I cannot say that. Just like I give Mr. Rudolf a book and say he's . . . 'You're one of the best attorneys,' but he's lousy."

When Dr. Lee stepped down from the stand, no one at the defense table would look their celebrity witness in the eye. They offered no celebratory handshakes. No pats on anyone's back.

47

The next witness called by the defense was Faris Bandak, a Ph.D. specialist in biomechanics, the study of forces and motion on living things. He prepared a flashy video to enhance his testimony.

The video was too stylish by far—the animated model wore black nail polish, and black lipstick on an otherwise blank face. It also had problems in its content. The lift chair so prominent in all the photographs of the stairwell at Cedar Street was not present in the film. Its presence at the scene gave the initial impression to investigators that Kathleen was disabled.

The computer-generated woman was shown leaning forward and holding the railing before she fell backwards—in direct contradiction to the laws of physics. It did not demonstrate any movement that would cause Kathleen to get blood on the soles of her feet. The pratfall seen in the animation would have caused bruising on the buttocks of a real woman. Kathleen had no such marks. And if the impact on the doorjamb was the first, as shown, the blood evidence found there would not have existed.

On cross-examination, Freda Black gave her most

effective performance up to this point of the trial. "What experience do you have in scalp lacerations?"

"None."

"Thyroid cartilage?"

"None."

"No research that you've done personally?"

"Do I have to build a 707 to know how to fly one?" Bandak was cocky now, but in a few minutes, Black would have him stammering like a schoolboy.

"So how many autopsies have you attended before?" she asked.

Bandak gave a rambling answer that included his experience in live surgeries with animals and children.

"Sir, I didn't ask you about surgeries and I didn't ask you about animals. How many autopsies have you attended where the ultimate opinion of the pathologist was that an adult person died because of a beating death? Any?"

"None."

"Not having that experience and not being a forensic pathologist yourself, you come to this courtroom and tell this jury that Dr. Deborah Radisch, who actually performed the autopsy, is just dead wrong about this?"

"Well . . ."

"That's what you told them, correct?" Black pushed.

Bandak stammered out his objections to being paraphrased and justified his interpretation of the biomechanical evidence. Black jerked him back to the question at hand: Did he disagree with Dr. Radisch's testimony that the lacerations were inconsistent with a fall?

Bandak stuttered his way through his responses as

Black lobbed one direct response after another at him. He tried to discredit Dr. Radisch's expertise, but left the impression that he didn't believe his own testimony.

He was still rambling on when Freda Black interrupted, "Do you remember my question?"

Then Rudolf interrupted her. "Objection. Argumentative."

"Assuming it is not argumentative," Judge Hudson said, "overruled."

"Sir, my question was, would you agree that a person that's actually there, whether it's a doctor or pathologist or even someone in your position actually there visualizing a person's body, looking at their wounds, feeling their wounds, measuring their wounds, looking at all the different things on their body—Would you not agree a person with that vantage point could really have an advantage in making a decision in a case like this?"

"[. . .] Not on the cause, not in the causation."

Freda asked Bandak to get up from the stand and use the Kathleen doll and acrylic model of the staircase. He held the doll awkwardly, like a man caught playing Barbie and trying to deny it. She asked, "Can you show us another scenario of what might have happened? Such that she received those injuries in the stairwell?"

Bandak bumbled through a clumsy response. Black then switched to photographs of the crime scene. Bandak held the photos before the jury box as Black fired a rapid series of questions. Bandak did not fare well under the constant volley.

Black's attack then led to one big question: "How many lacerations do you contend she had to the back of her head?"

After a long pause, Bandak answered, "If you count it, you count it per, per hit she has, uh, uh, four lacerations. If you count it as individual slices, she has more. Individual—if each individual fork is counted, she has more. It's just a bookkeeping issue."

"So the number of lacerations she has is a bookkeeping issue?" Outrage screeched like fingernails on a chalkboard on the edge of Black's voice.

"Objection. Argumentative," Rudolf shouted.

"I think she's just asking a question," Hudson responded. "Overruled."

"What do you mean by that?" Black asked again.

Bandak gave a disjointed response about the different ways you could count the injuries.

"So the number of lacerations wasn't important to you?" Black asked.

After another aimless response from Bandak, Black asked, "So, what was the answer to my question, sir?"

Rudolf called out an objection.

"Three—three lacerations," Bandak answered before Hudson overruled. "By my way of counting."

After establishing that Bandak had billed $40,000 to Michael Peterson so far, Black let him go.

48

On Thursday, September 18, for the first time in weeks, coverage of the Michael Peterson trial was not on the front page of the local newspapers. The gale force winds of Hurricane Isabel had blown it to the back pages. That day, court was cancelled in advance and then a lack of electricity in the courthouse suspended the action on Friday as well.

On Sunday, Defense Attorney David Rudolf called District Attorney Jim Hardin. He informed him that he might call lead investigator Art Holland as a witness for the defense. Hardin knew Rudolf had an unwelcome surprise in the works, but he had no idea that legal steps were taken behind his back.

Earlier that day, David Rudolf requested an *ex parte* order from Judge Orlando Hudson. That type of order meant that no one—not the judge or the defense—would inform the state of its existence.

Judge Hudson granted permission to the defense to remove evidence found in the house at 1810 Cedar Street after a professional photographer had recorded it where it was found and its condition at the time of discovery. The order also required that if the defense wished to enter this item into evidence, they must first inform the state of its existence.

Monday did not get off to a good start. One of the jurors overslept. Connecticut State Police Officer Palmbach was scheduled for a return visit to the witness stand. His previous appearance was cut short by his need to return home. Now, his flight was delayed.

Court was finally in session an hour and a half later than usual. Palmbach took the stand to face cross-examination by Jim Hardin. "With respect to those three hundred crime scenes you have worked, how many of those, in your opinion, have been perfectly maintained from the instant the crime had been committed?"

"And by perfectly, the assumption is exactly that— one hundred percent? None, none of them are done entirely correctly." Palmbach admitted that the majority of them are prosecuted nonetheless. Hardin asked him how many times he had processed a crime scene where the residence was 10,000 square feet, and Palmbach granted that that was a large area to maintain.

Palmbach persisted in his allegation that luminol was sprayed at the bottom of the stairs, even though more than one witness had sworn it had not been done. He corroborated that he and Dr. Lee did not do any independent testing of the crime scene or evidence.

"What I'm saying is that we don't *per se* go through the same level of experimentation and documentation, because that's not our function," Palmbach said. "That's the function of the primary investigator at the scene."

"But you rendered opinions of what they did or didn't

do. And those opinions, in some respects, are one hundred and eighty degrees divergent from Deborah Radisch's, who said this death was due to blunt force trauma and not consistent with an accident. And one hundred and eighty degrees from what Duane Deaver opined to this jury, which was that these bloodstain patterns were consistent with a beating and not an accidental fall. You're aware of that?" Hardin asked.

"Yes."

"And you hold opinions that are one hundred and eighty degrees apart from Deborah Radisch's and Duane Deaver's in particular, right?"

"Pretty much, yes."

"And they are the people that did all of the work?"

"Or didn't do all the work," Palmbach said. "But, yes, were charged to do it."

"In your opinion?"

"Correct."

"Okay. Your Honor, I have no further questions of the witness."

Next, the defense called Clyde Andrson, a young man who had worked inside and outside of the Peterson home since 1999. He said he had never seen a blowpoke in the house and that the pool furniture was always by the pool—both statements contradicting testimony by Candace Zamperini.

But he also said that in 2001, he and Todd bought and put up the Christmas tree right after Kathleen died. In fact, the crime-scene videotape shows the tree already standing on the 10th. Kathleen and Michael brought it home on the Friday before her death.

On Tuesday morning, the defense leaked to the media that they would witness a *Perry Mason* moment. Excited whispers and grins rippled through the spectator section behind the defense table.

Rudolf called Art Holland to the stand. Waving the blowpoke the state had introduced into evidence, Rudolf asked, "This is a pretty light item, isn't it?"

"It's fairly light, yes, sir," Holland answered.

"Hollow?"

"Hollow."

"It bends?"

"Flexible," Art Holland said, nodding his head.

"Have you given any thought to what would happen to an item like this if somebody hit someone over the head—three, four, five times—hard enough to cause the lacerations on the scalp?"

"Probably mangled up," Holland answered. As the blowpoke questions continued, he sensed what was about to happen. He had expected it much earlier in the trial. He and the prosecution team had discussed it many times. Unless he was mistaken, the defense was about to produce its own blowpoke.

And Rudolf did not disappoint. With a flourish, he pulled out a plastic tube containing a blowpoke and some dead bugs. It was dirty, discolored and covered with cobwebs. Rudolf had ignored Judge Hudson's instructions to inform the state of this evidence prior to its introduction in court.

"See that?" Rudolf asked Holland.

"Yes, sir."

[. . .] "That's a blowpoke, isn't it? Do you know where it has been for the last twenty months?"

"No, I don't."

"This doesn't appear to you to be mangled, does it?"

"It's not mangled."

"It's not even dented, is it? Not even a tiny indentation?"

"It doesn't appear to have any dents," Holland admitted.

After identification by Investigator Holland, Rudolf requested permission to enter it into evidence. Hudson paused, expecting to hear an objection from the prosecution. Hearing none, he said, "It is allowed."

It was great theater, even though it violated the judge's order. And it surely excited everyone in the media. But the jury was not impressed. Many of them had already eliminated the much-ballyhooed blowpoke as a possible weapon.

Professional photographer John Rosenthal followed Art Holland on the stand. He testified that he arrived at the Cedar Street home on Sunday, September 21, around 2:30 in the afternoon, and shot photographs of the blowpoke in the two-car garage.

Freda Black attacked the defense's inference that the blowpoke had just been discovered after resting in that same place since before December 9, 2001. "Do you have any earthly idea of how long it takes for dust to accumulate on an object in a garage?"

"No," said Rosenthal.

"Do you have any earthly idea how long it takes cobwebs to form?"

"No."

"You don't have any earthly idea on how long it takes a bug to die in someone's garage?"

"No."

With that witness, the defense rested. No testimony was presented about the where, when or who of the discovery of the missing blowpoke. The defense omitted a lot of other witnesses, too.

In his opening, Rudolf promised the jury that he would call witnesses who would tell them about the Camelot-like relationship between Kathleen and Michael. He said he would call a doctor to testify about Kathleen's headaches and ocular migraine. He promised that Marines would testify about Michael's valor and leadership during battle. But not one of them made it to the witness stand.

49

The state began its rebuttal case by bringing investigator Art Holland back to the stand. He explained the search conducted in the cluttered, dusty basement and garage. He insisted that he looked for any type of object or weapon that could cause injury to a person. "That poker was not in the basement."

To combat the defense charge that the prosecution hid their suspicions about the blowpoke from them until jury selection, the state called Ruth Brown, an evidence custodian for the Durham Police Department, to the stand. She said that she brought out the state's exhibits for the defense to examine in October of 2002. The blowpoke was brought into the room in a box and it stuck out of the end of its container.

After the box was set on the table, she said, the blowpoke was removed from it and lay in clear view. In the six hours that the defense spent in that room, they never requested a close-up viewing of the fireplace tool.

Lori Campell took her seat before the court on September 24. She said that the last time she saw her sister was in July of 2001—five months before her death. On that visit, she saw the blowpoke by the fireplace.

On cross-examination, Rudolf questioned Lori's honesty, making it clear he did not believe that she had visited the Peterson home that July. Then he attacked her mother Veronica, implying that there was something wrong with her going to visit family just two months after the death of her companion Carl.

Rudolf whipped out one picture after another showing shots of the fireplace without the blowpoke. One photo included Clancey, the bulldog who died in 2000. That prompted Lori to point out that the circumstances of Clancey's death were suspicious.

When Rudolf finished his questioning, he walked away with not only his photographs but also with one of Kathleen that Lori had brought to the witness box. With a quivering chin, she demanded, "May I please have the picture of my sister back?"

Once again, Rudolf had pushed a family member of a victim a bit too far.

The next witness in the state's rebuttal case was a man with impeccable credentials, Dr. James McElhaney, professor emeritus at Duke University and an expert in injury biomechanics. Over the last thirty years, he had testified in over one hundred civil cases, but this was his first criminal trial.

He acknowledged that he knew Faris Bandak professionally and had reviewed his testimony. Then, Freda Black asked him, "As an expert in this field, do you agree or disagree with the opinion that he formed in this case?"

"I basically disagree with his bottom line opinion in this case."

"And why is that?"

"Because what information I reviewed in this case has led me to the other side of his opinion and that is that the injuries, lacerations, bruises and contusions, to my mind, are inconsistent with a fall down the steps, but are consistent with a beating with a blunt instrument. Most likely a round instrument. Whereas his opinion is, they are consistent with a fall down the steps."

"Now, as an expert in this field, tell us, please, on what you have based your opinion."

"I base these opinions, first of all on my experience in doing experiments that create lacerations to the head and also my experience in the study of injuries over many years," Dr. McElhaney said. He pointed to the thirty-three places noted in the autopsy where there were bruises, abrasions or lacerations. "Reviewing those, I conclude at least fifteen impact sites."

He explained that a straight, flat impact, does not create lacerations four to five inches long. Because of the curvature of the skull, the object that struck Kathleen's head had to move across its surface. A stair cannot move.

He stood before the jury with enlargements he made from autopsy photos and said, "I'm sorry I have to show you this, but I don't think you can really understand these lacerations without seeing the pictures here.

"We get a laceration when we hit it hard. And fast. Fast is an important aspect to this. [. . .] So if what strikes us isn't going fast enough, we don't get this splitting type of laceration." He explained to the jurors how the distance of the fall played an important role in the severity of the fall. Kathleen's first fall did have enough height to create the first laceration. "However, then she's already used up three feet of the five feet she can fall. There's barely—there's probably not—enough energy left to create the speed to create a second laceration on that fall."

On cross, Rudolf wanted to know how much money McElhaney was making for this consultation and testimony.

"Nothing. It just seemed the right thing to do," the doctor answered.

Ms. Black appreciated Dr. McElhaney's response to Rudolf about the money he was earning for his work on this case so much that she asked him again on re-direct and he responded, "Yes, I am doing this for free. I've put in about forty hours. I was willing to do it without compensation because it seemed the right thing to do."

During re-cross, Rudolf attempted to use Dr. McElhaney to discredit Dr. Saami Shaibani, the state's next witness on the stand, but made very little headway.

Shaibani had an undergraduate degree from Oxford in Material Physics, had taught at three Virginia schools—Lynchburg College, Liberty University and Virginia Tech—and was certified by the Department of Labor and the Department of Justice as an expert. He also claimed to have a research affiliation with Temple University as a clinical professor. He had testified as an expert in North Carolina in the field of injury mechanism analysis on nine previous occasions. The district attorney tendered him as an expert witness.

David Rudolf objected to Shaibani's certification as an expert because, he said, he questioned the veracity of his credentials. But Rudolf did not want to examine him outside the presence of the jury because it would only prepare him to give better answers in front of the jury.

"If Mr. Rudolf has information along the lines of what he has described," Hardin said, "that's obviously very serious. It would be something that needs to be dealt with before the jury hears additional testimony from the witness."

[. . .] "I have no intention of going forward with *voir dire* if it's outside the presence of the jury," Rudolf insisted.

After a brief back-and-forth between the attorneys, Rudolf said, "I withdraw my request! Mr. Hardin can put on his witness. I'm sure Mr. Hardin can find out from his witness what the truth is. It's his witness, not mine."

Bickering finished, Judge Hudson certified Dr. Shaibani as an expert. The physicist took care to explain to the jury the principles underlying his science. He explained the importance of one of Newton's laws of motion: "For every action there is an equal and opposite reaction." He also defined the two underlying principles in the science of injury, relative motion and energy management.

He explained his experiment protocol involving five subjects similar in size to Kathleen Peterson. They were tested in rigid falls and loose, floppy falls to chart the complete range of possible motion.

His conclusion was straight to the point: the sequence in the video is not possible by the laws of physics in a fall. There is not enough space; there is not enough time.

The human body—the pelvis, the knees—do not move as shown in the animation.

He showed the jury a still shot from the animation. "This picture really, really reinforces that something impossible is happening to the pelvis for those legs to end up going backwards there—back up onto that step. You cannot manipulate and bend and twist the human body in the real world. On a computer, you can do anything. But in the real world, you can't."

Showing another freeze-frame, he said, "I don't see any way that body could be in that position, at any time, without help. Somebody had to put it there. The law of physics doesn't let it get there naturally. [. . .] You'd have to dislocate your shoulder to have your head on step seventeen and have your elbow on step sixteen. It doesn't add up," he said, pointing to the lower steps where Kathleen's body was found.

David Rudolf began his cross-examination of Saami Shaibani with questions about his current position and past positions. Disdain dripped from the edges of every word the defense attorney spoke. Then, he moved in for the kill. He queried Shaibani about his position at Temple University while Michael Peterson tried, in vain, to suppress a grin.

He presented Dr. Shaibani with a letter submitted to a court at a trial in October 2001 from the chair of the Physics Department saying that Shaibani was not affiliated with Temple and should not state that he is. "I have to write this letter once a year because he is claiming that he has an affiliation with Temple which he does not have," he wrote.

"Today is the first time I've seen it," Dr. Shaibani

said. "The public defender mentioned a letter, but did not produce it."

"Well, after it was mentioned in open court by an officer of the court telling a judge that there was such a letter, did you think to yourself, 'Gee, maybe I'd better call Temple and get this cleared up'?" Rudolf asked.

"I don't believe everything an attorney says, sir."

[. . .] "When you testified in a murder trial in Washington, D.C., when someone's life was at stake, you lied about your affiliation with Temple, didn't you?" Rudolf pushed.

"No, sir."

Hardin objected, Hudson overruled and the attack continued. "Would you be surprised to know that as recently as yesterday, the associate university counsel, Virginia Flick, at Temple University, reaffirmed that you have no connection, no affiliation, no relationship whatsoever, formal or informal, except perhaps in your mind, with Temple University? Do you understand that? Are you aware of that?"

"I am not aware of that, no."

Rudolf asked the judge to tell the district attorney to inform state officials about the need for an investigation into perjury charges against Shaibani.

Hardin said if the judge wished to take up the defense motion to find that Dr. Shaibani had perjured himself, the state would not object. He would decide after trial about whether or not it would be taken forward. Hardin did not want to abandon his witness, but he knew if he did anything else, he could damage his case—and possibly allow a killer to go free.

"If the district attorney won't contact the attorney

general, then I want the court to do so," Rudolf demanded.

"Mr. Hardin knows his responsibility under the law," Judge Hudson said. "He is not ignoring your argument. He knows how to proceed. It is not for this court to tell Mr. Hardin how to do his job."

Then Hudson struck the testimony of Dr. Saami Shaibani, telling the jury that the witness had perjured himself in relating his credentials to the court. With that, the court day ended. Many jurors were frustrated, and uncomfortable as well. The public flaying of the witness by Rudolf was a distasteful sight to see. They found the testimony of Dr. Shaibani to be full of common sense and practical information that they could readily understand. They had wanted to consider it in their deliberations. Now they could not.

Investigator Art Holland bore the onerous chore of taking Dr. Shaibani to the airport. Holland was not convinced that Shaibani had perjured himself. None of it made sense. What he did see with clarity was a man destroyed, a career ruined. He wondered if this destruction was justified or if Dr. Shaibani was just another victim of Michael Peterson.

On Monday, September 29, Dr. John Butts, the chief medical examiner for the state of North Carolina, took his place in the witness box. He told the jury that he agreed with Dr. Radisch's opinion—there were blunt trauma injuries and seven lacerations.

He contradicted the testimony of Dr. Leestma. At the conclusion of his direct testimony, he stated that

Kathleen's death was not caused by an accident, but was the result of a beating.

A subtle transformation rolled across Dr. Butts' face as the cross-examination began. During direct testimony, his visage was serious, but warm and open. As he turned to David Rudolf, his eyebrows elevated a centimeter or two and a sourness washed over his face, giving him a look of weary cynicism.

Rudolf was respectful of this witness, but was not above attempts to manipulate him. He tried—and failed—to use him to compromise the capability and credibility of Dr. Radisch.

When Dr. Butts stepped down from the stand, the prosecution announced it rested its rebuttal case. The defense was ready for their surrebuttal. They called Investigator Art Holland onto the stand again.

The questions flung at him attacked Candace's honesty about cleaning the stairwell, belittled the amount of time the police spent in the basement, and mocked Agent Deaver's experiments once again.

Reporters in the courtroom quivered when Rudolf's questioning turned to the state's decision not to test the blowpoke for Kathleen's DNA. But that was not what made them want to burst out of the courtroom to flash an update. The revelation that the Durham police had done DNA testing of Margaret Ratliff to determine if Michael Peterson was her biological father created the frenzy. Since before the trial, a rumor that Mike was Margaret's father had rampaged through the city and on the Internet. Now, the negative results of the DNA test put that ugly lie to rest.

The questioning of Art Holland continued with both

sides focusing on the blowpoke mystery. Finally, the defense rested.

In the middle of Dr. McElhaney's testimony, one of the jurors, Dorthea Waters, had contacted the judge. Dorthea, the wife of fabled Duke University basketball coach Bucky Waters, informed the court that she was once a neighbor of Dr. McElhaney thirty years ago when they all lived in West Virginia.

The morning after the defense ended its presentation, the judge dismissed Ms. Waters. He expressed his regret and emphasized the lack of misconduct by the woman who had given thirteen weeks of her life to this trial. She was replaced by the first alternate, a 70-year-old man who was retired both from the Navy and from his job as a Durham but driver.

The next morning, another juror's head was on the chopping block. Wilford Hamm had spent the previous night in the Durham County Jail. He had gone to a mechanic to check on the status of repairs to his pick-up truck in an intoxicated state, with his red juror badge pinned to his chest. He was not pleased with what he was allegedly told and threatened to get a shotgun and shoot someone.

When the police arrived on the scene, Hamm had already departed, but they spotted him across the street brandishing a 24-ounce can of beer. Hamm, with a great deal of foul language, berated the officers and warned them that he was a juror in the Michael Peterson trial and, because of that, they could not mess with him.

The trial had taken its toll. After twelve years of

sobriety, Wilford Hamm had fallen off the wagon in a very public way. The officers took him to detention because of concerns that he would harm himself or others. However, no charges were filed and Hamm was released at 9:45 in the morning. A hearing was scheduled to consider his fate as a juror on the following Monday morning after closing arguments and before the instructions were given to the jury.

When that hearing did occur, Wilford Hamm was also dismissed. On the way out of the courtroom, he patted David Rudolf on the shoulder.

50

Throughout most of the trial, seats were available to anyone who wandered through the doors. On October 2, 2003, the difference was dramatic.

Michael Peterson's family and supporters jammed cheek to cheek in three rows behind the defense table. The family of Kathleen Peterson was out in full force on the other side of the room. Journalists with their notebooks and laptops bumped elbows as they took notes. Not another spectator could fit in the seats at the back of the courtroom. Michael Peterson wore a special token of good luck. He told his attorneys it was his "phoenix rising" tie.

As they all squirmed in their seats, David Rudolf, with a studied air of indifference, surveyed his audience as if he knew he was as ready as he ever would be. As if he knew he could not fail. Was it possible he was that sure of his case, or was he burying insecurity behind an air of nonchalance?

Rudolf began his closing argument by playing an audiotape of a portion of Jim Hardin's opening statement—the portion where he revealed the blowpoke to the jury. Rudolf told them that the weapon advocated by the state wasn't missing, it was just discarded. Still, he did not reveal any of the mystery behind the discovery.

Rudolf went on to dispute Dr. Radisch's testimony and to build up the opinions of the defense's biomechanical expert, Dr. Bandak. As he talked, he replayed the slick video of the fall.

He then moved to a discussion of the principles of burden of proof and reasonable doubt. He pointed out the imperfections in the justice system and the recent uncovering of numerous wrongful convictions across the state.

"What I want to do this morning and this afternoon [. . .] is to focus on the reasonable doubts in this case. Since we are in the age of David Letterman and lists of ten, I've come up with a list of ten."

First on Rudolf's list was: "The missing murder weapon isn't missing and it wasn't used in a murder." Second: "There is no credible motive—and you don't just decide to kill your wife for no reason." Rudolf argued, "Your common sense tells you you don't decide to kill your wife in a first-degree murder for no reason."

He accused the state of working backwards—charging Michael Peterson with the murder and then seeking a motive. "I am reminded of *Alice in Wonderland*," Rudolf said, waving the book at the jury. "There's a great little line when the Queen of Hearts is having a trial over the stolen tarts and she says, all of a sudden, 'Sentence first— verdict afterwards.' And that's sort of what happened here: Indictment first—look for the evidence afterwards. That is not how it is supposed to work."

Rudolf attacked the motives presented by the

prosecution. "Having failed to present a financial motive," he said, "the state moved on to the other standby, sex. I submit to you that the testimony about gay pornography and bisexuality was masquerading as a motive, but it was really an appeal to bias. What it really was, was an attempt to get to your emotions to say, 'Oh, Man. God, the guy is bisexual. The guy has got pornography on his computer. Yuck.' That's what was really going on."

Rudolf continued down his top ten list. "Reasonable doubt number three: Michael and Kathleen Peterson were happily married with no history of violence—and spousal abuse generally doesn't start with murder." Reasonable doubt number four: "Michael Peterson's grief and shock was sincere—and no one who was there disagreed."

Number five: "Kathleen Peterson's injuries are not consistent with a beating—no skull fractures, plus no other fractures, plus no traumatic brain injury equals no beating."

Rudolf waved the blowpoke in the air to punctuate point number six: "You don't beat somebody and let them crawl around and die of loss of blood after thirty or forty minutes. That's not what happened."

Number seven: The information and documentation from the scene is not reliable. "Sometimes it's referred to as 'Garbage in—garbage out.' Some of you may have run into that in your various fields of endeavor, but what it basically means is, the end product is only as good as what goes into making it. That's just good common sense."

Number eight: The state relied on junk science. "You

know enough about blood spatter now," he said. "You can tell whether he's lying or not. You don't need me. Just look at the picture." Rudolf then launched his attack on the work of Dr. Deborah Radisch. "Even reputable scientists can engage in junk science."

Number nine: "The state has relied on emotion, guesswork and conjecture." He defended the autopsy performed by the osteopath, Larry Barnes, who ". . . came to the opinion that she died of a stroke. What's his dog in this fight? Why would he care? Investigators on the scene in 1985 saw no evidence of anything suspicious. [. . .] What evidence is there that Michael Peterson had anything to do with that? None. Zippo."

Rudolf ridiculed the prosecution's reference to coincidences. "Found at the bottom of the stairway. So, what, is he the stairway killer? The serial stairway killer? He continued down the state's list making disparaging comments about each one.

"Most of you are old enough to remember the Kennedy assassination. And some of you may even remember all those weird lists of coincidences. Lincoln–Kennedy. Lincoln elected 1846. Kennedy elected to Congress in 1946."

"Objection to this, Your Honor," Hardin interrupted. "I don't believe any of this was introduced in the trial."

After an exchange of heated words between the attorneys, the judge sent out the jury. Judge Hudson viewed Rudolf's presentation and decided that he could display it to the jury but could not read off the whole list. Finally, Rudolf moved on to reasonable doubt number ten: "The state's investigation suffered from tunnel vision—indictment first—evidence afterwards. From

December ninth on, the police weren't looking for all the evidence and evaluating all the evidence. They were looking for evidence that confirmed their theory. And if evidence didn't confirm their theory, they really weren't paying any attention."

By now, it was 3 o'clock, the normal end of the court day, and Rudolf wrapped up his argument. "I want to give you an apology for a couple of things." He first mentioned that he did not deliver all the evidence he promised in his opening statement. "You can hold that against me," he said. "All I ask is that you not hold it against Michael Peterson."

He then admitted being too aggressive, too competitive and too long-winded. "I apologize if I have offended any of you. Again, hold it against me, but please, please, please, do not, in any way, hold it against Michael Peterson."

He asked them not to get sucked into the images created by the prosecution. "Has the state excluded, to a moral certainty, every reasonable hypothesis except that Michael Peterson beyond a reasonable doubt beat Kathleen Peterson to death with a blowpoke in that stairway? Because if they have not—if there is a reasonable hypothesis of innocence—then there is a reasonable doubt. And you must, under your oath, vote not guilty."

He emphasized the importance of their decision. He acknowledged the impact of the trial on their lives, then told the jurors the effect on them would be fleeting. "But what you do will stay with Michael Peterson, Margaret and Martha, Todd and Clayton, Jack, his brother, and Bill, and everyone else associated with Michael, for the rest of their lives. There will be no going back if you have reasonable doubt."

Once again, Rudolf played the 9-1-1 tape. Once again, Michael Peterson cried. The only times he cried during the trial were when this tape was played or when words written by or about him were read aloud.

"We ask you, after considering all the evidence in this case, to return a verdict that will speak the truth—a verdict of not guilty of first-degree murder."

With those words, court adjourned for the day.

51

As it was yesterday, every seat in the small courtroom was filled and the air was electric with anticipation. Many had longed for this day, but none more than the members of Kathleen's family, who sat on the prosecution's side of the room. Small smiles of hope crossed their lips. Small furrows of worry cratered their foreheads. This was the day they believed that the state would connect all the pieces of the puzzle and bring them the justice they so devoutly desired.

The judge took his place. The jurors filed in. Freda Black was center stage. Some had called her "the Dragon Lady." Many said her intensity was over the top. But to the families of victims in any trial, those attributes are a strong and lasting comfort.

She was the epitome of Southern motherhood—full of warmth, comfort and homilies for those in need, but with a tongue as sharp as a knife for those who deserved it. The pitiless lash of that tongue was about to fall with relentless determination on everyone connected with the case presented by the defense.

She paused to make sure the eyes of every juror were on her. She was angry and full of righteous indignation.

She knew loosing reins on these emotions would open her to criticism, but she did not care. She stomped on her caution and commenced a passionate soliloquy.

"Soulmates say these types of words to each other: 'I, Michael, do take thee, Kathleen, to be my lawfully wedded wife. To live together in marriage. I promise to love you, comfort you, *honor* you, keep you, for better or worse, for richer or poorer, in sickness and in health, *and forsaking all others* be faithful *only* to you, so long as we both shall live.'

"Soulmates make these types of promises to each other. Some of you may have made that type of promise to another person at one time in the past. Michael says that Kathleen is his soulmate. His lawyer told you that, yesterday. Did he honor her? Did he keep her? Did he forsake all others? And was he faithful only unto her? You all know the answers to those questions. The answer to every one of those questions is 'No.' " Her eyes flashed with a challenge no one could deny.

Black walked the jurors through the arrival of the first responders at 1810 Cedar Street and their realization that there was too much blood for a fall. She talked about their difficulties at the scene. They were unable to get any information from Michael Peterson. "Then there's Todd," she said with a disgusted curl on her lips. "He's the one with the attitude. He's belligerent. He won't follow simple instructions to be quiet. He won't stay in one place. [. . .] They've got Ben—well, Ben's drunk. Ben is just plain drunk. Ben Maynor," she repeated with a disdainful and dismissive tone usually reserved for the discovery of sugar ants in the kitchen. "They've got to contend with that drunk person. Then they—they've even got growling dogs to contend with. They've got a ten-thousand-square-foot house, and a lady—poor lady lying there, deceased, and it appears to them that she's been dead for some period of time, but then, they're confused about this call they've received. So that's what they start out with."

She then dismissed the defense allegation that the crime scene was contaminated. "Now to hear them tell it, there was luminol that was done in one portion of that stairwell. Well, if you believe that, then you're just gonna have to believe that Duane Deaver is just a *liar*." Ms. Black jutted her chin forward and raked the jury box with her gaze. "And he has no reason in the world to come up here and lie to you. So there's been no credible evidence that anything was done to alter that stairwell."

She told the jurors that what was important was what was done prior to the arrival of the authorities. "Nothing was really done to refute the testimony of Dr. Bouldin. I argue to you he's one of the most important witnesses that you heard from in this case. Dr. Bouldin told you that in his area of expertise—and he *is* a qualified expert with impeccable credentials—that the average time for those red neurons to be found would be two hours. That he's never seen anything in less than two hours. What that means to you is: Kathleen was unconscious for at *least* two hours. That gives Mr. Peterson at *least* two hours to do things, *before* the 9-1-1 call is placed."

In the audience, the ashen face of Caitlin Atwater followed every word of Freda Black's presentation. Her eyebrows tensed inward. Dark smudges beneath her eyes testified to sleepless nights. Her mouth was pulled so tight her pale lips seemed to disappear.

On the other side of the courtroom, a small smirk fought to gain possession of David Rudolf's face as he stared past Jim Hardin at the faces of the jury beyond him.

Black contended that in addition to Peterson's odd behavior of removing his shoes, he also tried to clean up, positioned Kathleen's body and attempted to wash his hands. "And somewhere he put a weapon. Was it the blowpoke? We can't be absolutely certain, and we're not required to be absolutely certain, but that weapon went somewhere.

"But now, why did he do all these things? And you need to keep in mind, we're not dealing with the average individual over here," she said, swinging her arm back toward the defendant. "We're dealing with a *fictional* writer. Some people even say he's a *good* fictional writer. He is a person who knows how to create a *fictional* plot. And in this case, he has tried to create one. He tried to sell it to the EMS workers. [. . .] He tried to sell it to his family." Black paused and looked hard at the jurors. "And in this courtroom, he's tried to sell it to you—a fictional plot."

Black turned her comments to Liz Ratliff and Rudolf's ridicule of the commonalities between the two cases. Then she moved on to other defense contentions. "Is he really a grieving spouse? [. . .] Why didn't he try to give her CPR? You ever ask yourselves that?" Black then turned to Peterson's email use in the hours after Kathleen's death. "Would you really be checking your emails if your spouse was lying out in the hallway with blood everywhere?"

Black questioned why Peterson did not help with the

funeral arrangements and why he boarded up the stairwell. "You don't find it strange that he has had his deceased wife's blood in his stairwell, right there? You all saw it. For eighteen months! Isn't that strange?"

The prosecutor then took aim at the star witness for the defense, Dr. Henry Lee, criticizing his attack of Deborah Radisch, his lack of a final report and the way he laughed and made jokes on the witness stand. "And Mr. Rudolf said that state experts had engaged in junk science. Well, what do you call spitting ketchup across the courtroom? Throwing red ink? What do you call that?" Bending from the waist, she leaned toward the jury, her chin jutting at them in defiance. "Does that seem scientific to you? I call that junk science. Spitting ketchup over toward the state's table."

Black pointed to Dr. McElhaney's testimony, which refuted the defense theory of a fall. "Now, who else did the defense bring to you? Major Palmbach." She said his name with as much revulsion as any Southern belle reserved for a carpetbagger. "Well, according to Major Palmbach, we need to brace ourselves in Durham, 'cause we've got problems."

Black summarized the state's financial testimony and then moved on to the most sensational of all witnesses, "Brad"—Brent Wolgamott. "Do you really believe that Kathleen knew that Mr. Peterson was bisexual? Does that make common sense to you? That it was okay with her to go to work while he stayed at home and communicated by email and telephone with people he was planning on having *sex with*? Does that make sense? 'Go on off to work, honey, I'm gonna be talking on the computer with some of my boyfriends.'"

She picked up the pack of pictures of Brad and waved them in the air. "He's got his picture—he's downloaded his picture, front-side up and backside up—naked."

Across the room, Mike Peterson's eyes twinkled and his lips pursed as he struggled to hold back that smile that wanted to dance across his lips.

"I asked Brad what they were gonna do. He told you. And I don't mean to offend anybody but he *did* say they were gonna have anal sex. Do you really believe that was okay with Kathleen? [. . .] The only reason that meeting didn't take place was because of Brad. It wasn't because of Mr. Peterson. He was fired up and ready to go. Even got the price right. [. . . T]hat's not the way that soulmates conduct themselves."

Freda Black brought her fiery argument to a close. Her high energy was still outwardly displayed, but around her eyes, weariness from the long fight had left its mark. "We do thank you. All of our lives have been disrupted. But it's worth it, to find the truth and to seek justice. Not just for Michael Peterson, to seek justice for Kathleen. She's the one that died a horrible, brutal death. Nobody deserves that. Not even a *dog* deserves to die like the way she had to die. Can you imagine the pain and suffering she endured? You can just look at the pictures of the back of her head and just try to fathom that thought."

She stared straight into the eyes of the jurors. She extended an index finger as she spoke, elongating the sentence for her last declaration. "Michael Peterson is guilty of first-degree murder."

Behind the prosecution desk, Candace Zamperini wiped away tears.

52

As District Attorney Jim Hardin approached the podium, a large blow-up photo of Kathleen was by his side. Dressed in his dark blue suit, white shirt and gray-and-white-checked tie, his pale face radiated determination. The length of the fringe brushing his collar made it clear that a haircut was not on the top of his priority list during this trial.

He spoke in a soft, slow, low-key voice. His North Carolina accent caressed each word he spoke. "There is only one question you have to ask yourself and then answer: Was this a beating or was this a fall? Was it a murder or was it an accident?

"We have said all along that Kathleen Peterson was murdered. And they claim it was a fall. We've claimed that she was brutally beaten by this man right here," he said as he pointed his finger at the defendant. "They claim that this was just some bizarre coincidence. But all you have to do is look at these pictures and you can make your mind up quickly."

He talked about the evidence that the defense did not present to support their contentions in this case. "The bottom line, ladies and gentlemen, is, it didn't fit into their nice little package. It didn't fit into the plan. Kathleen Peterson took too long to die for this to work.

"And how do we know that? Dr. Bouldin is a good example. He combines the best evidence. He says that the red neurons in Kathleen's brain could not develop unless she were unconscious and there's a significant deprivation of blood to her brain, and it had to take at least two hours. So, ladies and gentlemen, she had to lay unconscious for two hours."

Hardin dangled Michael Peterson's bloody shorts from his hand. "Do you think the defendant really was out at the pool? I mean, he's got a pair of shorts on and a tee shirt. Is he contending to you that he was out there for the couple of hours it would have taken Kathleen Peterson to die? It was fifty-one degrees. It was damp. Who in the world is going to stay outside at a pool smoking a pipe for a couple of hours in the middle of the morning in December and it's fifty-one degrees and it's cold and wet?"

Putting up a chart of Dr. Deborah Radisch's findings, Hardin ticked off the thirty-eight lacerations, bruises and contusions she found when she performed the autopsy on Kathleen's body. "How in the world can someone get thirty-eight injuries over their face, back, head, hands, arms and wrists from falling down some steps—even if there are two falls? There is absolutely no way that makes common sense."

Hardin defended the state's allegation that a deadly weapon was used—that whether or not it was a blowpoke was irrelevant. What is important, he asserted, was the totality of the evidence. "And in this case, what's one of the most important things they saw? The seven lacerations on the back of the head."

Like Black, he reminded the jurors about Lee's contention that there was too much blood for a beating. "He talks about the fact that the scene is very dynamic." The volume of Hardin's voice rose and passion tinged his tone. "You better believe there is a lot of motion and a lot of action in there. She was fighting for her life."

"[. . .] We contend to you that she was struck, that she went down, that she was probably down for some time. She began to bleed. And then she got up.

"And he realized it as he was going through the process of cleaning up everything and he had to continue the assault. Why do we say that?" Hardin gestured over his shoulder to the defense table. "They don't even dispute that Kathleen got up. There is no dispute about that at all from either side. The question is how she received her injuries."

The D.A. turned then to a description of the cleanup on the stairs. "Why in the world would a grieving spouse want to clean if he's just found his wife dead—dead in the stairs from a fall? Why in the world would you do that? You wouldn't. But if you wanted to hide something or cover it up, you would.

"There's a whole lot of blood here, ladies and gentlemen, and he realized there was too much blood. And he decided that he had to make it look like he had helped her by putting the towels up under her head."

Jim Hardin then explained the concept of reasonable doubt and why it did not exist in this case. He followed that with a justification for the charge of first-degree murder. "What we contend to you, ladies and gentlemen, is that he assaulted her. She went down. He continued to assault her and that's when the premeditation formulated."

Hardin speculated about the stresses that could have started the confrontation, including finances, work and, of course, Brad. "We will never know exactly what caused this conflict to occur. But we contend that whatever it was caused that initial assault, during the assault, he develops the intent to complete the act and to kill Kathleen Peterson."

He held a photograph before the jury. "This photograph is the first photograph taken of Kathleen at the autopsy table. This photograph at least speaks a thousand words."

He held up a picture of the stairwell. "Ladies and gentlemen, these walls *are* talking to us. Kathleen is talking to us through the blood on these walls. She is screaming at us for truth and for justice."

Hardin's voice turned soft and intimate, it sounded like a prayer. "They've said Kathleen Peterson died of an accident. We've said that she has died of murder and we ask that you return that verdict. Thank you."

When Hardin finished, the courtroom was as quiet as a chapel in the aftermath of witnessing a miracle.

THE VERDICT

"What you see in very bright individuals and people with similar backgrounds, you can compare to sociopaths, in that they use people, in that their life is a living book and that's why they come up with these great plots and sub-plots and happen to live them, too. Too many coincidences here for my psychological comfort."

—Jeffrey Gardere, psychologist

53

Jury alternate number three, Richard Sarratt, was eager for the dismissal that would allow him to restart a normal life. He had a list of chores to do that day—a trip to Lowe's and to Home Depot. He was scheduled for a ten-hour shift as an operating nurse at the Durham Veterans Affairs Medical Center the next day. He hoped to take off on vacation for a week after that. He was prepared to bolt the courtroom as soon as the instructions were done.

The judge read the 19-page document to the jury point by point. The moment of freedom was a breath away for Sarratt as the judge said, "At this time . . ."

Then David Rudolf was on his feet, "May we approach?"

At dispute was one more juror. The defense had received a call from a co-worker of juror Joanne Hairston. She worked at a bank where Michael Peterson was a customer. Before the start of the trial, she had allegedly been overheard making negative comments about the defendant and mocking him.

"I have heard information," the judge told Ms. Hairston, "that could affect your ability to sit as a juror."

A deputy escorted her from the courtroom. An astonished Richard Sarratt took her place. The one remaining alternate, Mary Bruckchen, a Kroger stocker, was dismissed. She told *The News & Observer*, "I think they will find him not guilty because of the reasonable doubt."

On the first afternoon of their deliberations, the jury took a preliminary vote. Four of the members were undecided, five voted guilty, four not guilty. They were, however, in agreement on one point: Kathleen Peterson did not die from an accidental fall down the stairs.

This group of men and women had bonded over the months they spent together. They complained each time they were sent out of the court and wondered just what information was being kept from them. They exchanged observations about the attorneys.

They pondered the poker face of Jim Hardin and decided what he lacked in charisma, he compensated for with integrity, humility, a calm demeanor and a methodical thoroughness. They also noted that toward the end of the trial, looking good was not his top priority—he had needed a haircut for weeks.

They talked about the demeanor and the wardrobe of Freda Black. She was an open woman whose emotions flared from her eyes. In no time, they learned to identify the exact moment that David Rudolf had pushed one of her buttons.

They wondered about the absence of a wedding band from David Rudolf's hand the last few days of the trial. Although they felt he was sincere, they also thought that he was a showboater with a penchant for last-minute theatrics. Maher did not give them much to talk about. Like Hardin, he appeared calm, methodical and thorough.

They talked about reading, hunting, fishing, jobs and children. They joked that if they were here for Halloween, they would all have to come in costume. And that maybe they would still be here to draw names and play secret Santa. In the preceding weeks they talked about everything except for the one question that brought them together: Was Michael Peterson guilty as charged? Now it was their focus.

On Tuesday, one juror fluctuated and now five were undecided. "Why are you undecided?" the others asked. "What can we do to help?"

They worked to chop away at the evidence to get to the core, where they knew they would find the answer. They set aside the Liz Ratliff matter—any attempt to ascertain Michael Peterson's guilt in her death would be a distraction.

They discarded the blowpoke. After viewing the stairway, they were not convinced it was the weapon anyway. They certainly did not think that the blowpoke Rudolf presented days before was *the* blowpoke. Too many questions remained. Who found it? Where did they find it? Was it really found just two days before it was brought to the courtroom?

They set aside Faris Bandak's video because of contradictions between the actions of the figure and the blood spatter evidence, and because it showed Kathleen down on the stairs, but did not demonstrate how she got there.

Although they respected Dr. Lee, his statement that there was too much blood for a beating did not make sense. Since he had not done any testing, they had nothing concrete to compare to Agent Deaver's work and because of that, they relied on Deaver's work alone.

Dr. Deborah Radisch's testimony about the autopsy rang as true as bird song at dawn. For many, she was the turning point of the trial.

Their biggest obstacle to reaching an agreement on the verdict was premeditation. Again and again, they referred each other to the vital sections of their instructions:

> [T]he defendant acted after premeditation, that is, that he formed the intent to kill the victim over some period of time, however short, before he acts.

> Neither premeditation or deliberation is usually susceptible to direct proof. They may be proved by proof of circumstances from which they may be inferred . . .

Wednesday was the tensest day in their decision process. They might have compromised on a second-degree verdict at that time if they could—but it was not an option. The deliberation room was filled with argument and tears. Still, it felt more like a family around the Thanksgiving table engaged in a charged debate than it did strangers forced together to make a weighty decision.

Durham County Jury Clerk Susan Cowen added a bright spot to that day. She left her office, where a gift from this jury—a certificate naming her "The World's Greatest Jury Clerk"—hung on the wall with pride. She went to the deliberation room and gave each member a pen emblazoned with "2003 Juror of the Year" and "5 Month Survivor" in memory of the longest criminal trial in Durham history.

At the end of that day, no one was undecided. The vote was divided right down the middle—six for guilty, six not guilty.

They returned to their homes that afternoon to discover a letter in their mailboxes. The envelope had a hand-written return address that did not contain the call letters of a television station. If it had, many would not have opened it.

The letter inside read: "It has been a long summer in the courtroom—and I know you have gotten to know your fellow jurors very well throughout the Peterson trial. I would like to offer an opportunity for all of you to come together again after you have decided your verdict."

The letter tried to weave a bond through their mutual experience with the trial, then continued with an invitation to a dinner on October 18. It was signed by Sonya Pfeiffer of WTVD–TV.

The jurors had some anger at the presumption that they would reach a verdict by that date. Their reaction, however, was nothing compared to the fireworks in the courtroom, where finger-pointing reigned.

When the dust settled, Judge Hudson sent a letter to each juror:

> *It has come to the attention of the Court that a reporter with a local television station has sent letters to jurors expressing an interest in meeting jurors after the trial is over. The reporter informed the Court that the letters were to have been sent after the jury had been discharged from the trial, and were mistakenly sent while deliberations were still underway. Please disregard this letter, do not respond, and do not let the letter influence your deliberations in any way.*

Thursday morning, Paul Harrison told his fellow jurors that he had made up his mind that Peterson was guilty. "I could look him right in the eye and tell him," he said. By the end of the day, emotions were raw and the vote was ten guilty, two not guilty. They all committed to go home and think about their decisions.

Richard Sarratt lay in the hallway of his home with his legs propped up on the steps to the second floor. He considered and reconsidered his decision. It was a fitful night for all twelve.

54

Only the deputy heard the muffled knock from inside the door of the deliberation room on the morning of Friday, October 10. He eased open the door and stuck his head in the room. Then he closed it and announced, "We have a verdict."

As if by magic, the courtroom filled with tense faces and curious eyes. Michael Peterson took his seat between David Rudolf and Tom Maher. Judge Hudson stepped up onto the bench. He spoke to the gathered audience: "If you think you're going to have difficulty accepting the jury's verdict, and you're going to make noise or do something else disruptive in the courtroom, I am going to give you the opportunity to leave. Right now. If you disrupt my courtroom while I am doing this, and you cause a scene, I'm going to have you arrested."

He turned to the deputy. "Bring the jury in. Tell them to bring all their belongings.

"Have you marked, checked, whatever, the appropriate places on the verdict sheet?" Hudson asked the forewoman.

"Yes," she answered and handed the manila envelope to the deputy.

He carried it to the judge. Hudson passed it over to Court Clerk Angie Kelly. With all eyes on her, Angie opened the envelope and slid out a piece of paper. "We, the twelve members of the jury, unanimously find the defendant to be guilty of first-degree murder, this the tenth day of October, 2003."

Margaret and Martha Ratliff collapsed on one another sobbing. The jurors ached for them. Many wanted to wrap arms around the girls and take their pain away. But their pain had not been born today—it had been two decades in the making.

David Rudolf called for a poll of the jury. Angie asked each one, "Your foreperson has returned for your verdict that the defendant is guilty of first-degree murder. Is this your verdict, and do you still assent thereto?"

Each juror answered, "Yes." Their mission fulfilled, the jurors left the courtroom.

Judge Hudson said, "Mr. Peterson, if you'll stand."

An expressionless Michael Peterson rose.

"You certainly do not have to be heard," he said. "Anything you want to say before the court imposes judgment?"

"I just want to say to my children," he turned around with a twisted smile and nodded at each of the children, saying, "It's Okay. It's Okay. It's Okay. It's Okay."

When Peterson turned back around, Judge Hudson delivered his sentence. "The defendant is imprisoned in the North Carolina Department of Correction for the remainder of his natural life."

The deputy slid the handcuffs from his belt and wrapped them around the wrists of the man who had earned a Silver Star and a Bronze Heart in the jungles of Vietnam, the novelist who had made the *New York Times* Best Seller List, the husband convicted of murder.

After ninety-nine days, *State of North Carolina* vs. *Michael Iver Peterson* had, at last, drawn to a close.

THE AFTERMATH

"All the strength I have, I owe to my mother."

—Caitlin Atwater

55

Eighty-three-year-old Veronica Hunt was at a friend's house for a luncheon and a bridge party. In the middle of their game, the telephone rang. "He's guilty! He's guilty! Turn on the TV!" sounded through the room.

She sat before the television set and watched her former son-in-law being led away in handcuffs. Her friends hugged her and cried in relief—they had all worried about a hung jury. One woman rushed home and grabbed a bottle of champagne so they could toast the verdict.

Veronica was pleased that the "obnoxious" Rudolf had gotten his comeuppance. She was glad for a measure of justice for her daughter. But Kathleen was still dead.

Candace Zamperini was teaching sign language at a school near her home in Virginia when her husband brought her news of the verdict. She was relieved, but felt a heavy burden of pain. She knew that people expected her to jump up and down in excitement. But there was too much sadness for celebration. She had lost her sister. And now she had lost a brother-in-law as well. There was no winner.

In appreciation, she had Stuart Johnson make replicas of the chimes hanging over Kathleen's grave. She gave them to Jim Hardin, Freda Black and Duane Deaver. She also donated a set to the First Presbyterian Church to hang in the small garden where the family met before the first day of the trial.

In Germany, Barbara Malagnino spent many sleepless nights waiting for the verdict. She was in the stables with her horses cleaning the stalls when her mother called her on her portable phone. "The just wrapped cuffs on his hands and are walking him out," her mother said.

Barbara could not believe it at first and then she was swept with strong feelings of sadness and relief. She shuddered, remembering once again that she had been so close to evil and had not been aware of it.

The district attorney's office received a call from their most notorious witness, Brent "Brad" Wolgamott. He congratulated them on putting a monster behind bars.

The same day the verdict was rendered, David Rudolf and Thomas Maher submitted a notice to the courts indicating their intent to file an appeal on behalf of their client.

Two Durham County Sheriff's Department deputies escorted Michael Peterson from Durham to Central Prison in Raleigh, the admission point into the state prison system for any male felon with a sentence of 10 years or more.

Just before 3 that afternoon, he entered a residential hall at Central in his prison-issued white tee shirt and gray pants. He now faced a physical and psychological examination that included substance abuse screening, an

IQ test and an aptitude test. Sometime within two weeks, he would be transported to the facility he would call home. For dinner that first night, the prison served fish, cole slaw and a grape-flavored drink.

Within a week, the determination was made and Michael Peterson was on his way to the Nash Correctional Institution, home to over 600 maximum- and medium-security prisoners. The fifteen-building complex in Nashville, North Carolina, is surround by security cameras, guard towers and ten- to twelve-foot chain-link fencing topped with coiled wire. Outside the barrier are fields of cotton, soybeans and sweet potatoes and a scattering of homes.

Peterson—now inmate number 0816932—was taken to his 8-foot by 9-foot cell with its bed and stainless-steel toilet, sink and two tables attached to the wall. He had use of a limited library and a computer with word processing software, but without access to the Internet. He would be allowed one phone call per week and up to three visitors at a time on Saturday and Sunday. One of his new neighbors was another client of David Rudolf, former Carolina Panther, Rae Carruth.

Five days after his arrival at Nash, the reality of prison life hit Peterson hard. He was in his cell reading during a free time period after dinner—a time when all the cell doors are left open. Convicted armed robber Larry Wade entered his cell. A few words were exchanged and then fists flew.

In handcuffs and shackles, Michael Peterson was escorted to Nash General Hospital where he received several stitches for his busted lip. He returned to the prison late that night. Both prisoners were removed from

the general population and kept locked in solitary cells
while prison officials investigated the altercation. With
only himself for company, Peterson turned 60 years old
on October 23—but he no longer had anything to
celebrate.

At the end of the investigation, Wade was given 60
days of disciplinary segregation, 70 hours of extra duty,
and a 6-month suspension of visitation, telephone and
canteen privileges. His possible parole date was pushed
back, as well—he lost credit for 50 good days. Peterson
received no additional punishment.

The day before Michael was assaulted, Brent "Brad"
Wolgamott was in the news again. He allegedly mas-
queraded as a dentist named Karl Smith and called in
prescriptions including hydrocodone, a narcotic, and
clindamycin, an antibiotic, to a Raleigh CVS Pharmacy.
Four counts of obtaining a controlled substance by
fraud or forgery were filed. Wolgamott surrendered to
authorities at the Wake County Jail that evening. Two
hours later, he was released on $1,000 bond.

At 11:30 the next morning, Raleigh police arrested
him again. Police say he allegedly attempted the same
scam at a Kmart Pharmacy. This time, he was held on a
$10,000 bond. Wolgamott claimed the stress and
embarrassment of his testimony in the Peterson case
drove him to it.

Michael Peterson filed an affidavit of indigency asking
the state for a court-appointed attorney to handle his

appeal. The form he filled out showed total assets of $1,297,000—nearly all in real estate.

On the other side of the balance sheet, his liabilities included $105,000 in credit card debt, a $300,000 loan from his brother, Bill, a $168,000 loan from his ex-wife, Patty, and $78,000 he owed the Internal Revenue Service for his 2001 taxes. A review of his tax return for that year revealed that Michael Peterson claimed an income that was far less than the amount listed on Kathleen Peterson's W-2 from Nortel Networks in the last year of her life.

The total amount of his liabilities was $1,408,000. In other words, Michael Peterson was more than $100,000 in the hole. For months, his defense team mocked the prosecution's allegation of a financial motive. They insisted their client had no money problems.

Judge Hudson denied Peterson's application, saying, "If you have $1.2 million in assets, you can find a way to hire a lawyer."

David Rudolf filed a new motion with the judge requesting that he reconsider his decision. It said that although Peterson claimed a net worth of $2 million, the cost of his defense depleted his resources—the actual cost of the trial was not given.

Judge Hudson reversed his ruling and declared Peterson indigent. Thomas Maher agreed to accept the position of court-appointed attorney at a state rate of $65 per hour. The state would also bear the cost—about $40,000—to provide a full transcript of the trial proceedings to the appellant.

Maher did not expect to receive that document from the court reporters before the summer of 2004. He knew his appeal would include arguments about the inclusion of evidence surrounding the death of Elizabeth Ratliff and the admission of the gay pornography. He needed to review the transcript, however, before determining what other errors he might cite.

Maher's faith in his client was unshaken by the verdict. "I find it impossible," he said, "to believe he would commit any first-degree murder, particularly not of someone he deeply cared for and loved."

Thomas Maher no longer worked with David Rudolf at the law firm where they were both employed throughout the Peterson trial. One week after that case ended, Maher resigned to set up his own practice.

Juror Kelli Colgan thought about the Peterson case every day. Any spare moment, it popped up in her thoughts. In the beginning, it ran through her head six or seven times an hour. It stirred up primitive anxieties similar to a child's fear of monsters under the bed. The intensity of these intrusions did not ease up until Christmas.

1810 Cedar Street went on the market with a price tag of $1,175,000. People all over Durham marked their calendars for the three-day tag sale of furnishings, artwork and books at the house one weekend in November. For a $20 ticket, interested parties could get a sneak preview of the items on sale on Thursday evening.

One of the sale organizers said that security guards would usher out anyone making disrespectful remarks about Michael Peterson. Of the nearly 500 people standing in line early on the first morning of the sale, many had slept in cars and vans on the side of the road to get a prime spot in the front. Before the sale was over, more than 2,000 people entered the mansion. Items sold for a low of 25 cents for a can opener and a high of $6,000 for Peterson's vintage Triumph TR3. Organizers told reporters that the total take from the sale was nobody's business.

Todd and Clayton Peterson, Margaret and Martha Ratliff and Caitlin Atwater shared in the proceeds from the sale. Any amount Caitlin received would be considered a down payment against the judgment anticipated in her wrongful death suit against Michael Peterson.

On the two-year anniversary of Kathleen's death, the asking price for the house dropped to $975,000. As of June 2004, it was still on the market, but the price was now only $695,000. Finally, at the end of July, the home sold for $640,000.

On Thanksgiving Day, Barbara Malagnino found a letter in her mailbox at her home in Germany from the Darmstadt police requesting that she contact them regarding the death of Elizabeth Ratliff in 1985. A murder investigation was under way.

Many friends of Michael Peterson refused to accept the verdict of the court. Former U.S. Representative Nick Galifianakis and businessmen and lawyer Larry Pollard brought forward their theory of Kathleen Peterson's death. They wanted her body exhumed to test the back of her scalp for owl DNA.

They believed Kathleen's death could have been the result of an attack by a barn owl or a great horned owl. In his letter to District Attorney Jim Hardin, Larry Pollard cited eleven points of evidence in support of the theory of an owl strike, including the number, shape and location of the gashes to Kathleen's head. He also noted his research into owl attacks on people in the United States.

Many wondered if Pollard was driven more by his past than by his friendship with Peterson. In 1960, his father was accused of capital murder. In the end, he was convicted of manslaughter.

Jim Hardin responded to Pollard's letter. "We appreciate your concern and consideration of this matter, but we remain fully confident that justice was indeed served in this case."

Appeal attorney Thomas Maher distanced himself from the theory and said it would not play a role in the appeal.

Lawyers Weekly USA, a national newspaper for small law firms, announced its list of the top ten lawyers of the year in January 2004. Only one prosecutor made the cut—District Attorney Jim Hardin. Upon learning of this honor, Hardin said the recognition should be shared with Freda Black and David Saacks. "The prosecution of the Peterson case was truly a collaborative effort," he said.

. . .

On January 15, Judge Orlando Hudson ruled in the wrongful death suit filed by Caitlin Atwater that Michael Peterson was civilly liable for his wife's death. Caitlin was not present in court that day. Her attorney, Jay Trehy, said that the amount of damages would be determined at a later date.

Although Peterson had a negative balance sheet, the decision was still meaningful, Trehy said. "If he ever wrote a book, a chapter, an article or anything and tries to make money out of what he's done, then Caitlin Atwater will be able to come in and collect on those assets."

Caitlin had other pending legal matters as well. After pursuing administrative remedies, her lawyer filed a suit in federal court in Greensboro, North Carolina, against Nortel Networks for the $384,166 of Kathleen's benefits that they'd paid to Michael Peterson. The suit contended that North Carolina had prohibited the distribution of money to the person under indictment for her murder. Trehy did not expect a result in the Nortel Networks situation until 2005.

Caitlin was fighting the Navy Federal Credit Union over the foreclosure on one of the Peterson homes. She claimed they had no right to loan $75,000 to Michael Peterson after he was indicted for murder and therefore had no right to claim the home in exchange for the unpaid debt.

Prudential Life Insurance released the payment due on Kathleen's life insurance to the courts, asking them to determine the proper recipient. In June 2004, the courts ruled that Caitlin and Fred Atwater would share the funds from this policy.

In mid-February, *Dateline NBC* aired a two-hour special on Michael Peterson. The promotional announcement mentioning Gräfenhausen, Germany, caught the eye of Donna Carlson Lindahl. She had lived there for four years.

She remembered the town with mixed feelings. It was there she had her good years with her daughter, Amy— the years before Amy's grade school teacher, Liz Ratliff, committed suicide. Since that day, Amy's life was a downhill spiral. She'd suffered from depression. She had a health crisis caused by overmedication. She went without any care for a time when her father left the military and the family lost their medical benefits.

Then, at the age of 14, Amy Carlson took her own life—following the escape route she believed her beloved teacher had used. Deep inside, Donna harbored an anger at Liz Ratliff for the damage her suicide inflicted on Amy.

Donna settled down to watch the show—her mind filled with memories of her daughter. It had been many years since Amy's death, but the pain was still alive. She hoped glimpses of the distant past would smooth some of the scars she bore.

What she saw, however, jolted her with renewed pain. This show was not just any story set in Gräfenhausen—it told the truth behind the death of Amy's teacher. It was not a suicide. Donna wondered who had created that rumor and if it had been spread by someone wanting to protect Michael Peterson.

Her anger was intense, but no longer directed at Liz Ratliff. Her sorrow now had a new dimension. In her heart, Donna was convinced that there was one more victim of Michael Peterson—her daughter, Amy.

On February 18, David Rudolf appeared in Orange County Superior Court. It was not in his usual capacity—he had been summoned for jury duty. The case involved a former UNC football player who was charged with raping a student in her dorm room. Rudolf was excused from the panel.

The three most tragic figures in the courtroom, Margaret and Martha Ratliff and Caitlin Atwater, attempted to pick up the pieces of their lives. Margaret returned to Tulane University in New Orleans. Upon her arrival, three letters from Michael Peterson were waiting for her in her mailbox. Martha returned to her studies at the University of San Francisco. Bill Peterson was determined to make sure the sisters were able to complete their educations.

Caitlin was back in Ithaca, New York, at Cornell University. She had not declared a major yet, but her studies focused on sociology and government. She hoped to go to law school when she graduated.

In March 2004, military investigators consulted with authorities in Durham. Like the German police, they were

opening an investigation into the death of Department o
Defense employee Liz Ratliff.

Later that month, an attorney representing Michae
Peterson was back in Judge Hudson's courtroom
Peterson wanted his Cartier watch, which the police ha
seized as evidence. The judge denied the request, ruling
that the state was within its rights to hold on to al
evidence while appeals were pending.

It would be a long time before the people of Durhan
would relegate this tragedy to the dustbin of old news.

AFTERWORD

"Psychology is based on probability."

—Michael Nuccitelli, forensic psychologist

I drove to Maplewood Cemetery after court one day. Peace settled around me as I entered the serene landscape spotted with majestic trees. Beneath one towering oak, I found the last resting place of Kathleen Hunt Peterson.

Above, in the branches of the tree, a set of wind chimes hung. As I reached the foot of her grave a breeze danced through the air and the sweetest sound ever heard tinkled through the air. It was almost as if a gracious hostess was welcoming me to her new home.

I paused there for a time thinking about the great light lost the day Kathleen died. All the while the chimes graced the air with a pure sound that offered comfort. I placed a small stone on her headstone, turned and walked away. As soon as I passed under the tree on my way to my car, the breeze died and the music of Kathleen faded in the air.

I looked back and waved to the woman I had never known and now never would. She remained a presence in the hearts of her mother, her daughter, her sisters, her brother and in all the many lives she had touched.

And now, she was rooted in my life. In the music of

the chimes, I heard her voice. And I promised to remember.

Before the trial ended, the verdict was a foregone conclusion in my mind. The medical examiner's report made it murder. The spatter inside the shorts made it Mike. All else was window-dressing.

But who knows how the twists and turns tormented the collective mind of the chosen twelve? They pounded through weeks of a prosecution case where, at times, they seemed to be in the jury room more often than in the courtroom as one *voir dire* hearing after another banished them to their sanctum.

The top-dollar defense team did not need to prove Peterson blameless—that is not their job. They needed only to etch enough question marks in the air. Still, it seemed odd that they did not present a single tangible witness who connected in a real way with the accused or the victim. Not one concrete witness mounted the stand for the defense—only professional experts.

No one took the stand to extol the virtues, the passions or the good works of Michael Peterson. Not a friend from his past. Not any of his neighborhood supporters and not one member of the family. Once the trial was over, it was still difficult to find anyone willing to spend a few minutes sharing a kind word on his behalf.

No one took the stand for the defense to testify about the events of December 9 or 10 or any day in the lives of Michael and Kathleen. Of course, the defendant avoided the hot seat—he had too many toxic elements in his life to survive the crucible of cross-examination.

What about the blowpoke that mysteriously reappeared? Neither the public nor the prosecutors nor the panel sitting in judgment knew anything about the provenance of that tool. No one spoke of where it was found. No one spoke of who found it.

Despite public opinion to the contrary, the legal system is no longer designed to find the truth—it is constructed to decide a winner. Although life and death lie on the line, many players in the courtroom see it all as a game where cleverness and ruse win the day. A place where a desperate desire to deceive means truth is to be avoided at all costs.

And what is the truth—the whole truth—about Michael Peterson? Perhaps it will never be known. As his good friend, Richard White Adams, said at Michael's wedding to Kathleen, "Michael is a man of mystery." He seemed to take great pleasure in this image.

More than one mental health professional on Court TV suggested that he could have Narcissistic Personality Disorder. If that diagnosis is true, it does answer a lot of questions in Michael's life.

The *Diagnostic and Statistical Manual of Mental Disorders* defines Narcissism as "A pattern of traits and behaviors which signify infatuation and obsession with one's self to the exclusion of all others and the egotistic and ruthless pursuit of one's gratification, dominance and ambition." As many as 75 percent of all narcissists are men. It is in the same family as Borderline, Antisocial and Histrionic Personality Disorders.

The art of deception is a hallmark of Narcissism. A person with NPD projects a false face to the world and manages all social interactions through this fictional self. People often become involved with a narcissist without having any awareness of who he really is.

He expresses surprise that society should hold him responsible and want to punish him for his actions. When faced with the judgment of others, he feels wronged and persecuted. It is rare for him to feel any re___t for what he was done or any empathy for his victi_.

He ____t to experiment sexually with multiple partners. S___ _ him is the ultimate act of objectification of another hu____ being. It proves his superiority and fuels his narcissi_ _.

He often embroiders the tales of his achievements and talents to gain acknowledgment of his superiority. His humor is sharp and biting, and cloaks a deep well of hostility and venom.

He draws to him people who offer positive affirmation. They are the source of his narcissistic supply. He desires to impress and manipulate them—and hold them tight.

But theories about the state of Michael Peterson's mental health pale in importance when compared to the future of three damaged young women. What will become of Caitlin, Margaret and Martha?

Many in the families of Elizabeth Ratliff and Kathleen Peterson ache from the severing of their relationships with Margaret and Martha. The two sisters, whether they acknowledge it or not, are bound to suffer from this estrangement, too. Will they ever renew the relationships that were once so important to them? Will the fear of possible abandonment forever create barriers that separate them from others?

And what about Caitlin? She is a strong young woman with an intense desire to succeed. Time will somewhat soften the pain she feels from the loss of her mother. But, after viewing how her mother was betrayed by the men she loved—one painfully, the other lethally—will she ever be able to develop enough trust to enjoy a close relationship?

Margaret, Martha and Caitlin. The road to recovery for all of them will be a long and winding one. Whisper their names in your hearts. Bless them with a world of healing and a universe of hope.